Case Studies in Constructivist Leadership and Teaching

Arthur Shapiro

A SCARECROWEDUCATION BOOK

The Scarecrow Press, Inc.
Lanham, Maryland, and Oxford
2003

A SCARECROWEDUCATION BOOK

Published in the United States of America
by Scarecrow Press, Inc.
A Member of the Rowman & Littlefield Publishing Group
4501 Forbes Boulevard, Suite 200, Lanham, Maryland 20706
www.scaroweducation.com

PO Box 317
Oxford
OX2 9RU, UK

British Library Cataloguing in Publication Information Available

Library of Congress Cataloging-in-Publication Data

Shapiro, Athur S., 1928–
  Case studies in constructivist leadership and teaching / Arthur Shapiro.
      p. cm.
"A ScarecrowEducation book."
Includes bibliographical references.
  ISBN 0-8108-4462-1 (hard : alk. paper) — ISBN 0-8108-4463-X (pbk. :
alk. paper)
  1. Constructivism (Education)—Case studies. 2. Teaching. 3. Educational
leadership. I. Title.
  LB1590.3 .S417 2003
  370.15'2—dc21   2002008133

$\circledcirc^{\text{TM}}$ The paper used in this publication meets the minimum requirements of
American National Standard for Information Sciences—Permanence of
Paper for Printed Library Materials, ANSI/NISO Z39.48-1992.
Manufactured in the United States of America.

These case studies are dedicated to those who have participated in constructing them: My wife, Sue Shapiro, whose comments and common sense helped with its realism and whose dynamic presence is evident across these pages; our daughter, Alana Michelle Thompson, and son, Dr. Marc Douglas Shapiro, significant contributors to who we are becoming and who we are—and who are visible in numbers of these cases; and to our capable students whose voices speak across these case studies. Without you this book could not be.

It is because modern education so seldom has a great hope that it so seldom achieves a great result.

—Bertrand Russell
Why Men Fight

Contents

Acknowledgments   ix

Part I: Case Studies about Constructivist Teaching

1   Passing Through: The Confessions of an Alienated Student:
The Case of Sue Sharp—Or, How I Ran a Diner, and
Still Graduated High School   3

2   The Constructivist Teacher: When a Substitute Teaches
Your Class (and Hasn't a Clue)   11

3   Creative Classroom Management: Better Involve the
Troops—Or, How I Managed to Teach Mechanical
Drawing without Knowing Anything about It   17

4   Crocodile Rock: Gateway to Emancipation
and Empowerment   25

5   How I Created a Supportive Culture in a Constructivist
Classroom or Team (How to Pull It Off, and Make It
Work for You)   31

    Appendix 5A: Constructivist Leader's Mental
Checklist   41

6   My Development as a Constructivist Teacher,
by R. D. Nordgren, Ph.D.   49

7   Leprechauns in the Classroom   59

8 Classroom Management—Solved 65

9 Looking at the Right End of the Horse: What
We Found in Swedish Schools Amazed Us—
IDEALIZED Constructivism 73

10 Practicing Constructivism in a Public ESE Charter
Middle School—With Difficulty,
by Phylicia L. Cartwright 81

11 From the Mouths of Students—Interactions
with Constructivism 89

12 A Typical Day as a Constructivist High School Teacher
and Department Chair, by Janet Richards 113

13 ESOL, Constructivism, and You—Constructivist and
ESOL Philosophy and Practice: Another Surprise 125

14 Freedom versus Control—The Scripted Classroom:
The High Cost of Control to Everyone
(Including Teachers) 149

Part II: Case Studies in Constructivist Leadership

15 A Constructivist Sports Program: The Case of Principal
Marc Douglas's Unusual Basketball Team 157

16 Beliefs, Myths, and Realities: A Case Study of a Rogue
Junior High: Transformation into a Model Middle School 167

17 Looking Up the Wrong End of the Horse: Our Testing
Mania—Viewpoints of Politicians and Practitioners
(and Maybe Kids): A Cheap, Fast Way to
Weaken Education (but It Sure Looks Tough) 185

18 How to Make Your School (and Your Classroom)
Work Better—Decentralize into a
Constructivist Approach 197

19 A Day in the Life of a Constructivist Principal,
by Leanna Isaacson 209

20 Moving Orange Blossom Trail Elementary School
toward Constructivism   223

21 Outside the Box: Three Team Leaders as Co-Principals   245

22 Our Evaluation Ritual Trap: And How to Spring It   255

23 The Rigid New Principal and the Constructivist Teacher:
Studies in Tension   269

24 Where Are the Students on Your School Board?
A Case Study of an Alternative School's Student
Board of Education   279

25 Designing Our Structures to Do Our Heavy Work:
What a Curriculum Structure Can Do to Make Our
Professional Lives *a Lot* Easier   287

Appendix 25A: Two Curriculum Committee Structure
Models and Suggested Rules for Operation   298

26 Developing and Running a Pupil Personnel Services
Council: Making Our Structures Work for Us   305

27 National Standards—The Good, the Bad, the Ugly   313

Part III: Research

28 The Latest Research (about Constructivism) Part I:
Different Approaches to Constructivism—What It's
All About   327

29 The Latest Research (about Constructivism) Part II:
On Instruction and Leadership   345

About the Author   365

Acknowledgments

John Donne said it best: "No man is an island."

And so, I wish to acknowledge the innumerable contributions of my family, my friends, and my colleagues, and those of our supportive society and culture to my education and development. You will note that four of these case studies are contributions from educators who have sojourned through the slings and arrows that pioneers receive in forging approaches to improve their teaching and administrative practice. I give considerable credit to their persistence, courage, and dedication to their profession and to their own and others' development.

A special thanks is offered to those contributors who described a day in their professional lives with cheerfulness and enthusiasm. They are: Leanna Isaacson, principal of Southwood Elementary School in Orange County, Florida, whose unbounded energy, upbeat nature, and thoughtful approach shine through her narrative; Dr. Rollin D. (R. D.) Nordgren, former assistant principal of Bloomingdale High School, in Tampa, Florida, who shares his professional development honestly and forthrightly; Janet Richards, department chair and teacher in Riverview High School, in Tampa, Florida, who reveals her innermost thoughts and feelings so that we can grow along with her as she handles the complexities of her day; Phylicia Cartwright, who taught in a public ESE middle school in Florida and is now teaching in a private elementary school, and who lets us know forthrightly about the pain with which she met difficult conditions and the courage she displayed in her professionalism and decision making.

Thanks to school psychologists Andrea M. Mowatt and Amelia D. VanName. When they circulated their "Constructivist Leader's Mental Checklist" to the class as their "Most Significant Learnings," fellow students called it brilliant. That it is. It is appended to case study five. It presents detailed techniques, processes, and ideas to implement constructivist teaching and leadership behaviors.

I also wish to thank Carol Totaitive, whose creativity is illustrated in the diagrams and tables that bear her initials.

Diana Treese deserves credit for her creative designs in making the complexities in case study twenty, "Moving Orange Blossom Trail Elementary School toward Constructivism," so clear and evident. The faculty and administration of the school share this admiration.

And, to the many people who contributed so much to the richness of the classes in which we all participated, of whom a number are quoted in the text as examples of the immense benefits of a constructivist approach to teaching and leadership, my gratitude and appreciation.

Thank you, one and all.

Part I

CASE STUDIES ABOUT CONSTRUCTIVIST TEACHING

I learned that a constructivist life makes one's dreams the *pedestal*, not the ceiling.

> —Jean Kern, gifted elementary teacher,
> Peace Corps and VISTA volunteer

Constructivism has become the reigning paradigm in teacher education in America today.

> —S. Hausfather, *Educational Horizons*

CHAPTER 1

Passing Through: The Confessions of an Alienated Student

The Case of Sue Sharp—Or, How I Ran a Diner, and Still Graduated High School

> Because management was responsible for 85% of all quality problems, management has to take the lead in changing the systems and processes that create those problems.
>
> —G. Edwards Deming

> For me, there is no life without autonomy.
>
> —Sue Shapiro, Counselor, Hillsborough Community College

> The people who get on in this world are the people who get up and look for the circumstances they want, and if they can't find them, make them.
>
> —George Bernard Shaw

THE CONFESSIONS START

"Every class in every school I attended violated my personality. My basic lifelong need for autonomy was never on anyone's horizon, let alone respected."

So spoke Sue Sharp, longtime counselor and instructor at a Florida community college. Sue continued to address her fellow students, "My classes were rigid, controlling, loaded with far too many teacher-made rules, constricting my autonomy, my freedom."

She then felt safe enough for a very personal revelation, "And I never really felt safe in my classes—until I came upon a constructivist class.

"My teachers usually wrote on my report cards: 'Does not apply her-self.' But they never realized that it was their rules and it was their rigid-ity that turned me off. It was the systems my teachers set up, usually to control us, that were the culprit. But, they never even came close to rec-ognizing that they had actually set up the structure that so stifled me."

Sue continued, "When I left my small high school, where I knew every-one, to go to one with fifteen hundred students, I hated it. So, I took ad-vantage of my anonymity and skipped classes to run a diner, where I was really valued. My last semester I skipped classes forty-three days out of ninety in order to work at my diner because it was so rewarding. So, I had a 1.6 grade point average—except for my AP (Advanced Placement) class, where the teacher showed me respect. So I paid attention—and got an A.

"I couldn't graduate from high school in a lot of states these days."

THE CLASS AS A SYSTEM

Sue then analyzed the way the typical class operates as a system, "The way the system (shades of Deming) works, is that when we are kids we learn all the norms, customs, and rituals that define a traditional class-room early on. I asked a four-year-old child of a friend to tell me about her nursery school. And she laid out the nature and routine of school-ing as cold as ice, including sitting at desks, breaks at appropriate times, listening to the teacher, etc. It is the only model that we ever ex-perience—and, it becomes the box into which we lock ourselves—even though it makes most of us unhappy. Still, because it is the only model we have seen and known, we inevitably create it in our own class-rooms—despite ourselves.

"It's like my feelings about my mother's negative and critical behav-iors. I absolutely swore I'd never do what she did, act out her critical neg-ativity. But, every once in a while, I hear my mother's voice emerging from my lips, much to my chagrin! I hear myself being picky and critical.

"My easy-going husband, much to his credit, only once called me 'Ellen' (my mother's name), and only twice in our eleven years re-sponded to my critical carrying on by saying, 'O.K., Big E.'

"It's the same with running our classes. Most of us didn't like the way they were run, traditionally—boring, repetitious, meaningless homework, whole class teaching in which some struggled to keep up and others just waited. But, we use the same model, the same strategies because they're the only ones we've experienced."

Sue then revealed another insight, "I even felt that most teachers make you feel stupid—and then I ran into a constructivist class—and blossomed!"

A CONSTRUCTIVIST CLASS

Autonomy

Sue pointed out, "The difference is phenomenal! My autonomy was respected. *I* was respected. *I* was listened to. The organizing vehicle was the small group, something I'd never seen before."

Safety

"The instructor also went to great lengths to make it safe. The norm (read, agreed-upon rule) was that everything said was to be kept in the room—in total confidence. And (I almost said, remarkably), no one ever broke that norm, because we all agreed upon it—and it was crucial to making our class safe for each other.

"Another norm was that there was to be no destructive criticism. Rather, every comment, every insight was viewed as contributing to the ongoing inquiry. So, all of our comments were viewed as valuable. We were respected, even honored. We even learned to take someone's comments or analyses, even if off-base somewhat, and ask what other alternative insights might be proposed or developed in our line of inquiry.

"All of us were used to—no—expecting to be criticized. But, no one was ever criticized. So, everyone felt safe after a while—and valued. As a consequence, everyone felt comfortable participating, although some of us took a long time to undo years of hiding."

Maslow

Sue commented upon the processes that developed in the class: "And, after a while, some of us began to realize that the instructor was basing a lot of his process and structure on Abraham Maslow's Hierarchy of Needs. For example, Safety Needs were Maslow's second Hierarchical Level, the first being Physiological Needs. We actually had groups bring in snacks during our breaks. The instructor ran high schools where kids could go down to the cafeteria or snack bar during their breaks or free time, just like the faculty. It made for a relaxing and supportive atmosphere.

"We had a student who was an investigative policeman in the class, who turned out to be quite a watcher. Finally, one evening, to our surprise, he said to a couple of us that the break was really not a break at all. He noted that after a while, he began to watch the processes going on the class, and he realized that what looked like a break was hardly one at all, since we often continued to talk about issues and readings we had just been discussing.

"Only after some time, some of us began to realize that he was right, that the break was somewhat of an illusion, since we talked a lot about the class itself, its processes, the concepts and ideas being discussed, coming up with ideas for our groups, traded ideas, and the like. We even challenged the instructor, who responded by saying that that was entirely accidental, totally unplanned (he always claimed that things just happened, that they weren't planned—but, after a while, we began to know better). We also began to realize that there was quite a lot of hidden curriculum being carried out without our realizing it—at first."

The Organizing Vehicle—The Group (and, Becoming a Learning Community)

"We also realized that the organizing vehicle, the basic structure of the class, the small group, supported Maslow's third Hierarchical Level, meeting Social Needs, since we became a tightly knit and very active group. You know, recently, educators have begun to talk about learning communities. So, one day we accused our instructor about pulling another fast one on us. We had unwittingly developed a world-class learning community without any fuss or fanfare or solemn, formal declaration or announcement that we were about to embark upon an experimental journey and would try to develop a learning community.

We had actually constructed one! His comment was that somehow it had happened by accident—we just lucked out.

"By this time we were watching intently to try to uncover other hidden (to us) classroom, curricular, structural, and process components. Belatedly, we also began to realize that we were in a social situation with a master motivator."

Social Needs

Sue continued with her analysis: "Since we worked as a unit both in our small groups and as a total group, our social needs were more than being met. In addition, the instructor, after asking for our approval, printed out a class list of everyone's name, address, and phone numbers (cell, home, work), and even e-mail addresses, so that years later I am able to contact almost everyone in the class, and especially those people and friends in my small group."

Esteem Needs

"As for Maslow's fourth Hierarchical Level, meeting our Esteem Needs, the class obviously focused on meeting those goals. Note that we established the norm of no destructive criticism, of valuing everyone's comments and analyses as contributing to the ongoing inquiry. People generally felt real good about the class and looked forward to its meeting every week. Most of us came to classes early and tended to loiter for some time after class because the class and all that occurred in it was so stimulating."

Sue ended, "This was the best class I ever had. I couldn't wait for Wednesdays to come. I looked forward to it all week. We all did."

SUE'S SUMMARY

Sue summarized, "My autonomy needs were met, those whose major needs focused around their being people people, including wanting harmony above all (the Abstract Randoms, in Anthony Gregorc's Personality Style Delineator's terms), had their needs more than met, with the small group forming the basis of the class's operation. Those few people who were the analysts had ample opportunity to operate in whatever mode they preferred, had their basic needs met, and discovered that their 'big picture' contributions were greatly appreciated. Similarly, those of us who need to move around and not be tied to a desk for long periods of time, as often occurs in traditionally organized classes, found the group work offered ample opportunity to learn in our preferred style, often kinesthetic in nature. For example, we developed projects of all kinds, which enabled us to move around in order to get materials, equipment, etc.

"People felt they and their personalities and learning styles were genuinely valued and contributions were honored, since we largely worked in groups on group projects to solve problems, or issues, or concerns we or others raised, or on articles we agreed to read. When the last class approached, most people presented their 'Most Significant Learnings' as group projects, but were upset that the class was ending. Still, the last day was a relief from the ritualistic insistence that we all have experienced as finals. We actually experienced no stress, we were all curious and excited about the presentations, many of which had lots of humorous pieces to them, and it really was a kind of celebration. Most of us asked what other courses the instructor taught.

"The instructor? He was also upset that the class was ending. The learning community had become a genuine community of people who cared for each other, who worked well together. During and after this class, we all made decisions about changing our teaching techniques, based on what was modeled for us every week. We were freed to decide to do it differently."

QUESTIONS FOR REFLECTION

Sue Sharp was able to play the size of the school to her advantage to become anonymous. And she noted that she was valued in the diner she ran. She also loved classes that were constructivist. Note that Sue, to this day, knows where all of her thirty-three classmates in her small high school are.

1. How could the principal and central office beat the problem of size in a large school?

    A. Sue spoke about the value of learning communities. Could a school decentralize into learning communities or other models of decentralization? What did she see as the benefits?

    B. Have you ever known of any decentralized plan? How did it work? What are the positives and negatives?

    C. What elements should they consider in designing a plan to deal with this situation?

    D. What role should the central office play? How is the principal to generate support for this enterprise?

    E. How could they approach the faculty to begin getting support?

    F. Into what key social systems should they start dropping seeds?

    G. Should they approach the teachers' union in their planning, and, if so, when?

2. How could they reorganize the school so that students like Sue would feel valued in school, and not have to go to other organizations to get their esteem needs met?

3. How could they begin to help the teachers move toward constructivism (that is, if they valued such a model)?

4. What could the central office do to help the principals discover the benefits of constructivist approaches?

    A. What kind of plan should they consider to accomplish that end?

5. What other factors and issues would you consider in your thinking? (Would it be useful to lay them out on paper?)

SOURCES

Benne, K. D. & Sheats, P. (1948, Spring). Functional roles of group members. *Journal of Social Issues 4*, 242–47.

Bradshaw, J. (1988). *Bradshaw on: The family*. Deerfield Beach, FL: Health Communications.

Deming, W. E. (1982). *Quality, productivity, and competitive position*. Cambridge, MA: MIT, Center for Advanced Engineering Study.

French, T. (1993). *South of heaven: Welcome to high school at the end of the twentieth century*. New York: Doubleday.

Gregorc, A. F. (1985). *Inside styles: Beyond the basics*. Maynard, MA: Gabriel Systems.

Gregorc, A. F. (1997). *Relating with style*. Columbia, CT: Gregorc Associates.

Lewin, K. (1952). Group decision and social change. In G. E. Swanson & T. M. Newcomb (Eds.), *Readings in social psychology*. New York: Holt, 459–73.

Maslow, A. H. (1954). *Motivation and personality* (2nd ed.). New York: Harper & Row.

CHAPTER 2

The Constructivist Teacher

When a Substitute Teaches Your Class (and Hasn't a Clue)

Anyone can teach.

—Anon

THE ASSUMPTION: ANYONE CAN SUBSTITUTE IN ANY CLASS, EVEN ONE THAT'S CONSTRUCTIVIST

As Alana Michelle left her middle school at 3 P.M. and hopped into her Maxima to teach her prep community college class, she wondered how the kids in the class reacted to her colleague, Marie Cross, the assistant principal in her middle school, who had offered to sub for two class sessions. Alana had explained to the class that she had to miss two sessions because her father was undergoing some serious surgery out of town, and Sue Sharp, her father's wife and teammate, had asked her to be on hand for the surgery and for a few days afterward. Actually, Alana insisted on going to the hospital, much to her father's surprise. Her prep class enthusiastically agreed, and Alana had picked one of the more mature (read, older) students to bring the scented markers, 24″ × 36″ newsprint, masking tape, and other materials they normally used.

Alana had also told Marie that the class was totally self-sufficient, knew the routines, such as having read the articles she and the class had agreed upon and knew what questions to ask to analyze the articles using the following Great Books format. This format entailed asking the questions: What were the main points the author(s) made? Were they valid? How could they be used today?

The format included using 24″ × 36″ newsprint with large markers to respond to these Great Books questions, working in small groups established the first day of the class. Roles were assigned so that a recorder recorded group ideas and someone else reported the group's thinking to the rest of the class. These roles rotated during the semester.

THE REALITY: A DASHED ASSUMPTION

Reaching the campus, Alana raced up the stairs and into the prep English area and found Marie in her office. Marie's response to the class was clear in her first comments, "Never have I ever met such a rude group in my teaching career!"

Blown away by such a comment, Alana was stunned.

Marie then added that by the second meeting a number of the students were absent, and that they were polite, but not warm and accepting. The class did not want to follow her directions, but pointed out that they knew the routines and were perfectly capable of carrying out the model that Ms. Michelle and they had designed and which they had so expertly implemented.

Alana expressed her amazement and thanked Marie for subbing. Well, Alana thought, the class certainly had the bit in their teeth. She had a hunch about the dynamics—but wanted to see how the class interpreted the scenario.

THE STORY UNFOLDS—WHO'S IN CHARGE? ISSUES OF TRUST, POWER, CONTROL, AUTONOMY, RESPECT, HIGH NEEDS FOR RECOGNITION—AND MASLOW'S HIERARCHY

As the students trickled into class, they warmly welcomed Alana, some with considerable delight, asked how her father and Sue did, and were quite pleased with the positive outcomes. They then made some comments that began to clear the air. They indicated that they were very friendly to Marie, that she was a very nice person, but that they could tell that Marie came in clearly not sure that they would or could do the work well. So, Marie wanted them to take notes from the reports, and when they indicated that each group's analysis was the notes, Marie did not seem to grasp such a procedure.

Someone opined that Marie appeared to have a personal agenda. They even offered someone in the class to transcribe the notes on a computer, bring in each group's response to the articles, and make enough copies for everyone (including Marie), but she still did not seem satisfied.

Distrust Leads to Resentment

The class felt they were not trusted, and became increasingly resentful. There was a lot more discussion, which led Alana to conclude that some even became highly offended—downright insulted! A number of people felt that Marie was interested in control, whereas Alana had no such needs and trusted the people to do their work, that Alana knew that they were responsible, trusted them completely—and treated them as adults in contrast to Marie's behavior.

"Well," Alana thought, "I've learned something—and so has the class."

Needs for Control and Recognition

Since many students usually hung around after class to schmooze, several noted that Marie seemed to want to be center stage, to direct things, and not let them operate in their constructivist manner. (Alana noted the comment and the use of the term, constructivism. They had gotten it—completely!) So some people got irritated and did not show up for the second class. But, Alana noted, everyone was here for this session, to which the response was, that she trusted them and liked them. Several pointed out that Alana's constructivist structure ensured that they and their autonomy were respected.

The consensus was that people were upset about a number of issues that Marie had brought into the classroom: her lack of trust in students, her unspoken and hidden needs for power and control, her hidden (to her) need for attention, and a grudging unwillingness to meet the students' expectations that their autonomy would be respected. They also saw clearly that Marie had great difficulty perceiving them as adults.

All of these issues offended every person in the class, particularly in comparison with Alana's attitudes and behavior.

SOME SURPRISING CONCLUSIONS: CONSTRUCTIVISM PLACES DEMANDS ON TEACHERS AS WELL AS STUDENTS

Students concluded that constructivist classes placed demands on teachers as well as students, and that teachers had to become introspective in analyzing their own needs for power and control and for recognition. They also stated that trust and respect seemed to be key attitudes in developing a healthy class atmosphere.

They noted that constructivism was not easy to pull off and that a lot of teachers needed what they laughingly called "attitude adjustments" to establish such an outcome. They also pointed out that Alana had been quite successful in establishing structures and processes to facilitate students' needs for autonomy, respect, and trust, among other needs. They further concluded that Marie did not meet Maslow's third and fourth Hierarchy of Needs—Social and Esteem Needs—and jokingly commented that that was a pretty good analysis for a bunch of people having to pass a prep class to take college English.

THE TEAM CONCLUDES

In Alana's later discussion with her teammates, Sue Sharp and Marc Douglas, they thought that the students were right on target, that teachers' unconscious needs surfaced in constructivism, as the students' analysis of the classroom processes revealed. The three also were impressed with the students' ability to use Maslow's Hierarchy in their analysis of themselves and the situation, and to analyze how a teacher with different, but not unusual needs, had been unable to utilize a carefully crafted classroom model and design. They also felt that perhaps Marie, with her needs, probably was even unable to perceive the constructivist model that Alana had worked so hard to design and implement. They felt that Alana should be pleased with the group's development intellectually, with their astute analysis of the complex situation—and with their increasing maturity.

"Well," summarized Alana, "I've been real successful. My model worked. But, just anyone cannot sub in a constructivist class, especially if they don't understand what it's all about. And not only that, they have to get their needs under control, or they won't be able to apply constructivist practices."

Her teammates echoed that conclusion.

QUESTIONS FOR THOUGHT—AND ACTION

1. What are the obstacles to team teaching or operating a successful learning community in any school, from K–12 to a community college to any college or university?
    A. Is a similar philosophy necessary to finesse unhealthy conflict, so that instructors will want to continue to team teach or work in the same learning community next year?
    B. Must the teachers have a similar philosophy? If so, based on what factors?
2. If a group of teachers decide to team teach or to work in a learning community, what policy should they develop about using a sub for a member who is absent for a short time? A long time?
3. We all know people who talk the talk. In a teaming or learning community, must everyone walk the walk for the enterprise to be successful?
4. What levels of maturity would you want in a team or learning community colleague? Would you use Maslow's Hierarchy of Needs to serve as a base? Gregorc's Personality Style Delineator?

SOURCES

Brooks, J. G. & Brooks, M. G. (1993). *In search of understanding: The case for the constructivist classroom*. Alexandria, VA: Association for Supervision and Curriculum Development.

Gregorc, A. F. (1982). *Gregorc Personality Style Delineator*. Columbia, CT: Gregorc Associates.

Gregorc, A. F. (1985). *Inside styles: Beyond the basics.* Maynard, MA: Gabriel Systems.

Maslow, A. H. (1954). *Motivation and personality* (2nd ed.). New York: Harper & Row.

Shapiro, A. (2000, May). Creating culture for a constructivist classroom and team. Tampa, FL: *Wingspan 13*(1), 5–8.

CHAPTER 3

Creative Classroom Management

Better Involve the Troops—Or, How I Managed to Teach Mechanical Drawing without Knowing Anything about It

The more actively students are involved in the learning process and take personal responsibility for their learning outcomes, the greater are the learning results.

—Todd M. Davis and Patricia Hillman
Murrell, *Turning Teaching into Learning*

MY CONFLICT—STARVING VERSUS WORKING AS A SUB

I had put myself through high school by working summers as a waiter in the resorts by Lake Michigan not too far from Chicago (and after school in other jobs, of course), and in college working as a union waiter in Chicago's famous Loop (read, downtown) hotels. In the summer, I worked at racetracks, country clubs, athletic clubs, and as many higher-end restaurants as I could. Now that I had finished my second degree, it was time to get a teaching job, but my mother was dying of cancer, which delayed my getting the thesis done. Too late to get a regular teaching job, I turned to subbing in Chicago's schools. But, what a comedown! My income virtually collapsed!

I was working every day, but I was down to one-third of my income from waitering. Fearful that I was going to starve to death, I accepted every subbing job, from teaching mathematics (my majors were in humanities and social sciences), to teaching any grade and any subject in any school from elementary to high school. One activity period I was supposed to teach knitting, another day German (my only German words were not appropriate for school), and another couple of days I taught in a school for bad boys (actually, they were pretty okay). After a couple of months of going from school to school, I managed to get a long stint teaching mechanical drawing in a vocational-technical high school in a decidedly inner-city location (that I discovered recently that my father had attended earlier in the century).

THE PROBLEM

The problem? I had never taken mechanical drawing—hadn't the slightest idea what to do.

But hunger overcame good sense, so off I went.

THE REALITY

The routine in the mechanical drawing classes was clear, as I found out by getting to the school before classes started, going into the lounge, and chatting up the teachers. The students would attempt to draw various pieces of equipment, often from photographs, or from actual pieces of equipment, and then come up to have their drawing evaluated by the teacher. The role of the teacher was to sit at his desk in the front of the room (notice that everyone thought that there was a front in the room) looking wise, or go around looking at the drawing and helping with constructive comments.

Sitting at the desk, or going around the room looking wise was out, since I had no idea what a good (or a bad) drawing looked like.

MY QUANDARY EXPOSED

Immediately, my ignorance was exposed by the first student to come up to have me evaluate his drawing. I looked at the drawing and picked up a ruler. The young man very kindly said, "Mr. Shapiro, here's how to hold the ruler." So, I stopped the class and said, "We have a problem. I don't know anything about mechanical drawing, but I sure want everyone to learn what we're supposed to. How can we figure out a way to make this class work?"

The class looked real interested, and asked about my background. So, I told them I could teach any of the social sciences or studies such as history, government, civics, and the like, but had no background in mechanical drawing.

SOLUTIONS

A Rotating Jury of Experts

We started coming up with ideas, some funny (just sit around and talk, to which one student said, "And how are we supposed to pass Mechanical Drawing 2 next year?") and some serious. The one that got everyone's attention was the idea of setting up a small jury of five or six students who would judge drawings and make constructive suggestions. Terms would be staggered, so that every week two would go off the committee and two others would join it for their three-week term. Talk about excitement! They were turned on!

One somewhat skeptical kid asked if we knew enough to pull this off. Interestingly, everyone said that we could learn, but that we'd have to hit the books.

Decisions

A whole bunch of questions poured out. Who would go on the jury first? How many would serve? (Five.) They decided that everyone should have a turn. How to choose? They decided to start alphabetically, which would be fair to everyone. And to be fair to the first two to go off, we added a week to their term.

They also wanted to know if they could work in teams on their drawing projects, to which I responded that that was their choice (but most did work alone). One student worried whether someone might let the others do the work and would goof off. The group indicated that if that happened, the pair or the group could change membership, and that no one would want to work with the goof-off. (Later, we developed a form to deal with that sort of scam [see figure 13.1].)

The Jury of Experts Functions

So, the jury of experts came up to the front, I shoved off to one side, and the work began. It was fascinating to listen to the young men talk about criteria for evaluating drawings. They decided that they needed to get at those first before they could evaluate anyone's work, so they discussed the criteria they needed to develop to do the job, and asked the class to pitch into the thinking. Soon everyone was heavily engaged in discussing the criteria to use in evaluating drawings. Various people looked up different books in the room, and some students even asked permission to go to the library to find other books and sources. They came back having checked out a number. (At the lunch period the librarian looked me up, and told me that she had been at the school for a long time, and no one had ever checked out any mechanical drawing books. She wanted to know what was going on, and, of course, I told her. She shook her head and said that she'd be glad to help us out any way she could.)

By the next day, every class had formed their expert jury, and the other students began bringing their drawings up for evaluation. Soon, people were discussing the criteria and their application, so that what had been formerly (as they told me) a very brief encounter with the teacher in which they were given a grade or a suggestion or two, now became a discussion, sometimes of considerable length. I never noticed any acrimony, just interest and different people coming up with different interpretations, or different viewpoints or perceptions.

Since I had started at the beginning of the week, by Thursday I began to realize that in every class students were almost all intensely interested, and even I could see that the quality had picked up considerably.

Going to the Library

By the next Monday, several of the youngsters had raided the public library for materials, such as journals on architecture, plans for construction, and the like. One had even gone to a construction site where his older brother was working on building an industrial building, and was able to get some sample discarded plans.

Since I was new to teaching, I asked a couple of much older men teachers (they must have been in their early forties) if it was okay to shop at a grocery not too far from the school. Both said that shopping there would put a human face on someone that most kids feel fairly remote from. They both felt that it was good idea, that if I was comfortable, I probably would see some of my kids working and could shmooze with them.

The two also warned me not to walk too close to the outside railing of the stairs until the students got to know me and like me. They told me that an angry student might decide accidentally, of course, to drop a stool on my head. Needless to say, I was very (no, extremely) careful to stay close to the inner stair wall, since I didn't feel that my mop of curly red hair was strong enough to cushion such an impact.

An Odd Problem (for Me)

One problem worried me, though. One rather heavy young man seemed to put his head on his drawing table and would doze at times. Of course, I took this a bit personally, wondering how I could reach him. A couple of the students on the jury picked up my concern, and quietly let me know that he did that in every class, and was really retarded. Of course, I thanked them, was relieved, but still concerned. I was able to talk with a guidance counselor, who looked up the student's record and let me know that he really should not have been in the program, since his mental level was too low to benefit from the class. The counselor said he'd look into the situation. I felt that the kid was not getting much out of the class, but seemed accepted.

PROGRESS

By the middle of the second week, the drawings were considerably—no, really—improved over those at the start of my stint. People were working hard, the air was serious, talk was informal, and no one seemed to kid around or get off task. I was having a pretty good time, and no one from the administration bothered me or told me to get lost.

By the beginning of the third week, a couple of the original jury moved off, and the next pair moved on. Earlier, they had cleared off the teacher's desk and had lots of magazines, drawings, updated evaluative criteria spread all over. I had cleared off, too, and was busy reading stuff, and was participating with the jury and with groups of kids on criteria for decisions about quality, next projects, and the like. Time on task was high, fooling around was low, almost nonexistent, interest was high.

By the middle of the third week, the teacher working on Mechanical Drawing 2 and 3 caught me in the cafeteria and asked what on earth was I doing with my classes. I couldn't figure out what he wanted, so I asked him what he meant. His reaction floored me. He said that the students in the classes I was teaching had gotten so far into their curriculum, that they were in danger of finishing Mechanical Drawing 1 even before the end of the semester, and some were actually close to the second-year material. He asked me to slow down whatever I was doing, so that he could teach the second year of the subject, and not have the kids too advanced.

My reaction in retrospect was somewhat hilarious, since I told him that since I really had no background in the field, I didn't know enough to slow things down.

Eventually, the administrators found a sub who had background and experience in the subject—so that my stint ended.

MUSINGS ABOUT OUR SUCCESS

Ownership, Respect, Trust, Delegating Responsibility

Somewhat later, I realized more clearly what had happened. The students were given ownership—and they ran with it. They also were treated with considerable respect—and reacted positively, since we were working on Maslow's fourth level in his Hierarchy of Human Needs, Esteem. As a consequence, they became highly motivated.

They also liked working in pairs or with slightly larger teams of three. Maslow's level three consists of meeting Social Needs. Both the jury of experts and the small teams met this level strongly. And look at the power of peer pressure—and respect that the students clearly realized.

Maslow's second Hierarchical Level, Safety, was in operation almost from the beginning. Early on we set up the norm that all evaluations would be serious and helpful. We agreed that no one wanted his feelings hurt in this process. So, we agreed that every evaluation would be serious and constructive—and not personal. Later, I realized we were being facilitative.

WHAT DID I LEARN?

- How to utilize the talent in the class
- Treated like adults, with respect, people would become highly motivated
- To trust kids
- To trust myself
- That working in teams and groups was a great idea—and, maybe—just maybe—was a way to organize my classes—any class
- That I had learned how to let go, and give students ownership and responsibility
- That feeling safe was essential—no, indispensable—to teach effectively
- That Maslow sure was useful (and that if I were imaginative, theory could be the basis of highly effective practice)
- That teaching sure was exciting, stimulating—and fun
- And I didn't starve

QUESTIONS FOR THOUGHT—AND PRACTICE

1. Since this was early in my teaching career, what suggestions could you make to improve the classroom operation?
   A. Note that I continued to follow the model used in the classroom that almost every person worked *alone*, everyone was treated as an *individual*. I hadn't realized yet that I was working in a sea of social systems. Would you suggest that things could be improved if the students could work together? In pairs? In larger teams, perhaps of four? Why not three, or five?

B. If so, how would you think about the composition of the membership of the jury of experts?

C. Should they be drawn from teams? If so, what criteria would you and the class develop to ensure fairness of participation?

D. What measures would you and the class take to make sure that everyone would have a chance to participate over the course of a year?

2. What other questions would you expect the students to raise? What would you?

SOURCES

Davis, T. M. & Murrell, P. H. (1993). *Turning teaching into learning: The role of student responsibility in the collegiate experience*. [Abstract]. Washington, DC: George Washington University, 1993 ASHE-ERIC Higher Education Reports; Report 8.

Johnson, D. W. & Johnson. R. T. (1987). *Learning together and alone: Cooperative, competitive, and individualistic learning* (2nd ed.). Englewood Cliffs, NJ: Prentice-Hall.

Kohn, A. (1987, October). It's hard to get left out of a pair. *Psychology Today*, 53–57.

Lewin, K. (1952). Group decision and social change. In G. E. Swanson & T. M. Newcomb (Eds.). *Readings in social psychology* (pp. 459–73). New York: Holt.

Maslow, A. H. (1954). *Motivation and personality* (2nd ed.). New York: Harper & Row.

CHAPTER 4

Crocodile Rock

Gateway to Emancipation and Empowerment

But first you gotta get their attention.

—Old farm joke

THE USUAL RITUAL DANCE

So there I was, teaching to a class who weren't there!
Actually, they were there—physically.
But, they weren't there—emotionally, or mentally.
What they were doing was acting out a ritual:
    You (the teacher) lecture.
    We pretend to listen.
    And, we take notes.
    We turn in a paper or two or more.
    We take *your* midterm.
    We take *your* final.
    You give us a grade.
    We don't learn a damned thing!
It was a ritual dance.
This drama played out the first time we met.
And the second.
I fumed.

WHAT TO DO?

So, I checked it out with my trusted advisor and counselor—my wife.

We came up with a creative idea. We decided I'd do a ritual dance, also—but, literally. I brought a tape of Elton John's *Crocodile Rock* to the third session. About a minute before the class was supposed to start (and by that time most people [about thirty-five or so] were there chatting happily—and loudly), I started playing the song on a boom box—loudly. And I boogied like I was having a lot of fun.

The noise of lots of people trying to talk over each other slowly subsided—at last a dead silence, while I chugged around.

I finally looked at the class.

"Oh, I brought the music for the dance."

Dead silence.

"Oh, since you're going through the motions, dancing through this class, I thought I'd bring the music."

Dead silence.

"Funny thing, I respect you more than you do. This class can help you become a much better administrator and supervisor—and the opportunity is being thrown away!"

Still dead quiet.

DEBBIE

[Debbie, a shy young woman who had been in a previous class takes up the events.]

Well, I knew he didn't like what was going on, but it was a large group and most didn't seem to take things (their professional education) seriously. The first night everyone agreed to the few norms suggested: Since we are adults, everyone is responsible for his or her own learning. The instructor brings in materials (and students were urged to do the same). We read the articles and/or chapters. Everyone participates in the small group discussion (we were organized into groups of about five to six people). About halfway through the class, we indicate what our most significant learnings were, using any format we choose. At the end do the same.

But, much to my surprise, it was pretty clear that most people were just going through the motions—as I've seen done in many classes, but not in his classes. I say much to my surprise because in the last class, we worked real hard, and learned how to implement theories, concepts, ideas to improve our professional practice.

But, I couldn't get my group to function, either, and to take responsibility. (At that time I was real shy and not assertive.)

I wondered what he would do. (Only later did *I* realize that I had a responsibility.)

CROCODILE ROCK

At first, when he started playing *Crocodile Rock*, I froze. I had no idea what he was up to. But, since people were talking and socializing, they really didn't pay much attention to what was going on for a while. Slowly, they began to hear the music, which was kind of loud.

And they slowly stopped talking and began to look around to see where the loud music was coming from. They began to see him, paying absolutely no attention to the class, just boogying around. People slowly fell silent, mystified. Because I knew him from another class, I knew he had a game (actually, a scenario) going on. But, I was mystified, also. Frankly, it was scary. I'd never seen any instructor do anything like this, or close to it. Later, I realized it was quite risky—for him. Finally, he looked up and told us essentially that we were engaged in a ritual dance. He then asked us how many of us respected most of our principals and vice principals.

No hands.

"How are you going to be any better than they are? They've taken some of these classes. By magic?

"How many of your administrators are really knowledgeable about administration, supervision, and designing world-class curriculum?"

A few responses—very few.

"Do you respect those?"

The few nodded.

"So, how are you supposed to earn the respect of your teachers once you become an administrator or supervisor?

"You, yourselves say that you have to be knowledgeable to earn any-one's respect. How are you going to do that? By just going through a ritual dance—and not coming to grips with the theories and ideas, first to learn them—and then to use them?"

DEBBIE

I finally got up my nerve to say, "People who've taken this class with Art tell me that we'll be able to pass the F.E.L.E. from it alone." [The F.E.L.E. is the Florida Educational Leadership Examination, which must be passed to become certified as an administrator or su-pervisor in the state.] He said, "Look, it's my job to make sure each one of us grasps the concepts, theories, frames of reference, ideas essential to become effective in our field—and, to use them in your professional practice. But, *you* have to become engaged. If you/we want to make a difference, if we want to earn respect, we simply have to become knowledgeable. Otherwise, we'll be like most of our principals and vice principals, which we ourselves say are not worth respecting."

And to me (Debbie), he said, "I appreciate your taking a risk to speak out.

"In short, knowledge, ideas, best practices empower us to function better, to make better decisions (decision making being the guts of ad-ministration and supervision), to be a lot better than most of adminis-trators for whom we have such contempt.

"So, what are we going to do? We have to read the writings. Then, ask, do I understand what the author(s) are saying?

"Next, are the ideas valid?

"How can I/we use them today in my/our practice?

"And—then—use them, daily."

DEBBIE, AGAIN

It was obvious.
We buckled down.
Had a terrific class.

all given respect for their contribution to the classroom and to education. With a safe environment in which to express their viewpoints and personalities, people become relatively comfortable and stress-free.

The Capstone—"Today, I Learned"—And, "My Most Significant Learnings"

Another device is to conclude every class session with the sentence stem, "Today, I learned . . ." with all responses valued and accepted. Generally, people learn that they are respected both personally and professionally.

The Self-Actualization level is difficult to define and, therefore, to assess. Thus, it is presumptuous to focus on achieving this level. It is noteworthy that rarely do people feel damaged or hurt. People feel that they have learned a great deal (as can be seen in the assignments, "My Most Significant Learnings in This Class . . ." collected at midterm and at the semester's end). Neither format nor content are specified, and within that open-ended design interesting productions develop, including video and audio tapes, songs constructed on key class themes, socio-dramas, skits, poems, newspaper formats, and normal papers. In order to point out the myriad outcomes people report, I publish examples for the class (while protecting anonymity) to illustrate the variety of significant learnings. Numbers of people have indicated that one or more of the theories, exercises, and insights from the class have changed their lives. Chapter 11 presents samples.

OTHER DESIGNED MOTIVATIONAL FACTORS

Chart Paper, Great Books–Type Questions

Other design elements related to the motivational domain include the use of 24″ × 36″ newsprint by the small groups to respond to the following questions adapted from the Great Books program regarding each reading the class confronts:

1. What does the author state? What are the major points, assumptions, beliefs?

2. Are they valid?

3. How can I/we utilize them today in my/our professional practice?

How We Multiply Roles and Design Our System So Groups Compare Each Other's Work

As the groups attack the task, several motivational phenomena emerge from this designed structure. One norm designed to increase the number of roles operating is that the person serving as the recorder of the group may not take the role of the reporter. Another phenomenon that develops is that people do the assigned readings. Not to do so in a small group invites censure by group members, since work is hampered if assigned articles and chapters have not been read.

As groups finish, they place their newsprint on the blackboards in front of the class. Inevitably, virtually all people in the other groups look at the work to compare and contrast it with their own product. This validates the value of students' input, fosters their continued contribution, and assures students of the worth of their work. The presentations of each small group to the total class expands discussion to a larger group process in which metacognition develops, a key transformation that the model structures. At the end of each class, the newsprint text is typed, and copies are given to each student at the following session.

INSTRUCTIONAL DELIVERY SYSTEMS/VEHICLES

A Constructivist, Interactive, Experiential Classroom

My approach is to design a constructivist classroom (Brooks & Brooks 1993), interactive in nature, based on experiential learning rather than a lecture format. The theoretical basis for these elements lies in the fields of education, social psychology, and group dynamics, including work by such theorists as John Dewey (1938), Kurt Lewin (1952), Herbert Thelen (1949), George Herbert Mead (1934), Peter Berger and Thomas Luckmann (1966), Jacqueline Brooks and Martin Brooks (1993), and others. Taking the viewpoints from Mead and Berger and Luckmann that the reality of the classroom is socially constructed, I design the structure to produce the greatest impact upon participants (in a classroom with small groups as the primary vehicle, every person participates, no matter how alienated or shy).

Creating the Culture and the Elements of the Constructivist Classroom

Previous comments on using Maslow indicate various components of the culture I design. Satisfying the Hierarchy of Needs comprises a series of such design elements. People who feel safe in a classroom tend to become more creative and express their viewpoints more readily than if they feel attacked and threatened. Similarly, people have clear social and self-esteem needs, which, when satisfied, result in a more productive classroom.

When a classroom break involves food provided by a small group, students also meet some of Maslow's needs and become more energized. (Obviously, in a K–12 classroom with a traditional structure this is usually not possible, although some teachers can pull off reward parties at times.) Additionally, some discover that often the break is not a break—it becomes a time when people informally discuss insights into ideas, generalizations, and articles on which groups have worked during the first half of the class.

Lewin and the Value of the Small Group

Lewin's work (1952) was the basis for my decision to use the small group as the organizing vehicle for the classroom. Lewin's experiments demonstrated that decisions to change attitudes and behavior are considerably more pronounced when participants make them *publicly* in a small group. Additionally, a much larger number of people will honor a commitment they make publicly in a small group more frequently than they will from being urged to change their behavior in a lecture. Lewin next experimented by comparing two treatments with new mothers in terms of feeding their newborns orange juice and cod liver oil. The first treatment was to have a nutritionist talk to each mother on a one-to-one basis to instruct them to feed their babies the two healthy foods. The second treatment was to ask another group to make a commitment publicly in a small group to use the orange juice and cod liver

oil. The latter was far more successful in its impact on the women's behavior in carrying out their commitment.

Thelen's Theory of Least Group Size

Another design element rests on the value of developing different
roles in small groups to maximize participation and buy-in. Thus, Thelen's work (1949) on the Principle of Least Group Size becomes relevant. Thelen noted that work groups generally should not exceed seven
members in order to avoid duplication of roles. Thus, regardless of how
large the class is, we operate with small groups. Add people to the
class, make a new group (but be sure to mix the newbies into existing
groups).

Developing More Norms

Another norm (read, custom) that develops is that input from class
members (due to their diverse backgrounds) often leads to enhanced results. Additionally, with focused structuring, the class begins to grasp
the idea that they can establish the norms and the culture of this class,
as well as that of their own classes and organizations. Group bonding
is facilitated by using small groups as the mechanism for instruction.
The class often becomes a sounding board and a support group to improve understanding of and use of the concepts and theories in the students' professional practice and personal lives.

My approach may be summarized in part by Todd Davis and Patricia Murrell's (1993) statement: "What the recent research on student
learning has concluded is that the more actively students are involved
in the learning process and take personal responsibility for their learning outcomes, the greater are the learning results."

An Emergent Curriculum as an Element

After taking an appropriate amount of time at the first meeting for introductions to enable people to feel welcome and comfortable, I ask what
participants want to learn in this particular class. They respond first on paper individually, then in small groups on newsprint, which they then pre-

sent to the entire class, where we compare and contrast each group's product. After the end of the first class, the students' "What Do We Want to Learn" is printed and then handed out at the beginning of the second class.

The syllabus I have previously drawn up is given to students after they indicate their interests and needs. My syllabus contains a rationale, an overview including purposes of the course, my assumptions, and tentative objectives and concepts. While student responses are quite similar to the syllabus, the door is kept open to bring in resources in which students indicate an interest as the class develops, in addition to the selected readings I have provided. Thus, each class generates its own curriculum based on the ongoing development of their needs and interests. At its best, it is teaching to the moment.

Removing Fear and Threat

Another design element in the classroom culture is focused on removing fear and threat. To do that, we make a contract in which students agree to read all materials and to participate. Since some people are shy, participating in the small group is a key process. Interestingly, in every class people state strongly and with some surprise that they learn more with these norms since they do not feel threatened or forced and since they participate in the design of the class and of the curriculum. People often integrate some of these practices into their own classrooms with highly positive results. They note that their classrooms change significantly as they adopt key elements from these design elements.

Structure, Structure, Oh, Where Is the Structure?
(A Kingdom for Some Structure)

Because my approach is theoretical and conceptual, and is relatively informal, some students who are rigid in the beginning (Gregorc's CS personality, or the Myers-Briggs ISTJ) may not perceive the underlying conceptual structure and so may feel uncertain and insecure in the process. Therefore, at the beginning of every class we develop an agenda based on the previous week's assignments. When students make inquiries about concepts/problems, appropriate articles/materials are provided on the requested topic. In each semester, therefore, an emergent curriculum evolves. In order to sensitize the students early to the conceptual structure, I ask if a structure exists, and if so, what is its nature. Of course, I never indicate my own perceptions.

Shticks

Actually, I deny that there is a structure at all. People who are intuitive soon realize that a game is going on. What is a shtick? A game, an act, with a good-natured, fun aspect to it. Comedian Rodney Dangerfield used just such a shtick when he joked, "I don't get no respect."

Another shtick that's fun to claim is that the class has no hidden curriculum. Again, those with intuition catch on and enjoy it when the people who are Concrete Sequential (CS) (usually engineers, draftsmen, bookkeepers who like details and facts, are highly organized, always on time, and not intuitive) are unsure.

More Design Elements: Bloom's Taxonomy

Bloom's Taxonomy provides another element in the construction of the classroom. My intent is to model working at the higher cognitive levels. Therefore, the design element sentence stem "Today, I learned . . ." and the requirement to turn in "My Most Significant Learnings in This Class . . ." at midterm and at the end, emphasize the higher cognitive levels (application, analysis [compare and contrast], synthesis [develop a plan], and evaluation). Interestingly, this design element structures a focus on continual analysis and evaluation and leads to altering the curriculum should the students and the instructor feel the need. When appropriate, a short lecturette format may be utilized.

I also tend to utilize personality and learning style instruments such as the Gregorc Personality Style Delineator in classes when students indicate an interest, and where they are appropriate to the purpose of the course. The impact of learning about their own and others' styles, and accepting and respecting the differences of others' personality and learning styles can be profound. They learn that people with different styles are not behaving to annoy them, but that they are acting normally for that personality style. An opportunity is provided to examine the impact of their learning styles on their teaching styles, and can lead both to personal and professional change. In short, this can provide an opportunity to make different choices based on their new knowledge and to accommodate others' learning styles.

SUMMARY

This theoretically and conceptually based design, a carefully created constructivist classroom, learner- and problem-centered, discovery-based, experiential and small group–based, is focused on both content and process. Its many levels of strategies are carefully planned. Theoretically based content is structured to maximize its usefulness for professional practice. Assignments are often made to facilitate students to utilize the concepts and theories in practice, to elicit results from the class, and to develop suggestions to improve understanding and use of the concepts and theories. I model the design elements (at first hidden from the students) for the students to discover and then to use in their own professional practice.[1]

NOTE

1. Based on an unpublished paper "Creating Culture for a Constructivist Classroom" (Shapiro 1995), submitted for the Teacher Incentive Program, State of Florida. Published by Society for Applied Anthropology (SfAA) in *Global–Local Articulations* (Shapiro 1996), and *Wingspan* (Shapiro 2000). See Sources.

QUESTIONS FOR IMPROVED PRACTICE

1. Which of these elements would you think would be the first you would choose if you decided to move into a partial constructivist model?
    A. How would you increase safety needs? Does establishing the norm of confidentiality in the class facilitate this? What else can you think of?
    B. How about meeting social needs? Would trying to work in small groups facilitate this?
    C. If you do, would you work with the class about setting ground rules before breaking into groups?

2. Would you decide about what expectations of behavior (norms) and task outcomes are important before you start forming groups?
   A. What about who goes into groups? Can friends?
   B. What about the permanence of groups? Can people move around? How will this affect their security and the quality of the work?
3. What control needs do you have? (We have to be honest with ourselves—the people in the class will pick this up quickly [as they did with Marie Cross in chapter 2 "The Constructivist Teacher: When a Substitute Teaches Your Class (and Hasn't a Clue)"].)
4. What about meeting esteem needs? What can you do to avoid offensive criticism? Does any criticism hurt feelings? How can you and the class or team or school be supportive, even of ideas that are off the mark? Does treating every contribution as valuable help?
5. Have you thought about how you and the class can establish constructive norms? If you're an administrator, how can you help establish this for the total faculty? For a department, grade level, or administrative unit?
6. How can you help remove fear and threats?
   A. Would people feel comfortable revealing themselves? Do you want this? Are you comfortable with people revealing things about themselves. Are you comfortable revealing yourself? What first steps can be undertaken to facilitate people revealing themselves? Does it start with you?
7. How can unnecessary structure, rules, and regs be removed?
8. Are you comfortable in expanding the decision-making role of students and/or faculty? If not, why not? If so, how can this be facilitated?
9. Does a constructivist model attract you—or, scare you? If so, why? (Growth takes risks.)
   A. Can you take risks? If you cannot, neither will your students, or your faculty.
10. How will you handle the conflict that normally occurs among groups?
11. When you look at a class, a faculty, any group, do you see individuals—or, do you see social systems?
12. Can you think of any more questions I missed?

APPENDIX 5A

CONSTRUCTIVIST LEADER'S MENTAL CHECKLIST

The following sections have been designed to assess one's readiness to participate in a group as a constructivist leader. The checklist was developed to assist the constructivist leader in answering the question, "Am I ready to facilitate group process?"

Component One: Personal Readiness of the Facilitator

1. I have developed an understanding of my personality characteristics as well as my typical interaction or communication style in groups.
2. I have developed an understanding of others' personality and communication styles.
3. I accept and respect other personality styles.
4. I understand how to communicate with a variety of personality styles.
5. I am prepared to set the tone for effective group process by taking on the role of a facilitator even if my tendency to teach or lead is to do so in a role other than facilitator (e.g., more directive).
6. I understand that I must maintain an ongoing awareness of my own beliefs and values and use this self-awareness to promote an environment conducive to learning for individuals with similar beliefs and values as well as those with differing beliefs and values.
7. I understand my own learning style as well other learning styles.
8. I understand and am prepared to teach people with different learning styles.
9. I am prepared to model the essential underpinnings of Constructivist Leadership.
10. I am prepared to observe group process closely and to make decisions based on the observations to facilitate optimal group functioning.

Component Two: Structuring the Environment

1. The room design is such that it facilitates structuring for group process (adequate lighting, ability to control temperature, flexibility to arrange room, can accommodate workgroups).
2. There are enough tables and chairs to arrange participants into small work groups (maximum of seven members per group).
3. Chairs are strategically placed near the various workgroups to allow the facilitator easy access to individual groups.
4. An area is made available for the presentation of food and beverages.
5. 24″ × 36″ newsprint and writing implements are available.
6. There are plenty of nametags or name cards.
7. Relevant, interest-driven reading materials have been copied for distribution.

Component Three: Setting the Tone

1. Creating a Safe Learning Environment:
   - Group members are asked to learn about a person in close proximity
   - Ample time is afforded for introductions (introduction of another group member and self-introductions) during the first two meetings
   - Confidentiality is established (members are asked to agree that "it is safe to speak in the group" because "what is said in the group, stays in the group")
   - The facilitator encourages and supports risk-taking and sharing of personal information
   - The facilitator makes it known that "all contributions will be valued"
   - The facilitator models acceptance, respect, and validation of individuals and varying viewpoints
   - Although high expectations and a sense of personal responsibility are clearly communicated, anxiety is reduced through acceptance of situations impeding group attendance and timely arrival to the group

- Through a collaborative discussion of evaluation methods and ownership for learning, the learning environment becomes less threatening
- Refreshment breaks allow for informal sharing of information, development of more intimate relationships, and the establishment of a safe community

2. Addressing Social Needs:
   - Participants are arranged in small work groups
   - Small and large group interaction/discussion is emphasized
   - A list of names, phone numbers, and addresses is compiled and distributed to group members to promote networking during and after group sessions (The facilitator's information is included in the same format and is placed in alphabetical order, within the list of group members, to establish and promote balanced power.)
   - It is made clear that refreshment breaks, in part, provide a more relaxed atmosphere for socialization and "bonding" of group members

3. Fostering Motivation (Making It Relevant):
   - The facilitator asks key questions to promote input and shared decision making regarding arrival and dismissal time, assessment format, relevant content, and group goals
   - The facilitator accepts and manages student responses to develop a sense of ownership by group members
   - Individuals are asked to write their goals/objectives for the class
   - The facilitator indicates that all contributions are valuable and should not be dismissed
   - Groups are requested to compile the individual goals on newsprint
   - Group goals are posted, presented, discussed
   - The facilitator compares and contrasts goals and points out the similarities of groups as well as the diversity and creativity both within and across groups
   - Group goals are compiled and distributed at the next meeting
   - The compiled list of goals is used to develop a syllabus that best meets the unique needs and interests of the group

- As group members raise questions, the questions are used to guide group discussion and when consistent with the goal of the group, are used to guide the selection of relevant reading material
- Group members are told that they are responsible for their learning
- The routine participation in workgroups establishes the implicit norm for advanced preparation of the individual prior to meaningful engagement in group activities
- Individuals are given choices about the format and content of the midterm and final and are told that they are responsible for demonstrating their "most significant learnings in the class" either individually or with a group

4. Satisfying Esteem Needs:
   - Group members are given multiple opportunities to express ideas
   - The facilitator communicates that varying viewpoints are encouraged, accepted, and valued
   - Contributions are honored by connecting ideas shared in class with relevant content information
   - Sharing of ideas and relevant personal information is promoted by thanking individuals for sharing and by providing positive feedback when contributions are made
   - A constructive versus destructive criticism norm is encouraged, modeled, and reinforced
   - Formal recognition (positive feedback and applause) is provided for each small-group contribution

5. Meeting Physiological Needs:
   - A refreshment break is scheduled
   - When possible, groups are scheduled at an optimal and convenient time for learning/working
   - Movement and group interaction are incorporated to reduce restlessness, inattention, and physical discomfort

Component Four: Instructional Format
1. An agenda is posted each session and at a minimum, includes information to be covered, group work time, group

presentation and discussion, the refreshment break, and the phrase, "Today I learned . . ."

2. Group-generated goals and areas of interest expressed by group members guide the topics selected for coverage in the group.

3. The facilitator selects readings relevant to the goal of the group and based on the interests expressed by group members during the previous meeting.

4. Individuals are assigned tasks (e.g., reading) either in class or before class to prepare for group work.

5. Individuals are constantly encouraged to watch group dynamics, to relate observations to key concepts covered in the course, and to develop an awareness of the interrelationship between leadership and group behavior.

6. Individuals and groups engage in a variety tasks to promote self-awareness.

7. The following questions (adapted from the Great Books program) are posted:
   • What does the author state?
   • What are the major points, assumptions, and beliefs?
   • Are they valid?
   • How can we utilize them today in our professional practice?

8. Individuals are arranged in small (no more than seven members) work groups.

9. Work groups discuss and organize responses to the posted questions.

10. Work groups present their responses to the entire group.

11. Individuals then have the opportunity to comment on or question information presented by work groups.

12. The facilitator interjects as necessary to make salient key points, to link newly introduced concepts to previously covered concepts, and to prime group members for future learning experiences.

13. The facilitator consistently encourages and models acceptance of the contributions.

14. The facilitator acknowledges the difficult nature of sharing information and thanks individuals for sharing feedback, insight, and relevant personal experiences.

15. Group members are given ample time to eat and to engage in conversation during a refreshment break.
16. Group members are invited to use the phrase, "Today I learned . . . " to articulate a concept or insight they have gained from that particular group experience.
17. When applicable, the group is assigned a task to prepare for the next session.
18. Understanding and application of theory, activities and insights is facilitated by:
    - Small- and large-group participation and discussion
    - Opportunities to share what has been learned using the sentence stem "Today, I learned . . ."
    - Observation and discussion of group process
    - Observation and discussion of facilitator's actions and comments (modeling)
    - Tasks designed to increase self-awareness
    - Engagement in the midterm and final projects emphasizing one's "most significant learnings"

Component Five: Monitoring Group Process (Watch & Listen)
1. Is the environment safe and relatively stress free?
    - When asked about the norms of the group, do group members express that they feel comfortable discussing opinions, asking questions, sharing personal information and giving/receiving feedback?
    - Are group members demonstrating a sense of safety by revealing personal information, asking questions, taking risks, expressing opinions and giving/receiving feedback?
2. Are relationships developing?
    - Do individuals appear to be engaged and interacting with one another in a comfortable manner during (small-group) work sessions?
    - Do individuals appear to be engaged and interacting with one another in a comfortable manner during the refreshment break?
3. Are individuals accepting responsibility for their learning?
    - When asked about the norms of the group, do group members state that individuals are responsible for their own learning?

- As the facilitator moves about the group, does it appear that group members are prepared and contributing to the group process?
- If issues arise within the group, does the facilitator encourage self-correction among group members?
- Are roles developing as indicated by the actions of the individuals within groups (e.g., engagement in discussion, rotation of responsibilities for writing, and presentation of ideas to the entire group)?
- Do individuals ask and answer questions?
- Do individuals produce a thoughtful midterm and final project reflecting active participation in the learning process?

4. Are individuals and work groups demonstrating knowledge as indicated by:
   - Discussions in work groups
   - Listening and participation in small and large groups
   - Observations of individuals and group dynamics
   - Content of work group presentations
   - Large group discussions
   - Individual questions and comments
   - Responses associated with the sentence stem of "Today I learned . . ."
   - Content of presentations of "most significant learnings" projects

Note: Checklist developed by Andrea M. Mowatt, Ed.S., and by Amelia D. VanName, Ed.S., in 2002. The checklist reflects concepts published by Dr. Shapiro and addressed in the course.

SOURCES

Berger, P. L. & Luckmann, T. (1966). *The social construction of reality*. Garden City, NY: Doubleday.

Bloom, B. (1956). *Taxonomy of educational objectives*. New York: David McKay.

Brooks, M. G. & Brooks, J. G. (1993). *In search of understanding: The case for the constructivist classroom*. Alexandria, VA: Association for Supervision and Curriculum Development (ASCD).

Davis, T. M. & Murrell, P. H. (1993). *Turning teaching into learning: The role of student responsibility in the collegiate experience.* [Abstract]. Washington, DC: George Washington University. 1993 ASHE-ERIC Higher Education Reports; Report 8.

Deming, G. E. (1982). *Quality, productivity, and competitive position.* Cambridge: Massachusetts Institute of Technology, Center for Advanced Engineering Study.

Dewey, J. (1938). *Experience and education.* New York: Macmillan.

Ericson, E. H. (1968). *Identity: Youth and crisis.* New York: Norton.

Goffman, E. (1967). *Interaction ritual: Essays in face-to-face behavior.* Chicago: Aldine Publishing.

Goodlad, J. (1984). *A place called school.* New York: McGraw-Hill.

Gregorc, A. F. (1982). *The Gregorc Personality Style Delineator.* Columbia, CT: Gregorc Associates.

Herzberg, F. (1966). *Work and the nature of man.* Cleveland: World Publishing.

Johnson, D. W. & Johnson, R. T. (1984). *Circles of learning: Cooperation in the classroom.* Alexandria, VA: ASCD.

Kroeber, A. & Kluckholm, C. (1952). *Culture: A critical review of concepts and definitions.* Cambridge, MA: Harvard University Press.

Lewin, K. (1952). Group decision and social change. In G. E. Swanson & T. M. Newcomb (Eds.). *Readings in social psychology* (pp. 459–73). New York: Holt.

Linton, R. (1955). *The tree of culture.* New York: Vintage Books.

Maslow, A. (1954). *Motivation and personality.* New York: Harper & Row.

Mead, G. H. (1934). *Mind, self, and society.* Chicago: University of Chicago Press.

Myers, I. B. (1962). *The Myers-Briggs type indicator.* Palo Alto, CA: Consulting Psychologist Press.

Shapiro, A. S. (1995). *Creating culture for a constructivist classroom.* Teacher Incentive Program, State of Florida.

Shapiro, A. S. (1996). Creating the culture of constructivist classrooms in public and private schools. In *Global–Local Articulations.* The Society for Applied Anthropology (SfAA), 1996 Annual International Conference, Baltimore, MD.

Shapiro, A. S. (2000, May). Creating culture for a constructivist classroom and team. *Wingspan 13*(1), 5–8.

Thelen, H. A. (1949, March). Group dynamics in instruction: The principle of least group size. *School Review,* 139–148.

Tyler, R. (1949). *Basic principles of curriculum and instruction.* Chicago: University of Chicago Press.

CHAPTER 6

My Development as a Constructivist Teacher

R. D. Nordgren, Ph.D.

Life can only be understood backwards,
But it must be lived forwards.

—Søren Kierkegaard

MY (VERY) SLOW BEGINNINGS

It was not until I worked with student teachers at a professional development school that I realized that my methods of teaching were greatly different from most others. Having student teachers allowed me to leave my classroom periodically to visit other teachers and to discuss with my interns their experiences visiting other classrooms. My style of being a facilitator of learning rather than a dispenser of knowledge was not widespread among my colleagues at a middle school that was in partnership with a local university. Despite this partnership, my colleagues' classrooms did not reflect what I had learned at the university as effective learning. This explained why university professors kept sending visitors and interns to me. I knew it was not because I was the most dynamic teacher at my school. In fact, I was far from it. Some of my eighth-grade students called me "Mr. Monotone" or "Mr. Game Show Voice," the latter referring to my attempts to alleviate the monotone problem.

My style developed over a period of years, in small but significant increments. It was not until the end of my doctoral studies that I realized there was a name for my methods of teaching and my educational philosophy: constructivist. My major professor had recently published a book on the subject (Shapiro 2000) and, although I had modeled my style in part after him, I was not aware that the term constructivist existed.

SOCIALIZING US NEWBIES: TO GO FORTH TIMIDLY— AND STAY THE SAME

My student teacher internship was miserable; my supervising teacher worked laboriously at squeezing out, then destroying everything I had learned at the university about effective teaching methods. She would not allow me to do anything but "stand and deliver" the curriculum that she and the district had developed. My only consolation was knowing that someday I would have my own classroom where I could do what I wanted.

Once I had my first teaching job, I spent the first two years trying to fit in with the other English teachers at my new high school (VanMaanen & Schein 1976). In the beginning of the year, we would meet to decide what novels each English level would read so that there would be no overlapping of content. We certainly did not want the same novel or poem being taught twice! Our objective was to cover the curriculum, not for students to gain deep understandings about literature and writing.

All four of us new English teachers met with the veteran teachers to see how our department preferred we *presented* the subject matter. We rookies surely did not want to "rock the boat" for fear of 1) being ostracized by our peers, and more important, 2) not passing our beginning teacher program by the administrator in charge of us that first year. Consequently, my classroom looked like the other eighteen English teachers' classrooms in the school: stand and deliver, keep the students silent so as not to bother the room next door.

As new schools opened in our district, my position was cut, causing me to be placed in a new middle school. This was where I had wanted to be in the first place. I always believed that pre-adolescents would better accept my corny humor. The summer before starting at the middle school, the district required those of us who were new middle school teachers to be trained to teach at that level. "What did I need to know about these kids?" I asked myself. They were just a little less knowledgeable than the high school students. I would simply "dumb down" my lesson plans.

AWAKENINGS

At the training, we wore funny hats, sang songs, and essentially had fun. Another high school teacher said to me during a break in our week-long training, "I don't know what this has to do with training us for the middle school, but if they're willing to pay me a week's salary to be silly, I won't complain." It was only after a semester with my eighth graders did I realize why we were asked to wear hats and sing songs: middle school students did "goofy" things; therefore, we teachers needed to not take ourselves so seriously. I found that this allowed me to build relationships with my students, relationships that enabled me to understand their learning needs better. This was my first step to becoming a constructivist teacher: finding and attempting to meet individual student's needs through relationship building.

Three Steps

Between semesters of my first year at the middle school, I read Nancy Atwell's *In the Middle* that advocated the use of reading and writing workshops. In these workshops, students were allowed to read and write anything of their choice. This, Atwell proclaimed, motivated students to read and write. The next year, I implemented the workshops and the students did indeed read more and write more often. Allowing students to make their own choices about their learning was the next step in my development as a constructivist teacher.

With students reading and writing on their own, I promised that I would take no more than ten minutes at the beginning of each class for a mini-lesson on grammar, punctuation, or spelling. The rest of the fifty-five-minute class would be spent facilitating the learning of students. My role changed from knowledge dispenser, a role that I had detested, to that of facilitator of learning.

This changing role was step three in becoming a constructivist educator. Students were not objects whose heads could be opened and into which knowledge could be poured. I found that being the "guide on the side" rather than the "sage on stage" allowed me to become closer with each child, becoming more of a mentor and coach, motivating them individually to do their best work. I would no longer be the center of the classroom; I wanted visitors in my class to come in and quickly see that students were the focus of the class, not I.

Still Another Step

About that time, I began taking classes toward a master's degree in educational leadership. I wanted to go into administration some day so that I could have an influence in changing whole schools into following my quickly developing philosophy of teaching, which stressed student choice and child-centeredness. One of my professors, who would eventually be my major professor in my doctoral studies, was a true constructivist and taught his master's courses in curriculum in this manner. On the first day of class, he asked us what it was we wanted to learn and how we wanted to structure the class. I was not too surprised that this tactic worked with graduate students (although most were startled), but could it work with my middle school students? I decided to try.

A Bold Step

In my third year at the middle school, I had my 160 seventh graders decide on the first day what it was they wanted to learn and how the class was to be structured. Knowing that a large percentage of students like predictability (Myers 1997), I had a carefully planned syllabus that I had given each parent who attended registration the week before school started. It specified what the students would be learning and doing during each of the thirty-eight weeks of the school year. This syllabus was essentially "for show." I was certain that my administration and the parents of the very conservative community that fed our middle school would not readily accept my new approach to teaching and learning.

Many of the students had seen the well-planned syllabus on that first day, probably expecting me to be very rigid, someone who would operate a tightly structured class. When I asked them what they wanted to learn, most, like the grad students, did not know how to respond. Was this the guy who wrote such a detailed four-page syllabus? I had to use all my powers of facilitation to drive out fear and coax them to open up to the point where each of the small groups could write their ideas of what they wanted to learn on the chart paper provided. I had also suggested that the students select their own groups, something they had obviously not been allowed to do in the past, as evidenced by the puzzled looks on their faces when asked to break into groups.

PAPERING THE WALLS

The initial results of these groups' work was a bit disappointing. Many students had said they wanted to do nothing, or wanted nothing but free time. Others were aware of my reading and writing workshops and liked the idea of being able to read what they wanted and write about whatever they desired. They wanted me to follow the syllabus I had developed. Each group had taped their chart paper onto the walls. At the end of my fifth class that first day, I had dozens of pieces of chart paper on the walls, so much so that my classroom rules were covered.

It was mandatory in our district that teachers post classroom rules, so I was a bit worried that an administrator might come by and not see these rules, rules I had quickly written knowing full well that I would change them as soon as the students had a chance to develop their own. I made sure that the next day would be spent having the students devise their own rules, leaving the "What I want to learn this year" chart papers as work in progress.

Students Making Classroom Rules

If you have never had students make the classroom rules, you are in for quite a surprise. They are much more severe in their choice of consequences for inappropriate behavior than an adult ever would be. I had to guide the students toward a rational set of rules; in the end, simplifying them to one just rule after assimilating all five classes' ideas.

"Respect others' right to learn" was all that was required from the students and it was agreed on the third day that when someone broke that rule, the class would have input on what should happen to the child. Severe cases, the students agreed, would be my problem. I said that I would call parents as part of my duty (I had by then surmised that writing an office referral only told the students that I was incapable of facilitating my own classes, thus, losing their respect). This simple system worked. Students were kept on task by peer pressure and by the fact that they were allowed to talk freely but quietly during class time.

Some Initial Results

As can be expected, the conversations of the students often were not about class work. Usually, I allowed this to happen and believed that they had a need to be social and would take their social time whether or not I allowed it to happen. I decided not to fight it and allow socialization to take place—as long as it did not interfere with others' right to learn. Rarely did an off-task conversation last long, as students would go back to what they were doing after a few seconds or minutes, without my admonishing them. I attributed this in part to my allowing them to be engaged actively in meaningful learning of their choice.

By the fourth day, I still had not resolved the problem of what we were to learn that year. Sure, they could follow my syllabus, but that was not developed by them; thus, they had no ownership, which could possibly keeping them from staying motivated throughout the year (Gott, Lesgold & Kane 1996; Glasser 1998). As most students liked the concept of reading and writing workshops, I went ahead with my plans, with one caveat: we would revisit the syllabus periodically to decide democratically if we should continue with it.

The students did not get tired of the syllabus, perhaps because it was based on student choice. They, of course, had the choice of what to read and write during the workshops, but at the end of each nine-week quarter, we would move into a literature unit. These units were two weeks long, centered on a theme such as "conflict," and required that the students create a project of their choice that was to represent their learning. I suggested collaborative projects, but some chose to create their own. Even those who worked on individual projects spent at least some time working with others on theirs or others' projects. As in the writing and reading workshops, I limited my direct instruction to no more than ten minutes per class period, not wanting to take away from their project time.

A MAJOR CAREER MOVE—AND UNHAPPY FINDINGS ABOUT TEACHING AND ADMINISTRATIVE PRACTICES

After six years in the classroom, I moved on to administration where I found that few constructivist teachers existed in the four different districts in which I worked. I also found that the official state teacher evaluation instrument was not appropriate for a teacher whose role was that of facilitator rather than knowledge dispenser. In fact, the first year I taught in the middle school, my class was using cooperative learning when an administrator came in for my annual observation using the state's instrument. She left after only a few minutes telling me later that she would come back when I was teaching. I gave her a "dog-and-pony" show a few days later with students taking notes from the overhead while I lectured. I alerted the students of the observation and that my teaching style would change back the next day. They were relieved.

As an administrator, I became frustrated with the high percentage of teachers who exclusively used direct instruction followed by seatwork. I was even more frustrated that this practice was rewarded by administrators and some school districts as this was deemed a good way to control students. At one high school where I was an assistant principal, I looked into the classrooms of every teacher during the middle of a randomly selected class period. Not surprisingly, I found that, not counting music, drama, or physical education, seventy-five teachers were either lecturing or having the students do individual seatwork, eight were conducting laboratories (either science or computers), and only two had students working collaboratively in groups. And this was a school with a very high reputation for academic excellence (it also served a very high socioeconomic population of students).

SOME INTROSPECTION—AND SOME CONCLUSIONS

My development into a constructivist educator was slow and came about mostly because I was willing to be different from my peers, to take risks. I also can attribute this development to my willingness to increase my effectiveness in the classroom, not being satisfied to merely making my life as a teacher as comfortable as possible. I knew that the traditional model of teaching with the teacher as knowledge dispenser was not effective, because I trusted the prevalent research that espoused that the teacher be a facilitator of learning.

As I gave my students more opportunities to make choices, the learning taking place in my classroom became more meaningful to them, and the classroom became a democracy rather than the usual autocracy where control of students is key. My constructivist methods, learning environments, and philosophy may have prepared my students better to live in a democracy that depends on citizens who make good choices for themselves and for society.

QUESTIONS

1. Why was Dr. Nordgren so unaware that his teaching approach deviated from his peers?
2. Why did it take so long for him to become a constructivist teacher?
   A. Did he have any role models?
   B. Is the pressure to be the same as everyone else present in every organization?
   C. What strategies can we develop to avoid arousing antagonism?
3. Can we find other brave souls to join together into a social system to protect ourselves?
4. What role models would you use in in-service programs to facilitate people moving into constructivist teaching?
   A. With which social systems would you start?
5. Note that Dr. Nordgren had no support in his efforts to become a better teacher. His development depended upon accidental events external to him. But, he prevailed. Why?
   A. What support systems would you establish to facilitate a planned outcome?
6. How comfortable are you in inviting classes to participate in making the rules (norms)?
   A. Why? If not, is it your need for control? Is it lack of trust of the good sense of the students in your class?
   B. But, if you are comfortable, why is this? What is your level of trust in people? What was R.D.'s? Did his change?
7. What further questions would you ask?

SOURCES

Atwell, N. (1987) *In the middle: Writing, reading, and learning with adolescents.* Upper Montclair, NJ: Bynton/Cook.

Glasser, W. (1998). *Choice theory in the classroom.* New York: Harper Perennial.

Gott, S. P., Lesgold, A., & Kane, R. S. (1996). Tutoring for transfer of technical competence. In B. G. Wilson (Ed.). *Constructivist learning environments: Case studies in instructional design.* Englewood Cliffs, NJ: Educational Technology.

Kiersey, D. & Bates, M. (1984*). Please understand me: Character and temperament types.* Delmar, CA: Promethius Nemesis.

Myers, I. B. (1995). *Gifts differing: Understanding personality types.* Palo Alto, CA: Davies-Black.

Shapiro, A. S. (2000). *Leadership for constructivist schools.* Lanham, MD: Scarecrow.

VanMaanen, J. & Schein, E. H. (1976). *Organizational careers: Some new perspectives.* London: Wiley.

CHAPTER 7

Leprechauns in the Classroom

Who knows, they may even catch a leprechaun.

—Jean Kern

THE PROJECT

Jean Kern, who later became both a former second-grade teacher and Peace Corps worker, wanted to stimulate some action and excitement in her second-grade class. Having made the journey from using a model of tight control and trying to dominate the teaching/learning process, she knew that the kids both liked doing things (called "active learning" these days), and learned much better by being actively involved in their learning than when she controlled (or tried to control) everything in the classroom.

For this project Jean decided to utilize Whitehead's three phases of lesson planning to organize the enterprise: Romance, Precision, and Generalization.

To be sure, however, Whitehead noted that one can design lessons so that we can experience Romance in both other phases. Similarly, lessons can be developed in which Precision is present in the other two phases, as well as Generalization in the Romance and Precision stages of the lessons. Obviously, Jean did exactly that.

GETTING STARTED: THE ROMANCE—STIMULATING INTEREST AND EXCITEMENT

What to do to jazz up St. Patrick's Day? And to make it a genuine learning experience, rather than the usual superficial pass of green cookies and little green hats over the holiday. Where she worked, a lot of people had come over in the middle and late nineteenth century from the "Auld Sod." So, the community had been having a lot of fun celebrating St. Patrick's Day, with parents coming to school, seeing the kids make hats and costumes, put on skits about St. Patrick, and share in eating big shamrock-shaped green sugar cookies.

But, thought Jean, that's pretty superficial. Committed to active learning where the kids actively created, designed, implemented, and evaluated projects, she thought about various projects that could be fun and yet would provide some deeper understanding of Ireland and its culture.

Using Mythology as an Organizing Principle

Since mythology seemed to be important in the historical development of Ireland, she thought that concentrating on leprechauns, as well as rainbows, pots of gold, shamrocks, luck, granting wishes, and other Irish myths, might be the way to make things exciting and simultaneously provide insight into the nature of the holiday and its mythology.

WHITEHEAD'S SECOND PHASE, PRECISION

They started out by having the kids study all the major mythology of the country in historical times. The kids virtually looted the libraries of the school and the community of relevant materials.

She then asked the kids if they wanted to work in groups (which they did), each taking a myth as their first focus. As they reported about their myth to the rest of the class, Jean noticed that while their interest grew exponentially, its major focus increasingly was on the leprechauns. Asking why this occurred, they responded by saying that the leprechauns were little people (even being called that), and so were they.

The Project

So, as the groups immersed themselves studying the other group of "little people," Jean thought that she could kick up the interest even more by creating a culminating experience. She asked the class if they wanted to build traps to catch the leprechauns when the "little people" visited the room the evening before St. Patrick's Day when no one was around. (They were pretty shy.) The kids' excitement grew even more.

But one sharp young, red-headed lad asked why would the "little people" come to the classroom? After serious discussion, they agreed that the leprechauns loved big green sugar cookies, but their appeal would increase if the cookies were shamrock-shaped since shamrocks were so important in the Irish culture and to the "little people." They would bake big shamrock-shaped green sugar cookies the day before and leave them for the leprechauns, who would show up the evening before when no one was around (they knew that the little people were shy around "big people") and would eat the cookies that the kids would bake and leave out.

And, they would be caught in the groups' traps. But, they decided that since the leprechauns loved privacy, they would talk with them to find out more about their private lives and some of the myths, and then release them.

By this time, motivation was astronomical.

MORE PRECISION

The kids, with enormous interest and excitement, immersed themselves in studying everything they could lay their hands on about leprechauns: their physical appearance; their habits; their homes; their customs; what were their preferred foods; what did they usually wear—and why was green so important; what did they believe—their myths; the language they spoke; their history; and how they related to each other.

The Parents

Naturally, this interest was communicated rapidly to parents, who amusedly began to become involved in all sorts of projects. As the class organized itself for the Big Day, certain parents found indispensable responsibilities delegated to them. One of the most important, of course, was that one group of the designated adults found that they had the privilege of baking large green sugar cookies for the day before—and another group of parents was honored to bake the cookies for the actual St. Patrick's Day festivities.

Costumes

The class also decided that each child was going to make his or her own costume for the increasingly exciting festivities, and that each child would get a prize for his or her costume. The class decided that everyone should get a prize, since if only a few received awards, those who did not get one would have their feelings hurt. So, they decided to forego any prize categories.

Each group focused on the physical nature of their subjects, since if they were going to make traps, they had to know a great deal about their size, weight, and so forth. They had to know how strong leprechauns were, otherwise the "little people" would be able to break out of their traps and be gone before the kids could chat with them.

The project proceeded apace, with excitement rising as the Great Green Day approached. Parents found themselves involved in the details and dynamics of building traps, although each was physically built by its respective group in the classroom. The industrial arts teacher (the middle school and high school were adjacent) found himself increasingly involved with tools, materials, and techniques for making and assembling the traps. Interestingly, all the groups designed and tested models first to see if their ideas were realistic.

As the traps began to be assembled, numerous real-life tests began to be planned and carried out, with subsequent modifications to the traps, amid heavy discussion of all sorts of phenomena. At the end of the day before, the cookies were placed out (many in the traps), the traps were set, and the kids left.

Results

As the kids excitedly arrived at the school, Jean had them gather near the classroom where they exclaimed at their costumes (as did the parents and other school personnel), and then they rushed into the room. What did they find?

The traps had been kicked over, many cookies were eaten—but some were only partially eaten. But the most exciting thing was the little green footprints that were visible going across the floor, up the walls, and across the ceiling. While the kids expressed disappointment that they didn't catch any "little people," they thought that their work was great fun. They also concluded that the "little people" were pretty smart to avoid all the traps and yet were clever enough to eat the cookies.

The kids had a wonderful time, wolfing down big shamrock-shaped green cookies and Irish soda bread that a couple of parents baked as a treat, and gulped green punch.

GENERALIZATIONS (OUTCOMES)

Jean thought that the constructivist project that she and the kids developed generated a lot of outcomes:

- The kids had fun
- They were actively involved
- The kids felt that they learned a great deal
- Parents were delighted, and so were the teachers and other kids
- She thought that the consideration the kids displayed for the comfort of the yet-to-be caught "little people" was admirable (and said so to the kids)

Academic outcomes:

- Reading and literacy understandings and skills
- Library skills
- Mathematical understandings and skills
- Historical research, understandings, and skills
- Cultural understandings and sensitivities

Interpersonal understandings and skills:

- Group skills, such as cooperating, becoming more sensitive to others' feelings
- Kids learned to work even better in their groups (they even agreed to work with other groups for the next project to get to know other kids better)
- Small and large muscle skills
- Relating to parents over meaningful projects, and involving parents in them

Jean decided to see if her kids would be interested in pulling off the project in the following year. They were—and they did. Who knows? They may even catch a leprechaun.

QUESTIONS AND SUGGESTIONS

1. What other imaginative projects could you design in which to engage your students as strongly as did Ms. Kern?
   A. One teacher with heavy student involvement decorated her entire room as though it were an underwater grotto, with plants, papier-mâché fish, amphibians, and mammals. She had the kids research legendary figures, as well.
   B. How would you publicize your efforts?
   C. In one school the students built very large papier-mâché dinosaurs, which were placed at the entrance to the building.
   D. How would you involve administrators? Parents?
   E. One Latin teacher developed an entire Latin Festum, with Roman plays, costumes, and so forth.
   F. Your turn.
2. Zingyness pays off.

SOURCES

Davis, T. M. & Murrell, P. H. (1993). *Turning teaching into learning: The role of student responsibility in the collegiate experience.* [Abstract]. Washington, DC: George Washington University. 1993 ASHE-ERIC Higher Education Reports; Report 8.

Whitehead, A. N. (1929). *The aims of education.* New York: Macmillan.

CHAPTER 8

Classroom Management—Solved

Me: So, you want to learn how to manage your classroom?
Class: Sure
Me: Watch

—Arthur Shapiro

ESTABLISHING YOURSELF AND SIZING THINGS UP

Yesterday, when I walked in early into a colleague's classroom to sub, no one except one small young woman close to me bothered to pay attention. "Strange," I thought. And mostly all (about eight) were seated around tables far from the front.

So, I called out, "Hallo, out there," but most people didn't catch on. So, I sat down with the small woman, found out what she taught (first grade) and asked her how the class was run. People were given various reading assignments, which they were to summarize on large chart paper, and then read to the class. I joked, introduced myself to everyone as he or she came in, made small talk, and tried to get the lay of the land. People, coming in after work, did not seem to be very excited.

THE HOOK

One serious man, as I circulated around and chatted with all and sundry, said that he wanted to learn how to manage a classroom. Of course, I immediately checked with him about the assignments, which were the same as the small woman had indicated were on tap. They seemed to be covering a lot of different articles for that session, mostly dealing with writing objectives, plus a couple of other topics.

Since I didn't know anyone, I asked them to introduce each other (this avoids shy people being embarrassed at telling about themselves). And I introduced myself.

The young woman was joined by another woman about her age, and both felt equally that the article they were supposed to summarize was insufferably boring. I knew that the article was useful in writing objectives, but they didn't seem to perceive this.

STARTING

I managed to get everyone to move to tables closer to the front (note that the classroom organization was such that there was a front) and everyone got busy writing on the chart paper, but I thought that they were just copying quickly. One of them noted that they usually went over the copied major points quickly.

Watching what was going on, I asked myself if people were grasping the meaning of the articles, and then anything about using them, or, were they just going through the motions. They put their summaries of the articles on the blackboard, but the speed at which they wrote and their lack of interaction convinced me that they weren't even getting at Bloom's comprehension level. I thought that they were just memorizing, a strategy which is useful for passing a low-level test, but not very useful in learning to write halfway decent objectives. And, they weren't very engaged.

Not much energy, not much interest, not much focus.

MOTIVATING AND ACTIVE LEARNING

So, I asked them if they wanted to learn how to write really good objectives, that we would do this in two parts, the second featuring a take-off on a parlor game, to which they responded very positively.

Although they had an article on writing objectives and another on Bloom's Taxonomy (each group was going to report on only one article), they just summarized the articles. They didn't seem to grasp the idea that they could actually write an objective, and equally didn't seem to grasp the relationship between objectives and Bloom's *Taxonomy of Educational Objectives: Cognitive Domain*. I gave them some basics (the two necessary parts of an objective [behavior and content], and the two optional [conditions and level of proficiency]), and told them to practice writing three or four examples, only concentrating on the two necessary parts. Each group got busy after finding out that any subject and any grade level was just dandy. (Why throw limitations into their activity?) Students produced three to four each, most of which contained one or two of the optional parts. Of course, I walked around to every group, and made positive comments. They seemed to be getting more interested—and building up more energy.

Increasing Roles

Then, we increased roles. We agreed in the groups that the recorder should not be the reporter, so that the teacher could increase roles in the classroom, which is one way to increase active learning. (Note that we set the ground rules early on—by getting the groups to do this, you get buy-in.)

People had done a pretty good job of writing the objectives, and after each group reported, we applauded them and their work. As they reported, I asked the people to figure out which part of each objective was behavior and which part was content—and underlined each part in a different color. This tended to slow things down from the rapid pace of getting through the assignment. Each group's objectives were right on target, and they appreciated the public appreciation of their accomplishment.

During the time they were writing the objectives, I dashed to my office and got the parts of the game together. It was a takeoff on paper bag dramatics, in which people reach into a paper bag to draw out roles. (People did not seem to know this parlor game, but did know "improv" theater and had heard of "Second City" as improvisational theater.)

THE GAME—AND ITS IMPACT

They had a diagram with appropriate verbs for each level (e.g., list, explain, apply, compare and contrast, plan, evaluate) of Bloom's Taxonomy, but obviously it wasn't taking, so we went over the six levels, with examples, and they seemed to be getting it. I then went around to each group at their table and had them reach into the bag and pull some item out (a little pamphlet on "How to Speak Southern," a tin box of Band-Aids, some dried and very salty mud from the Dead Sea, a bicycle horn that squawked, a Care Bear, a Christmas ornament, a little bottle of vitamins, etc.). Their task was to write an objective using their object on each of the six levels of the taxonomy.

Well, the interest jumped; people really got engaged. Of course, I kept circulating, and when asked a question, reflected it back, asking what they thought. It seemed to me that they were on target, and started to enjoy what they were doing. One group finished after a time, put up their chart paper with its results, and started chatting. So, I went over and quietly asked them to watch another group's discussion across from them and figure out what was going on. This group was getting into it, discussing, developing different viewpoints, and really working hard. One member of the group that had finished thought that the other group might get out of hand, so he suggested that I go over and see what was happening.

I did this, listened, realized that they were having a good discussion regarding whether an objective was on Bloom's second or the fourth level, said nothing, and walked back to the first group. One of them noted that I had said nothing, but that the group seemed to be working hard and trying to figure things out. I asked them if I should have intervened (about which they weren't sure).

Eventually the second group put up their results, and so did the other two. Each group's reporter then read each objective, and one at a time and slowly the groups responded regarding whether each was on the claimed level. Interestingly, each group produced six objectives with the appropriate parts and right on the level they claimed. I reminded them just before we started that this was practice and a learning experience, and they were pretty relaxed about it.

The class was really very pleased about their success. I asked them if they thought they needed another practice session, but they really felt that they had writing objectives under their belts. I asked them how long it took, and they indicated that it took them only about an hour.

Note that with four groups, they essentially practiced writing each level four times, for a total of twenty-four different objectives, providing a considerable amount of practice for everyone.

THE LECTURE (INACTIVE LEARNING)—WHAT A DIFFERENCE

We took a break, and then one man from a group wanted to carry out his assignment, which was to give a lecture to the group on something they were supposed to have read.

I sat beside the man who had indicated that he wanted to learn how to manage a classroom, and said to him that he might be interested in comparing and contrasting the difference between the group work and the lecture. He watched carefully as the man, who was obviously popular and had a fine sense of humor, lectured, realizing that the group lost interest rather rapidly, slumped in their chairs, became inattentive, and displayed less than rapt attention.

The lecturer admonished people to pay attention but did not have a great deal of success. He, of course, knew that the lecture couldn't compare with the active learning, and when he finished after about twelve minutes, said so.

ANALYSIS—COMPARING AND CONTRASTING

Then I asked the man who wanted to learn something about classroom management to tell the class what he wanted to know. He obviously trusted me, and repeated his question to the class. The group then compared and contrasted the active group learning with the lecture.

In the active group learning they were entirely engrossed, discussed things thoroughly, had a good time, and really learned to write objectives on six levels. They pointed out that the lecture dealt with the first or second levels only and they felt it was ineffective. We then had a discussion about the relative positives and limits of the lecture method and compared it with the active learning they had experienced.

One outcome they concluded was that they had to watch the processes going on in the class, or they would be clueless and really would not be effective. They felt that they had to watch to see if students were engaged, and how to get them involved. In short, they realized that process was pretty important if they wanted to be effective.

I thanked the student who was interested in learning about classroom management because I indicated that it focused my actions. He was quite pleased at the recognition, and so were the rest of the people.

They were pretty excited by now.

ENDINGS

To finish off the class (read, end the session), I gave them a sentence stem: "Today, I learned . . ." and asked them to complete it (not giving anyone eye contact to avoid embarrassing anyone). After a moment or two, people began to respond. One person indicated that if you involve people in a group, you get more interest, especially if they report to the group.

Another compared and contrasted the effectiveness of the lecture with the active learning stimulated by participation in the group, noting that the lecture couldn't compare. A discussion ensued, which led to people concluding that even a good lecture had a limited time span of effectiveness, whereas I had to call a halt to the discussion to end the class.

Another (the student who was interested in classroom management) said that he learned more in tonight's session than in most entire courses. Particularly, he noted that the teacher actually didn't say a lot, but facilitated by asking questions, approving the interactions going on almost by body language, such as nodding. He was particularly interested in the instructor's conscious decision to let go as well as to let things play out, trusting both the process and the good sense of the students.

I told them that I appreciated their confidence and trust, and hoped that they would try some of the techniques and processes we analyzed and developed in the class. A number of people hung around and chatted, some socializing and some planning activities for the next session.

MORE QUESTIONS

1. What would you do to develop a better teaching/learning model?
2. What would you do to establish yourself?
3. What would you do to get the attention of the class?
   A. Would you try to get one or two of the social systems engaged at first?
4. How would you keep the attention of the class and its social systems?
5. What do you think of using, "Today, I Learned . . ." at the end of the session?
   A. On which of Bloom's cognitive levels can "Today, I Learned . . ." focus?
6. How much of your classroom work is focused on the higher cognitive levels, starting with application?

SOURCES

Bloom, B. (Ed.). (1956). *Taxonomy of educational objectives. Handbook I: Cognitive domain.* New York: McKay.

Brooks, J. G. & Brooks, M. G. (1993). *The case for constructivist classrooms.* Alexandria, VA: Association for Supervision and Curriculum Development.

Chrenka, L. (2001). Misconstructing constructivism. *Phi Delta Kappan 82*(9), 694–95.

Davis, T. M. & Murrell, P. H. (1993). *Turning teaching into learning: The role of student responsibility in the collegiate experience.* [Abstract]. Washington, DC: George Washington University, 1993 ASHE-ERIC Higher Education Reports; Report 8.

Geocaris, C. (1996–1997). Increasing student engagement: A mystery solved. *Educational Leadership 54*(4): 72–75.

Glatthorn, A. A. (1987). *Curriculum leadership.* Glenview, IL: Scott, Foresman.

Phillips, D. C. (Ed.). (2000). *Constructivism in education: Opinions and second opinions on controversial issues. Yearbook of the National Society for the Study of Education: 2000, Part 1.* Chicago: National Society for the Study of Education.

Shapiro, A. S. (2000). *Leadership for constructivist schools.* Lanham, MD: Scarecrow.

Shapiro, A. S., Benjamin, W. F., & Hunt, J. J. (1995). *Curriculum and schooling: A practitioner's guide.* Palm Springs, CA: ETC.

Tyler, R. (1949). *Basic principles of curriculum and instruction.* Chicago: University of Chicago Press.

CHAPTER 9

Looking at the Right End of the Horse

What We Found in Swedish Schools Amazed Us— IDEALIZED Constructivism

I. FUNDAMENTAL VALUES AND TASKS OF THE SCHOOL
Democracy forms the basis of the national school system.
. . . each and everyone working in the school should encourage respect for the intrinsic value of each person as well for the environment which we share.
. . . this is achieved by fostering in the individual a sense of justice, generosity of spirit, tolerance, and responsibility.

—Swedish Curriculum for the Compulsory School, LPO 1994

Facilitating is burned into their brains.

—R. D. Nordgren, American Educator

EXPECTATIONS

So there we were, assorted American educators flying to Sweden to visit their schools, roughly four months after about forty Swedish educators visited ours. A motley group (elementary, middle school, high school, and university teachers and administrators, a national principal-of-the-year, a dean of international studies, a physician/professor from the Colleges of Medicine and Public Health), every one of us was secretly convinced that not only did we know a lot more about developing excellent schools, but that we really could teach the Swedes a lot about doing that (although we would have to be very diplomatic about our considerable educational expertise, and be careful not to offend them with our wisdom and superiority).

After the requisite period most of us needed to overcome jet lag, all of us peeled off to schools we were scheduled to visit. Our group took a train to a smallish city of about fifty thousand—Katrineholms.

LOTS OF SURPRISES

First of all, virtually every Swede from seven years up speaks English, not a painful, halting English, but an excellent rendition (lots of youngsters came up to practice with us). Second, their public rail, subway, and bus system transcends anything in the United States. It's omnipresent, clean, inexpensive—and works! And it goes everywhere. We still hadn't concluded that the Swedes really knew what they were doing educationally or in every other sphere we became aware of, but that came in due time.

Before visiting the schools, we were welcomed and treated like royalty by the superintendent and his staff and by members of the school board, one of whom (surprisingly, to our American thinking) was the vice mayor who was strongly committed to the schools and to education.

Also surprisingly, there was absolutely no pumping up of the schools, no glitzy presentations, no pointing-with-pride, no pretense. This, we were not prepared for. Everyone was down-to-earth, modest, talked seriously, and never bragged about their schools. None of our group was sent to visit so-called elite schools.

VISITING THE ELEMENTARY SCHOOL: MORE *BIG* SURPRISES

The next morning we visited an elementary school, which was set in a park-like campus rectangle in a blue-collar neighborhood. As we approached the school, we noticed and were surprised by a number of things. The school did not consist of one large building, as virtually every elementary school I've ever visited, but it was composed of several buildings in a campus with trees, lawns, playgrounds, and recreational areas on the perimeter of the campus, ringed by apartments across the streets.

As we crossed to go into one building, we Americans stopped and gawked. Of the approximately 125 bicycles lining the west side of the building, only about 25 or so were locked! We actually counted the few locked bicycles, a strange sight for American eyes. As we entered the building, we saw everyone's shoes lining the perimeter of the rooms. When we asked several kids if they had trouble locating their shoes, they looked mystified. Apparently, no Swedish kid thought of making off with someone else's shoes.

Moving on, we were unprepared for more surprises. None of the several male teachers wore ties or jackets (despite the fact that they knew were coming). And the kids called them by their first names; even the littlest kids were quite comfortable doing that. They even called the superintendent by his first and middle name, or by his three initials. The faculty often referred to him by his initials or by an affectionate nickname, never "mister."

Kids were busy everywhere! We never saw one kid cutting up, nor any child not working, although once in a while a kid might look out of the window for a minute. We never heard any teacher correct any kid. We also found out that our American colleagues-in-arms never had that experience, either, whether they were in other elementary schools, middle schools, secondary schools, vocational schools, or colleges. One American, who was doing a dissertation on the Swedish schools and was there for quite some time, reported that he saw a couple of kids horsing around, but they stopped after less than a minute and went on about their work. The teacher watched for a moment, yet never felt he had to do anything. Kids were self-starters, and usually busy—very busy—absorbed in their work.

PLANNING BOOKS—A MAJOR KEY

Back to the Kids

Children early on pointed out their Planning Books to us, which were pretty obvious since they were on a string on the side of their tables (which were large enough for several kids to do group work together). When we asked about the Planning Books, the kids told us that at the beginning of the school year, they and the teachers individually worked out their goals for the entire year. Then, every Monday morning of each week, each child worked on his or her Book developing his or her plan for the week—what each wanted to learn in each area for that week.

They said that they and the teachers perceived that the teachers' jobs were to facilitate the kids' accomplishing their goals in the school. R. D. Nordgren, the one in our party who later decided to do a dissertation on the Swedish schools, remarked, "Facilitating is burned into their brains."

We Americans had a difficult time concealing our astonishment!

RESPONSIBILITY AND TRUST

The Swedes had set up a system that resulted in every kid becoming responsible for his or her own learning! Was this constructivism, or what?

Well, how did it work?

Kids were virtually always busy, often working in groups, mostly on various projects, occasionally alone. The faculty had set up one room where kids could work alone—the "Quiet Room"—where conversation was not permitted. This norm was invariably followed—no one talked at all.

In another room, classical music was playing rather softly, while kids gave each other back massages in turns. We never saw any horseplay, only kids working seriously. Several children as young as seven (the usual starting age for school) came up to us and chatted in English, some practicing their English skills, others asking questions, sharing what they were doing with us. They were very friendly, although some were a bit shy. We asked a number of them about their teachers' roles, to which their response was that they saw the instructors as facilitating their learning, as helping them carry out their (the students') plans. We saw teachers interacting with students, helping students on a one-to-one basis or in groups. We never (nor did any of our American party) saw whole class teaching in elementary, middle, or in secondary schools. Similarly, this did not occur in vocational schools.

The Planning Books generally dealt with students' goals to learn Swedish, English, science, mathematics, social studies such as geography, community studies, environmental studies, and the like. In their role as facilitators, teachers most often spent their time working with small groups of kids as their vehicle to achieve the kids' goals. (Again, this constitutes the fundamental vehicle of constructivist education.)

We also thought that more adults were on hand than in U.S. schools, although they maintained that staffing patterns were similar.

MORE TRUST

At about 10:20 A.M. or so, all students went outside to play and the faculty went into a lounge of a sort, had a snack, and chatted with each other and with us. The significance of that was not lost on us litigiously conscious and risk-aversive Americans. When one of us asked about safety and liability, the faculty responded by saying that if someone needed help they would respond. They were mystified when one of us mentioned concerns about liability, until one of the teachers responded that the community trusted them to take care of work with their kids.

Students had the freedom to come and go as they wanted. They went into different rooms to work on things with different groups, or to work alone, or to change to another project. No one kept track. It was obvious that they were trusted by the faculty, and, in turn, trusted each other. And that might explain why the teacher:pupil ratio appeared so much lower than ours. Kids were free to move about to accomplish their goals and to go wherever they felt they needed to go—and they did. So, fewer kids were in the various classrooms at one time. They went about their business and went where they decided they needed to be. A little responsibility goes a long way.

RESPECT

Respect was another clear outcome of this social system. Teachers and students simply respected each other, which was apparent in all their interactions and behavior.

TEACHER ROLES

In the Swedish system, a major teacher role is to support the students. This seemed to have a considerable impact on student resourcefulness and independence, since much of the work was being done without teacher or adult supervision. This also turned out to be true in the secondary schools and in the vocational schools. The teachers' role of facilitator was operative in the secondary schools as well.

MORE CONCLUSIONS AND COMPARISONS

Our colleagues who visited middle and secondary schools emerged with the same observations and conclusions. Students and adults there displayed the same behaviors. Teachers and students appeared quite comfortable in their settings, with students being as self-motivated as those in the primary school we visited. When one colleague asked why secondary students came to school (in Sweden, secondary school, which starts at about fifteen or sixteen, is voluntary), students replied in all seriousness that it is their responsibility to learn. So, they do. And virtually almost all go to secondary school, about 98 percent.

DISCIPLINE

How about discipline and fighting? When one of us Americans, seeking to dig underneath this Nirvana, asked a secondary principal about kids fighting, the latter looked startled. Finally, after some thought, he responded that they had had a fight in the school about three years ago. Another secondary principal replied to the same question (note our concern for control) by saying that they had a student fight earlier that year, but because they did not know what to do, they called the police.

Teachers felt perfectly comfortable having kids work without supervision to the point that in the vocational schools with large and potentially dangerous equipment, students were often unsupervised while adults worked with small groups of young adults or with individuals. Americans were astonished when they realized that the teachers often were not even in the same room. Again, it took some time for us to become aware that students often took off to different parts of the school in their focus on their work. The Swedish vocational curriculum contains seventeen different curricula to prepare students for college and for the world of work. One of these curricula is entrepreneuring. Students are expected to set up a small business, which they support by getting a loan from a bank.

They build and develop the business and at the end of secondary school, they can continue with their own business or repay the bank loan.

The Swedish educators who came to America were extremely excited by the prospect of finding how we pulled off our educational programs in entrepreneuring, which they assumed were extensive and omnipresent.

What did they find? No examples.

They were really quite shocked.

We claim to be a nation of entrepreneurs and we extol it. We brag about our great American creativity in entrepreneuring—but we do almost nothing to teach it.

PULLING IT TOGETHER

In retrospect, the Swedish national curriculum focuses on and fosters democratic values, as noted in the quote beginning this chapter. The tasks of the schools are to foster democratic values. With this focus on values and process, rather than content, they have moved strongly toward a constructivist school system.

With the testing mania growing ever more powerful weekly in America (as Ross Perot's industrial-based and bottom-line accountability juggernaut crashes down through our schools) and being supported by a president who urges testing every year for every grade starting in third grade, the American standards and state curricula now focus on mastering content.

Yet, in international comparisons, the Swedish kids do extremely well in mastering content, and exceed Americans in this respect.

AN AMERICAN DILEMMA: WE ARE LOOKING AT THE WRONG END OF THE HORSE

What did the Swedes who visited us discover about the basic values being practiced in American schools? Did they find us practicing democracy? Did they find trust? Did they find us practicing activities to lead to responsibility? Did they find us teaching entrepreneuring? Did they find kids being respected to manage their own learning (a tenet of constructivism)? What did the forty Swedish educators report they found about the basic value being practiced in the American schools? *Control.*

QUESTIONS

1. How can we make our schools more community-focused?
2. How can we change the culture of numerous politicians attacking American schools, instead of supporting them?
3. What can be done at the grassroots level to build more trust for the schools—and teachers?
   A. What strategies can major educational organizations utilize and unite in changing the attitude of Americans that the public schools are not very good?
4. Will developing more student decision making build more trust, more self-control, which in turn can assist with discipline?
   A. How do you build more responsibility?
   B. How do you build respect?
   C. Will such actions increase student responsibility?
   D. How can students improve their decision making without practice in making decisions?
5. How can we improve the process of facilitating kids managing their own learning?
6. What questions can you ask that may lead to improving American schools?
7. What can we do to deal with the simplistic notion that we can grade schools by test scores?
8. What suggestions did we make to improve the Swedish schools?
9. Finally, would you send your own kids to the Swedish schools?

SOURCE

Nordgren, R. D. (2001). *Shared power, trust, student responsibility, and global workforce competence.* Unpublished doctoral dissertation, University of South Florida, Tampa.

CHAPTER 10

Practicing Constructivism in a Public ESE Charter Middle School—With Difficulty

Phylicia L. Cartwright

Learners control their learning.

—Jacqueline Grennan Brooks and Martin Brooks,
The Courage to Be Constructivist

Know that your most worthy efforts will be scorned by your peers, for it is they who suffer most when you excel. If your actions and ambitions threaten them not, you're simply striving toward the insignificant.

—Attila, the Hun, on: There Is Another Day

ATTILA ON: THERE IS ANOTHER DAY

The radio went off as usual this morning at 5:20. I rolled out of bed and took a deep breath as I started to think about "my kids." I have two children of my own, but the kids I carried around in my heart and mind along with my own would be meeting in room 221 this morning as they have for the last nine weeks. The more I thought about implementing my lessons for the day, the more motivated I became, yet by now I knew there would be sorrow to follow.

Each new day brought many lessons for me as a first-year teacher. I would throw out the facts, model a few appropriate behaviors, such as ignoring inappropriate behaviors, making choices about responding to others' behavior in social settings, just being nice to kids, and letting the students "go to town" constructing knowledge in each of his or her own individual ways. Students, who have had behavior problems throughout their entire school careers, were astounded that they could make decisions, lead groups, organize material for sharing with the class, and illustrate small-group projects in ways they never believed they could.

MY BACKGROUND

Let me back up a bit and share some pertinent information. I am forty-one years old and recently graduated with my bachelor's degree in special education. My areas of specialization are learning disabilities and behavior disorders. I consider myself a constructivist and have a very difficult time coexisting with people who are punitive in the administration of behavior management for children.

SOME KEYS TO MY OPERATION

My class began each day with "good morning," and "how are you feeling today?" I really wanted to know! The students knew that I wanted to know and that I would take the time to listen to what they said. If someone had been through a traumatic experience (whether an adult thought it to be or not), I would take that into consideration when observing his or her actions in class. I never felt happier than when I was in that classroom!

But, a Different Philosophy

If I could have kept the students all day long it would have been wonderful. I knew each day that I would have to deliver them over to classrooms where they were intimidated, yelled at, threatened, and embarrassed. I could hear the teachers in the rooms I was sandwiched between making it very clear that they would *not* put up with any foolishness or disrespect. I would try to ignore it and focus on my own class but would develop a knot in my stomach as I listened to the wasted breath of the teachers permeate the walls as they berated the kids.

My students would ask me why the other teachers were so angry, and I would just tell them to "focus" on what our class was doing. How could they focus if I couldn't? I tried to palm off the old, "Every teacher has a different style of teaching" line, but only once. It troubled me greatly.

MORE KEYS—AND RESULTS IN MY CLASS

Becoming a Family

Our class became a family. Children with learning difficulties were encouraged to find their own special talent or gift and use it to help them in academic areas they struggled with. Those who needed to stand up to write were allowed to do so. Those who needed to talk everything through with someone were allowed to find someone in the class with whom they were comfortable to do just that. No subject was off limits, except for the behaviors of the other teachers. And the kids began to respect that limit after a while.

A Cloud on the Horizon

I sought counsel from an apparently veteran constructivist teacher, and was told in no uncertain terms to keep my "first-year teacher" opinions to myself. I was to do nothing that would damage the "constructed" image of the school that had been portrayed to the public and parents, in spite of the truth. I was led to believe that I was applying to work in a different type of school where children were treated with respect and dignity, in spite of veteran teachers' sarcastic remarks and attempts to intimidate other teachers.

Though I was a new teacher, I had already learned that the only way to facilitate learning was to ignore inappropriate behaviors, be willing to let them escalate, and then watch as they melted away. I practiced this with my own children, and I had observed the effectiveness of this method with some hard-core cases. Throwaway kids became my best friends, and most interested learners.

MORE SUCCESSFUL RESULTS

Getting Attention

In the mornings I would greet the class and wait quietly for their attention. It took a few minutes at first, but after a few days, students themselves were shushing one another. I would hear, "Be quiet, she is trying to teach." I would remind the students of why I was there each day. I would tell them how much I cared about them, and that their behaviors would not change that. I don't think they believed me at first, but the care I received back from them proved that they had become believers.

Language Arts and Kids' Learning Styles

Language arts is a battlefield for many children. The students in my class were allowed to select a place to sit in the room where they were most comfortable. Every Monday I would give my students a spelling packet containing various strategies and methods of studying the words. Every child was able to complete the packet by Friday, which gave me an opportunity to put an extra "A" in the grade book. The packets began an upward track for the students' self-esteem. They knew that even if they did not do so well on the spelling test, they still had a good chance of making a good grade.

It took a few weeks to determine the spelling and reading level of each student. I gave three tests at once during some of my classes. I let the students know that we never stop learning! I let them see me looking up words in the dictionary, and I told them never to be afraid to admit they did not know something. Even the most confident students in the class began to realize that we are all in this world together.

Success in Writing Essays!!

Essay writing was as simple, in most cases, as telling the students that they could write! No one had ever told them that most writers' material was pulverized and spit back out before it ever became a published work. I began to receive calls from parents, in very emotional states, calling to tell me that their child had never written before. These parents could not believe that their children had written five-paragraph expository essays in a matter of a week.

It was a humbling experience to know that just a few teacher-made outlines, colored lines in paragraph form and some fancy bordered paper from a local store could encourage such results. Some of the topics chosen by the children were not in my schema, but I let them teach me about them. Students seemingly obsessed with certain television programs were allowed to write about them. Boy, did I get an education!

These students were motivated! I remarked with positive feedback on each and every paper. I only requested one sentence per paragraph to start off, but I was flooded with information in written form. These children could pass any essay test the school system wanted to throw at them. The good news is that the test never came up during class.

Storm Clouds Appear: The Teachers' Social System Begins to Criticize

The better the behavior became, and the more my students produced (while often laughing and having fun), the less popular I became among certain teacher populations. The students would say, "We don't want to go to the next class 'cause she hates us!" It appeared as though the other teachers had never interacted with students who had behavioral problems stemming from a consistent inability to succeed. The rigid and domineering orders would be barked out in a manner that begged further defiance from the students. Often, totally unreasonable punishments would be given for talking back or not having your right shoulder against the wall while standing in line. Students who had great difficulty writing would be told to complete five apology letters: one to his or her parents, one to each of the three teachers, and if another adult was present, they would get the fifth one.

Even the head of the department, who held a doctorate in special education, refused to acknowledge the damaging effects of this method until I mentioned the obvious futility of the task. I could not believe that people, whom I had respected and worked very hard for, were further damaging students' abilities to succeed. After I expressed my concerns, the letter writing stopped for a while.

Parents wrote notes to the teachers asking why their children were being asked to read out loud in class, when clearly they struggled when reading the directions for an assignment. I would assure parents that I was not asking this of the students, and they would quickly say, "We know *you* are not doing it, but the others are!" Parents wondered why they didn't receive midterm progress reports from the other two teachers. I made the terrible mistake of taking it upon myself to computer generate a report for each child, including a few handwritten lines to share some of the students' successes. I was doing for my students what I wished someone had done for my own child.

I felt great compassion for the students, even when they acted less than perfectly. I felt no pity for the teachers, especially those who had years of experience in the classroom. Why choose a career that provoked you to wrath each and every day? When I asked this question, I was quickly reminded that these children were in need of better parenting, and that disrespect would not be tolerated while in their classrooms! One of the teachers even went as far as to say that it was a shame we could no longer take out a stick and beat them, as in the "good old days." This remark might be expected from one who had been teaching far too long, but a young, first-year teacher blurted it out!

Next, Isolation

I was not supposed to be able to teach without getting angry! Teaching without behavior issues in my class made me a target for punishment. I was not a part of "the team" anymore. I noticed that the other teachers avoided me while talking and laughing together. We had only two meetings that included all three of us, and one of them was to distribute my share of IEPs. I knew what was going to be expected of me as a teacher. I could not figure out why they griped about doing the job they were hired to do. If I did not expect to document, and sign students' planners daily, I would never have considered working in a school where this was an absolute must for the children to learn organizational skills.

When important people (prospective investors) were paraded around our school to see the wonderful teachers in action, I would stand amazed as the other teachers would don their flowing, chiffon-like, personas. Suddenly, they were the quintessential champions for all children. As soon as the observers were gone, students who dared to misbehave listened to the standard threat of what would happen if they ever embarrassed them in front of visitors again. Positive learning rarely resulted from a day in these teachers' classrooms.

Our facility was advertised to be one of specialized learning. The contract I signed at the beginning of the year was one of a *constructivist* environment, not a *constructed* facade. Finally, after realizing that students were going to suffer even more if I exposed the undignified, dysfunctional manner in which they were being taught, I prayerfully decided to resign, knowing that the act alone would topple the apple cart.

My heart was broken, the students cried, but the principal quickly ushered me out of the school, so that no one would ask any questions that I might get a chance to answer.

The other teachers in the school who share my feelings about teaching applauded my actions. They said that they wanted to do exactly what I had done, but they feared the repercussions. Parents have found my phone number in the book and called my home to tell me that they knew something was wrong, and that now they could address issues with boldness on behalf of their children.

I know there is a special place for me to teach. Until the time comes that I find such a place, I will homeschool my own child, and tutor as many so-called throwaway kids as I can.

POSTSCRIPT ANALYSIS

Critical mass is a key in influencing change in any organization. Do you have enough people to hold onto their beliefs and practices when the slings and arrows begin to fly? Obviously, Ms. Cartwright did not have enough critical support in an ESE setting where behaviorist approaches were the majority. Often, this has been the fate of innovators, of which many will leave the system in frustration, as they encounter hostility of peers and administers.

Ms. Cartwright concludes:

A few days later, I reflected upon the resignation letter I had read to the principal:

> This letter is to inform you of my resignation as of the end of the October grading period as per my contract, signed on June 12, 2001. I believe I am within my contractual rights to do so at this time.
>
> This decision has been made after realizing that I was hired to work diligently to enable learning-disabled students to learn appropriate social skills as well as meet their individual academic needs through multiple learning styles. The environment I am working in is not representative of one that supports efforts to complete this task. Yes, we have technology, but students are suffering! Teachers who yell and threaten are supported, while those of us who are not intimidated by discipline problems and take the time to model appropriate behaviors, are treated badly.

Parents have made remarks about the improvement in their child's class work, and about finally feeling like they have a teacher who cares about them. Students are learning in my class! It breaks my heart to leave. I thought this school was going to be a place where students would be treated well, in spite of teachers' egos. This is not the case.

Thank you,

Mrs. Cartwright

B.S. Special Education–Learning Disabilities/Behavior Disorders

QUESTIONS

1. What would you advise people who are highly in favor of an educational practice to do in interviewing for a position?
   A. Would you suggest that they visit the school or district first?
   B. Would you suggest that they talk to key teachers in key social systems ahead of time to determine if they would have success in using their ideas and practices?
2. How accepting are schools that largely deal with special education students to philosophies that veer from behaviorist approaches?
   A. How about magnet schools for the gifted?
   B. What about schools for the arts? Other models?
3. What is the reaction of peers to colleagues trying for national board certification if one is the only person in the building trying for such certification?
4. What slings and arrows can anyone expect for practicing an innovation alone?
   A. Therefore, is it better to find at least one partner to form a social system of your own, which can help resist pressures and criticisms, which will certainly emerge?
   B. How do you find such allies?
5. What steps would you take to develop support?
   A. How about your own social systems?
   B. What about administrators' social systems?
   C. What other program in the school depends upon recruiting students (such as industrial arts), who often do not have required programs? Can they become allies?
6. What further questions would you develop?

CHAPTER 11

From the Mouths of Students—
Interactions with Constructivism

In this class I learned to trust myself.

—Student

INTRODUCTION

When my wife asked me what were the most memorable responses to the question I always ask in my classes—"What are my most significant learnings in this class?"—one of the best answers was "I learned to trust myself."

The Process in the Class

A little explanation about the process we use in my classes will explain why this series of case studies can have such a huge range of reactions from students, ranging from insights regarding content to process to emotions and to themselves.

At the end of every class period, people respond to the sentence stem "Today, I learned . . ."

Twice during the semester—about halfway through and at the end—students respond to "My most significant learnings in this class . . ."

No format is required or suggested, nor are any conditions placed upon students. People have written songs, parables, and poems. Others have developed skits and put them on videotape. One woman did a mime act. A small museum could be filled with the many presentations hanging on my walls and from my ceilings.

A FEW BEGINNING QUOTES TO WHET THE APPETITE

So, here goes. I'll repeat a few from chapter 22 shortly, since they are so insightful.

On Understanding Oneself

A somewhat random woman, who had just been promoted to be an assistant elementary principal, grasped my arm and said intensely:

> I never understood why I did the wacky things I do until I got into this class. I never understood anything about personality styles until I took this class. I never understood why my husband and I clashed and he became so angry at times. You helped me make my marriage more effective. We now understand each other.
> You made me believe in myself. —Kate Blackburn

The Gregorc Personality Style Delineator (1982) was one tool used in this woman's class. It proved a lot better than a Swiss Army knife. Another woman's quote: "This class changed my life." She was referring to the Gregorc. Later, we married. (Some change!)

INSIGHTS INTO HOW THE CLASS OPERATES

Ten Commandments for a Constructivist Classroom

    I. Satisfy Basic Needs: Comfort, Food
    II. Everyone Is Equal: Respect
    III. Value Differences
    IV. Discussion = Insight
    V. Why Create Pressure? We're All Professionals. Think, Speak, and Interact Freely
    VI. Everyone Is Involved
    VII. Useful, Recent Articles/Information
    VIII. Have An Underlying Plan for Quality Performance and It Will Happen

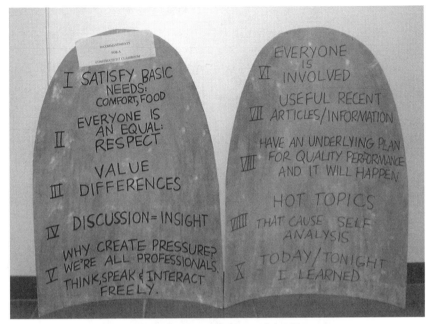

Figure 11.1   Ten Commandments for a Constructivist Classroom

IX. Hot Topics That Cause Self-Analysis
X. Today/Tonight I Learned . . .
                                            —Alex Dworzanski and Tim Hodak

The most thought-provoking articles, for me, were those introducing
W. Edwards Deming and his plan.—Robin Thompson

A Basic Theory Implemented in the Class

I've read Maslow in two classes, but I never figured out how to use it
until this third class with you. Now, I know how to use it.
Thanks.—Andres Fernandez

It probably wouldn't have occurred to me to put the day's agenda on
the board to ease the students' anxieties . . . I really liked the "Today, I
learned . . ." technique. I plan to use that in my own classroom in order
to get feedback from students.—LaMark Stillings

Figure 11.2   Maslow and Constructivism

The *Most Significant Learning of the Semester* is that process is as important as any outcome (content).—Jane Moerschbacher

How I Became a Real Teacher—or, "That Set Me Free"

Learning, if it is truly to serve our need to become more complete, more human, and genuinely happy, must somehow set us free to be all that we naturally are. Learning, therefore, is significant if through it one experiences the exhilarating joy of being set free.

I experienced that exhilaration during our discussion of the Gregorc Personality Profiles. I had somehow become conditioned to believe that a good teacher is highly organized, efficient, ordered, and in total command of every situation. In my experience as a student I would always point to teachers with that Concrete Sequential personality as good teachers. It was easier, it seemed, to learn when expectations and goals were clearly marked. I thought considerably less of teachers who taught with a more random style that demanded of me spontaneity, participation, and student discussion.

Figure 11.3   The Flower of Constructivism
—Phylicia Cartwright and Challen Mancione

My first few years as a teacher have been marked with the frustration of trying to be my image of a good teacher without a personality that fits that description. I was often discouraged because I was not running a sequential classroom. . . .

Our discussion of the different personality styles for teaching and learning showed me two important things about myself *that set me free.* First, I reflected on my experience as a learner and saw that the most valuable, practical, and meaningful things I have ever learned came from random learning situations where I could be myself and was pushed to contribute my creativity. Although I earned high grades in sequential classrooms, I remembered that experience as tortuously boring and I realized that I have used very little of the knowledge I had accumulated in those classes. I looked at my experience as a teacher and realized that when I tried hard to be sequential, I was actually tortuously boring. When I taught with my personality and used my personality to encourage my students to be open, outspoken, and free, wonderful learning had taken place. I cannot measure the effectiveness of that learning with tests and grades and summative evaluations, etc.

But it sure is a lot of fun! —Father P

Most Significant Learning

CONSTRUCTIVISM

Cooperative and collaborative learning methodology

Organization is established without order

Needs of learners are identified, valued and met

Safe learning environment is paramount

Trust between instructor and student and among students

Respect for opinions and ideas other than your own is critical

Unconditional acceptance of others and their ideas

Concepts are focus of instruction rather than isolated facts

Teamwork between learners

Instruction focuses on connection between facts & new understanding

Variety of learning styles are accommodated

Individuals construct his or her own meaning

Student-centered curricula customized to student's prior knowledge

Model of learning based on the student's own search for meaning

Nadine D. Mescia, M.H.S.

Figure 11.4   Most Significant Learning

More on Teaching Techniques

Teaching without a lecture makes everyone feel equal. The discussions are more open and each person contributes.

This grouping style, instead of traditional lecturing, made me accept other people's ideas and strategies.—Jeremy Coleman

You learn how to trust your own judgment.—Chris Novak

If an organization wants to improve its quality, it must change its entire culture.

It is important to know the reward orientation of subordinates, as many management groups incorrectly guess employee reward orientation, consequently adding to low morale and productivity.—Jerry Jones

In matters of education, curriculum dwells at the heart of the system.—Ann Lee

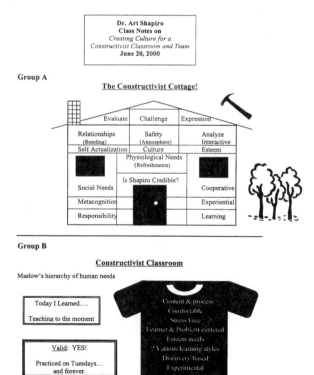

Figure 11.5   The Constructivist Cottage

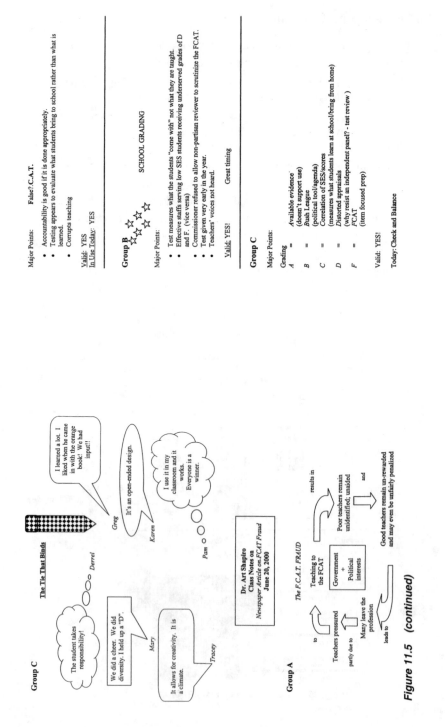

Figure 11.5 *(continued)*

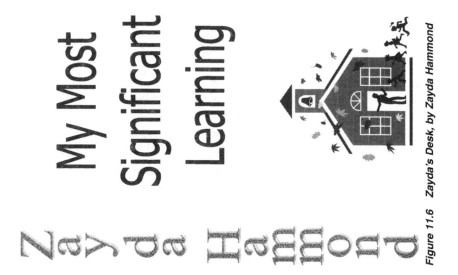

Figure 11.6   Zayda's Desk, by Zayda Hammond

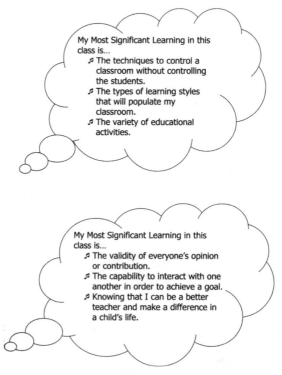

Figure 11.6   (continued)

It has opened my eyes to another way of teaching, instead of the "I talk, you listen" traditional way. I found I learned a lot sitting with my peers and exchanging ideas, and it's sometimes amazing how different or similar our thoughts are and both extremes can be advantageous in different situations.

I'm not a very social person and by the end of the semester if I have spoken to two people in the class that's a big number for me. This class has been set up in such a way that has helped me feel comfortable. Through the food and the phone number exchange I was able to interact with almost everyone in this class. This class has allowed to us to speak freely of our personal lives, which is not the norm in most classrooms.

My career goal is to be a guidance counselor for high school students and from now on I will try to find ways to make my students feel as comfortable as I did in this class when they have to speak to me about anything.

I would also like to thank my group for their support and insight in our weekly task and especially Mistie for always keeping us laughing with her creativity. I am going to miss you guys.—Monette Scott [Note: I hand out a class list to everyone with name, address, phone numbers, and e-mail (with permission, of course).]

My most significant of all learnings is that I am not perfect, nobody is. The children will not expect to be perfect and nor should I. If a lesson does not work out . . . move on to one of the back-up lessons!—Mistie Adkins

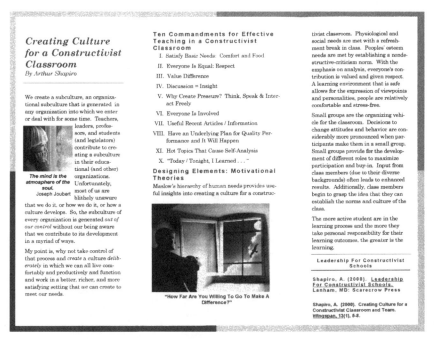

Creating Culture for a Constructivist Classroom
By Arthur Shapiro

We create a subculture, an organizational subculture that is generated in any organization into which we enter or deal with for some time. Teachers, leaders, professors, and students (and legislators) contribute to creating a subculture in their educational (and other) organizations. Unfortunately, most of us are blithely unaware that we do it, or how we do it, or how a culture develops. So, the subculture of every organization is generated *out of our control* without our being aware that we contribute to its development in a myriad of ways.

The mind is the atmosphere of the soul.
Joseph Joubert

My point is, why not take control of that process and *create* a culture *deliberately* in which we can all live comfortably and productively and function in a better, richer, and more satisfying setting that *we* can create to meet our needs.

Ten Commandments for Effective Teaching in a Constructivist Classroom
   I. Satisfy Basic Needs: Comfort and Food
   II. Everyone Is Equal: Respect
   III. Value Difference
   IV. Discussion = Insight
   V. Why Create Pressure? Think, Speak & Interact Freely
   VI. Everyone Is Involved
   VII. Useful Recent Articles / Information
   VIII. Have an Underlying Plan for Quality Performance and It Will Happen
   XI. Hot Topics That Cause Self-Analysis
   X. "Today / Tonight, I Learned . . . "

Designing Elements: Motivational Theories
Maslow's hierarchy of human needs provides useful insights into creating a culture for a constructivist classroom. Physiological and social needs are met with a refreshment break in class. Peoples' esteem needs are met by establishing a nondestructive-criticism norm. With the emphasis on analysis, everyone's contribution is valued and given respect. A learning environment that is safe allows for the expression of viewpoints and personalities, people are relatively comfortable and stress-free.

Small groups are the organizing vehicle for the classroom. Decisions to change attitudes and behavior are considerably more pronounced when participants make them in a small group. Small groups provide for the development of different roles to maximize participation and buy-in. Input from class members (due to their diverse backgrounds) often leads to enhanced results. Additionally, class members begin to grasp the idea that they can establish the norms and culture of the class.

The more active student are in the learning process and the more they take personal responsibility for their learning outcomes, the greater is the learning.

Leadership For Constructivist Schools

Shapiro, A. (2000). **Leadership For Constructivist Schools.** Lanham, MD: Scarecrow Press

Shapiro, A. (2000). Creating Culture for a Constructivist Classroom and Team. **Wingspan, 13**(1), 5-8.

"How Far Are You Willing To Go To Make A Difference?"

Figure 11.7   How Far Are You Willing to Go to Make a Difference?

A Life-Changing Experience

The most significant learning throughout this semester thus far has been the Gregorc Personality Styles Assessment. My life has been structured since I can remember, and I believe it has been due to achievement. I always had to be the best and failing was not an option. Since I was a child, my father has instilled in me to be the best and there is no second place. So in order for me to achieve success I became anal, orderly, and independent. I am not angry with my father for instilling in me hard work and values because I have achieved much in my life thus far, but at the cost of high blood pressure, headaches, and a very anal lifestyle. I had a turning point in my life when asked "What in life is perfect? Why are you striving for something that you will never achieve?" Nobody in my life has ever broken that down to me like she did and I will forever be indebted to her for that. Right there and then I vowed to change my life style one day at a time.

The Gregorc has also changed the way I deal with my staff and realizing that everyone is not like me and I cannot deal with all of them the same way. I will try to utilize their individual skills to help better their performance.—Donavan Outten

Today I learned what type of person I am, and why I tend to react to certain situations the way I do. We took the *Gregorc Style Delineator* and it opened my eyes to differences between people, and what makes each

"Final" by Phylicia
for
"The Genious"
December 1, 1999

Figure 11.8   Oz Is Out There Dorothy

Finally! Aims, goals and objectives make sense. I aim to teach teachers how to teach, without the teachers knowing they are being taught. My goal is to model the teaching strategies and methods used in this class. The objectives are: to have a sound curriculum, engage students in productive, yet seemingly unstructured group activities, and make each individual know that they are valued and important beings.

This semester I learned:

- How to become aware of other people's styles, and blend them with my own
- How to be conscious of a hidden curriculum, and learn from it
- How to incorporate my strengths and talents into facilitating others
- How to incorporate great skills of others into my own way of thinking
- How to write a lesson plan that will be most effective
- How to write curriculum (that really blows my mind, I did it!)
- How to like Bloom, he use to give me a stomachache
- How to stretch, learn, and grow, painlessly
- How to be my own best friend, and a resource for those who need me
- How to collaborate with people, who are much more educated than myself
- How to relax and enjoy a course, while learning is naturally taking place
- How to discuss an issue in class without offending anyone
- How to keep on going in spite of personal issues, and hurts
- How it feels to be encouraged by a professor who exemplifies everything you want to be

Thanks for making my first semester interesting, fun, and easy to remember. I hope to always be in touch throughout the years.

Sincerely, Phylicia Cartwright

Figure 11.8   (continued)

tick. . . . I realize that this test can be used in the classroom, to determine the type of students I am dealing with for the year. I will be able to realize why they react the way they do in my class. I feel this will help me when dealing with fellow teachers, thus improving our relationships. . . . Thanks to your wife, I feel I have grown as a person.—Sean Farrell, Teacher of the Gifted

A Major Insight

My most significant learning has been what I have learned about myself. . . . All my life I have done things for other people. . . . I also hate to see people around me struggle. I have tried so hard to keep other people from having to struggle, that I often have ended up in hard times myself. Many people have taken advantage of me. After class on the day we took the Gregorc personality test, I vowed to myself that I would not let people use me any more. . . . There is a fine line that determines whether or not you are just treating people kindly or letting them use you as a doormat. I have finally, at the age of 21, determined where and when I draw that line. Thank you so much for the test.—Angela Robin Collins

This was a comment made to the class:

I took the Gregorc about ten years ago, and it changed my life. I realized that I was engaged to the wrong person, and broke it off almost immediately. I realized that she was not right for me. I just got engaged to someone who is a better fit for me. And, it's working.—Andres Fernandez [Note: They did get married about a year and a half ago—and, it is working.]

Figure 11.9   My Most Significant Learnings, by Donna Hodnett

ON THE NEXT PAGE YOU WILL FIND MY MOST SIGNIFICANT LEARNINGS. I APPROACHED THIS ASSIGNMENT WITH A DIFFERENT STYLE. INSTEAD OF WRITING PARAGRAPH AFTER PARAGRAPH I DEVELOPED A CHART. WHEN I FIRST SAT DOWN TO START THIS ASSIGNMENT MY MIND WAS RACING WITH IDEAS, THOUGHTS, FEELINGS. IT CONFUSED ME ON HOW TO SET THIS ASSIGNMENT UP. BUT ONCE I STARTED, THINGS FELL INTO PLACE. THINGS STARTED TO FIT TOGETHER LIKE A PUZZLE. IN ONE WAY OR ANOTHER EVERYTHING SEEMED TO BE RELATED. THINGS SEEM TO BE COMING TOGETHER. I THINK THE REASON WHY IS BECAUSE WE ARE ALWAYS DEALING WITH HUMAN SITUATIONS. IT ALWAYS COMES BACK TO THE PERSON. THIS CLASS HAS REALLY OPENED MY EYES TO A LOT OF NEW WAYS TO LOOK AT DIFFERENT SITUATIONS AND PEOPLE. THANK YOU.

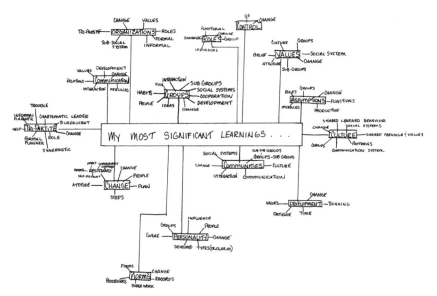

Figure 11.9   (continued)

Using a Countdown Format

My Most Significant Learning Experiences Countdown

Since I am unable to focus on just one learning experience, I have decided to share my significant learning experiences in countdown format . . . [some omitted].

And taking the Number 8! position—I've developed several colleague friendships and built on other colleague friendships that will continue to have meaning beyond the semester . . .

Then in the Number 7! slot we have—Structure doesn't need to appear structured. I recognized that the class environment was extremely safe and that in that atmosphere learning through challenging, evaluating, analyzing, thinking outside of the box, venting, listening, questioning, etc., can occur.

I realized there was a rationale to using the small group process, and that strategy has value. I also think it was helpful to be in a group which stayed constant over the semester, which allowed for everyone to share roles. . . . By maintaining group composition, we self-monitored the sharing of roles. As instructor you did not have to take responsibility for assigning leadership.

I realized that the "today I learned" provided a good method for closure to each class session and also an opportunity for simple class closure. I'll use this strategy with groups I teach.

I felt like a professional in this class.

And next as Number 6! —There is value to recognizing the social functions of the school . . .

We're halfway there in "Significant Learning Countdown." Here we go with the TOP 5!!!

Taking the Number 5! position—Finally, I can make sense of curriculum development.

Then, not to be forgotten in the Number 4! slot we have—There is value in understanding the different ways people process, communicate, and work . . .

And now as we get more profound, in Number 3! we find—There is value to questioning what seems like a given and looking at things through multiple lenses . . .

Not to be outdone, we have Number 2!—You can learn more from listening, than from talking . . . and here we are. You're about to learn my top learning experience.

The Number 1! learning experience of this semester is—It is important to develop a personal mission and philosophy . . .

This class has supported this personal process.—Saybra Chapman

A Rap (one stanza):

We're diverse but we're positive, that all that's at stake
Together with culture a great climate we make.
Strong relationships, communications benefit us all
It's really important for the three-year haul.
—Pam Sudzena

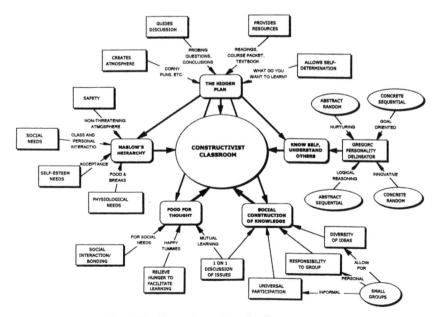

Figure 11.10 My Most Significant Learnings So Far

Dealing with Fear and Apprehension

Apprehensive and confounded about the course work and requirements, I found that after the first class session I could afford to get rid of
my consternation and anxiety. As the overall purpose, goals, and objectives of the course were (discussed), it was clear that this was going to
be an interactive class with everyone actively participating and contributing to the learning process.—Derrick Brown

Of all the time that I have spent with you in class and with others, I
have learned more about people during this course than in any of the
courses I have had. . . . I learned that size and scale of schools are important. Big is not always better. A decentralized school affords teachers
and students a clear sense of purpose, participating, and belonging. Communication is enhanced between teachers, students, and one another. Just
as Wal-Mart has owner-employees and high production, smaller schools
also generate a feeling of ownership, where everyone is needed to make
a healthy community effort. As a result, there is an overall higher level
of self-esteem, empowerment, and satisfaction.—Mary T. Shapiro

The 10 Things My Classmates Should Know

#10. What did he actually want us to learn this semester? A little bit
of everything. But most of all, hold your ground during an intellectual
battle.—Carlos Zometa

What is the answer to the so-called problem in education? I have to won-
der if there was really a problem in the first place. . . . It seems that politics
have invaded our schools and now there is a problem.—Jeanine Romano

On Active Learning

My experience with developing a curriculum has been limited to a few
staff development sessions at my school. The session we had . . . on developing a curriculum was the most interesting session all summer for
me because I would really get to develop a curriculum with other professionals in my group and we were all interested in doing it.—Acie
Jenkins [Note: I asked if they wanted to develop a curriculum.]

Several groups responded with Jeopardy Game take-offs.

My Most Significant Learnings

By

Kelly Ready

Curriculum and Instruction
EDG 4620
Professor Shapiro
February 25, 1995

Independent thinking and acceptance of responsibility were my most significant learnings in the first half of Curriculum and Instruction. Interestingly, I thought I knew these things before I began this class, but it was not until the instructor challenged me to think for myself that I realized I did not even know where to begin.

I have been a student in the Florida school system for twenty-one years. During this time I have always done exactly what the teachers required. Sometimes I did the opposite of what they required due to my rebellious nature. (Would you ever have guessed?!) The point is they made all the suggestions, evaluations, and decisions, not me. I can now see I grew increasingly dependent on the suggestions and decisions by the "experts" I believed them to be. Classical stimulus response scenarios were taking the place of intellectual developments throughout my classes and in my life. I would be become anxious about an assignment and rush to the teacher for help who would essentially plan and execute the assignment for me. The assignment was a reflection of the teacher's perceptions and beliefs, not mine. At the times this happened I felt good, relieved that I had finished my assignment. When the assignment was returned with an "A" and the comment, "Good Work!," I felt empty and depressed without knowing the reason. Now I realize I felt depressed about a good grade because I knew I did not deserve it. Thousands of assignments later, my self esteem had become practically nonexistent.

In the class for which this paper is written, there is no syllabus except for the one created by the students. As intrigued as I was by this concept, its inherent responsibility made me anxious -- after all, taking an active part in the learning process was a foreign experience.

1

Fig. 11.11   *My Most Significant Learnings, by Kelly Ready*

When an assignment is given, Professor Shapiro does not provide his opinion until after the students give theirs. Because we work in small groups and express our ideas in a written format, I am compelled to participate and give my opinion on different topics. The group members rely on each other's opinion in developing the material for class discussion.

When I asked the teacher, "Tell me *exactly* what you want regarding the paper on hidden curriculum," he consistently and humorously tossed the question back to me. He refused to give me an opinion regarding the contents of a suitable paper. While I did not feel comfortable (I was in fact scared.), the challenge proved to be rewarding. However, when he told us about the assignment concerning our "most significant learnings," I once again unknowingly tried to make him tell me "exactly" what he expected. His reply was, "What do you think your most significant learning was; what do you want to do?" His answer irritated me at the time. I was angry for having registered for this class. It was then I realized I had for years been asking people to think for me. For the first time in a scholastic environment, I was required to think for myself.

I edited this paper many times. I wrote about different types of personality styles in the classroom, different teaching styles, behavioral objectives, hidden curriculum in the classroom, having fun while learning (NO! Such nonsense!), and many others. The ability to think independently and to accept responsibility for my feelings and actions however, were the invaluable lessons I learned. Though I believe all of these things are important, the latter concepts will carry me through life and assist me to persevere and succeed in my endeavors. I feel comfortable completing an assignment on my own for the first time!

Fig. 11.11 (continued)

2

In my opinion independent thinking and accepting responsibility for one's feelings and actions need to become the foundation upon which curriculum is developed and instruction is presented. I will apply the methodologies I have learned this semester to my teaching practice. Hopefully, I can become as graceful and tactful in my display of curriculum and instruction as you are, Professor Shapiro.

3

I've learned to question what I do.—Enrique A. Boza

I've also really enjoyed having an arena in which to discuss education from a theoretical perspective. I find it fascinating to examine how theory manifests itself in actual practice.—Evan Cadmus

I learned that there is a hidden curriculum everywhere I go. (All I need to do is to focus in order to see it.)—Liz Cole, as her part in a group with Tiffany Van Cleave, and LaKeitha Robinson

Shticks

Note: I suggest to people that they develop a shtick (a signature, or a game, such as that used by comedian Rodney Dangerfield, with his "I don't get no respect").

The first thing I noticed when the constructivist professor walked into the room was he was definitely going to be cool. He wore a Pink Floyd tie and a fancy colored shirt.—Jackie Guarascio

Top 10 Things I Learned in Constructivist Class . . .
   10. Working groups are fun.
   9. A good environment makes creativity blossom.
   6. Good teachers earn respect.
   5. Relax . . . Let the students make decisions about the class.
   1. Dress flashy and make a fashion statement.—Mary Linkous

STRATEGIES OF CHANGE (A SONG)

Clamped, the system stomps on the efforts of the teacher
trying to create a spark.
Her students bored, the same old thing small-town culture
does not allow thought.
Youthful talk gets out of hand, feelings hurt.
Big daddy comes along and waves a big redneck stick.
CHORUS:
Melt the mold, break the bonds,
Let there be the dawning of a new day.

Carry then on to new life,

Set their feet on the higher ground of His love.

Change, you cannot change another person

he has to change himself, so ask

The questions that make him aware

of his own discontent, socializes the unrest

Empower small groups of the committed

And the influential

Let them shake and move, and there will soon be

the dawning of a new day—Ken DeVeau

My Most Significant Understandings of this Class
(or a concrete student's survival in an abstract prof's world)
by Jan Owen

Analysis and Change is one of the most unique education classes offered at USF.

Food is used to quickly and effectively break down barriers and enhance group functioning. Group activities are included frequently to reduce boredom and increase understanding of concepts.

The basic premise of the class is that everyone is a capable being and should be treated as such. Coupled with this is the primary belief that a good self concept is essential for all positive growth and development. Each student should be encouraged to grow and take risks and the classroom environment should be engineered to allow a student to feel comfortable as s/he explores her/his potential.

In order to create such an environment, positive reinforcement should be given for behaviors that move the student towards his/her potential and for the most part other behaviors should be ignored.

Besides the above observations, one of the most important and useful ideas for me was the concept that we are all in a state of transformation. This transformation can be positively enhanced by picking apart the process of change, identifying inhibiting factors and composing strategies for overcoming those inhibiting factors.

These are the positive concepts that I learned from this class and I look forward to implementing them in my own classroom.

Fig. 11.12   My Most Significant Understandings of This Class

This class brings it all together for me. This is the 1st class I can re-member where different theorists were not only talked about, but also ap-plied to practice—with examples. For instance, Lewin and his problem-solving techniques are excellent. I liked the items we did this week in preparation for class.

I have also learned to appreciate the Gregorc more than the last time I took it. It actually makes sense as I try to put it into practice more and more with people I deal with—I think I have a CR principal. He likes me around because I can accomplish paper trail items in one day; he is a month behind in due dates on—he is very much a people person. We get along well. I have also learned to appreciate and understand my husband better.

The modeling by you is extremely interesting, and I have tried to copy these behaviors in the meetings I have been in lately. I find that keeping a soft voice, probing questions, and a listening attitude helps a lot with children and adults. Thanks.—Molly Greer

Reflections

First, this is the very first course I've ever taken that has allowed me to learn about myself. Second, this course offers a first-hand exposure to process. The professor allows for on-site classroom experience throughout the entire course. Although I've previously sought to involve individuals in group processes, this course has provided me with many successful techniques which I am very excited about utilizing this fall.

My third most meaningful experience in this class relates directly to the manner in which the professor treats every student. This university is the very first facility in my eight years of college experiences where the graduate and/or doctoral students are treated with respect (and) the instructor displays a genuine interest in every student. The interests and concerns of the students are also his . . . he has never "put down" a student for an incorrect response. Rather, he very gently directs the students towards the correct idea. This enables the student to feel relaxed and to enjoy learning. . . . However, this is first time I've enjoyed learning since I was in elementary school.—Unknown

AND, LAST

What I should have learned in kindergarten but learned this year:

1. Structure is not control.
2. Embrace change: you will learn and grow from it.
3. If you write it down, put it on the wall, and look at it—you may just remember it.
4. An open heart will open the mind.

5. Food shared with friends nourishes relationships.
6. Life is the Olympics of existence, with a multitude of game and players.
7. Teaching is a partnership with the learner; learning is a partnership with yourself.
8. People speak different languages, and speak the same language differently.
9. People hear different languages, and hear the same language differently.
10. People live in different worlds, and live in this world differently.—Suzanne Gibson Wise, July 1994

QUESTIONS STUDENTS ASK

1. How can we change our schools from the inside?
2. How can we get support from many politicians who seem to be motivated to denigrate the public schools?
3. Why aren't educators more involved in making the decisions that affect education, rather than having noneducators take control and tell us what to do—and, by now, often how to do it?
4. How can I build support with and from my colleagues?
   A. How can I develop support in my social systems?
   B. What can I learn from other teachers who develop imaginative, constructivist projects and ideas?
   C. I have to learn how to build support from the administration. How can I do that?
5. How can I take charge and build the culture of my classroom and/or team? (Hint: Several chapters provide ideas and practical approaches, especially chapters 5 and 13.)
   A. How do you start?
6. This process in this class works. How can I pull it off so it works for me?
7. The Gregorc Personality Delineator seems to be cornerstone of what you do. Why does it work for you? (See chapter 13 for some ideas, among other cases.)

CHAPTER 12

A Typical Day as a Constructivist High School Teacher and Department Chair

Janet Richards

The Realities of a Chairperson's Life: Hurried, Harried, Harassed

—Chairperson

BUSY BEGINNINGS

I arrive at school at 8:00 A.M., my flex schedule (from 8:00 A.M. to 4:00 P.M.) agreed upon when I returned to teaching at the high school with Mr. Thorston, with whom I had worked for eight years at a previous school. I sign in at the main office and check my mailbox. On the way to my classroom, I am stopped by Chris (an On-the-Job-Training [O.J.T.] student), who starts complaining about his employer and how he wants to quit his job. I remind him of the procedures required and ask him to see me in my office before leaving campus today. I continue to greet several students, custodial personnel, and others in the outdoor courtyard and inquire about how their weekend went.

Arriving at my teacher planning office (TPA/Office, which is in between two classrooms) I check my phone messages—especially concerned with the secretary's report of who is absent. None of our teachers are out, so I begin by concentrating on my duties (as I see them) as the business department head. Because of our extremely large building and the separation of our teachers (one is located in the main office; two are in classrooms attached to our TPA; two are located on the second floor of the 500 building; and two are located in "the new" building), I look in on Sloan and Joan to say "Good Morning" and then call upstairs. Sam answers and all is fine with him and Sakeena. The same is true for Ruth, Kyung Hee, and Jack. (We have established a "buddy system" where teachers check on each other every morning and cover until I arrive. If anyone is out, I ensure that a substitute is there. Because of the enormous shortage of subs we [the instructors] usually have to cover until our principal's secretary arranges coverage.)

From the beginning, our department was established with the philosophy that we all are capable and successful professionals and that I am here to assist or help them with any needs or problems. That is why I do not require them to "sign in" daily, but to work as a team in order to cover each other. Since there would be no central area for "signing in," that would not require unnecessary additional time on their part.

I then log onto our school's intranet for communication regarding the daily schedule and so forth, and my "in school" and district e-mail. While doing this, Sakeena comes into the office looking upset. (Sakeena has taught two years at the junior high school, but this is her first year as a high-school business instructor. In order to help her transition, I asked Kyung Hee to serve as her mentor regarding curriculum and lab procedures. I planned to work with her on classroom management on an ongoing basis.) Sakeena updates me on a student discipline problem she had been working with and informs me that the father left a message that he wanted to meet with her and his son's dean that morning. Sakeena is nervous and concerned.

We review the actions of the student, her steps to correct and encourage positive involvement from the student, and the results. I assure her that she had done everything I suggested (and more), and I would be at that meeting for support. I arrange for Kyung Hee to cover Sakeena's class, Sloan to cover mine, and call the assistant principal to let her know to expect us at 9:45, the only time the father and the A.P. could meet. Sakeena expresses appreciation and appears to relax. I send her to start her third period and tell her to come get me at 9:40.

Homeroom

Just then the bell rings for students to go to homeroom. (Department heads do not have an assigned homeroom, so we can cover our department as needed, and if not, do "duty" in the halls during homeroom.) I grab my stack of student papers, hoping to get a few minutes to get some graded, and head for the "Fish Tank"—the open amphitheater in the middle of our campus.

I smile and encourage students to stop socializing and start heading to their homerooms to avoid being tardy. As the tardy bell rings, a few stragglers angrily pass by.

Some Quick Planning

I yell hello to our assistant principal of curriculum and he waves me over. We discuss the situation with my marketing teacher, Sally, being on maternity leave, and Joan's (one of our business instructors) maternity leave approaching. Our goal was to have Sloan cover as a temporary teacher for Sally in marketing and then cover for Joan after Erika returns. This would give Sloan experience teaching both marketing and business classes—in both of which she is certified. Due to complications with her pregnancy, Joan's doctor is now advising her to begin her leave a month earlier than first planned. This unforeseen development has made it impossible for our plan to work, and we briefly discuss options. As the bell rings ending the ten-minute homeroom period, Marty and I agree to meet after the department head meeting that afternoon to continue brainstorming ideas.

First Period

As I arrive to my classroom, I open the door, and "stand guard" in the hallway. I smile, laugh, and joke with students passing me in the extremely crowded hall. I welcome my students individually as they come into the classroom, asking them how they are doing, asking about their jobs, and so forth. Two students I don't know or recognize as friends of my students stop, poke their heads in, ask "Miss—what's this class?" I enthusiastically tell them "Marketing"—inviting them to come back and talk to me about the class, club, and program, but reminding them they can't be late to their class!

MY CLASSROOM

My students walk into our classroom, which is unlike many classrooms in the county today. It is unique due to its appearance and subject matter. For this is a marketing class, one that looks different, feels different, and will motivate students to their highest individual capabilities! Trapezoid and conference tables instead of individual desks; DECA banners; mannequins; digital display boards; display cupboards filled with trophies and scrapbooks; and three bulletin boards filled with pictures—one titled "Our DECA Family," one of our O.J.T. students at their job site, and one titled "Competition." Lots of *color!!!*

Safety Needs

Being a high Abstract Random (AR) personality (people's feelings are important, and I tend to react emotionally to most social situations), I understand how important it is for students to feel comfortable and safe in their learning environment. The climate of the classroom is crucial! All individual learning, as well as personality, styles are accepted and considered in everything I do. For example, my Concrete Sequential students who feel most comfortable with structure and routine will find bell work on the board when they arrive in my classroom. (They know the ninety-minute class schedule will be spent with fifteen minutes on bell work; thirty minutes on instruction; thirty minutes on DECA; five minutes on "wrap up"; and ten minutes on social time.)

Third Period

Third period comprises my Marketing II and III students, who are very familiar with each other and many greet with hugs, joking, and smiles. While students settle down and begin the bell work, I quickly take roll and enter tardies in our computerized tardy program.

Clara and Jeff are standing next to me, and I ask them please to give me a few minutes to finish. Jeff insists that he needs to use the restroom, and I remind him that we must follow the school's rule that no one leaves classrooms during the first and last ten minutes of class. I tell him to get his pass card from our "pass box" and fill it out for me to sign, so he'll be ready to leave as soon as ten minutes have passed. As he goes to get the "pass box," I see Clara is about to cry and she whispers she really needs to talk with me.

A Major Problem

I escort her quickly to my storeroom (which is the only place I can talk privately to students without being interupted by other students or other teachers) and ask her to give me five minutes to get the class going.

Today, Heather, who has aspirations to be an elementary school teacher, is scheduled to deliver the lesson over chapter 25.2 in a "classical style" (lecture/overhead notes) but will have her class assignment be a group project. I ask Heather if she is ready, and she is. Before she begins, I review the expectations I have while a student (or anyone for that matter) is in front of the class. I then inform the class that I need to leave at 9:40, but I hope to be back before the class ends. Mrs. Forrester will be in to "cover" for me, but they all know what to do. As soon as they are finished with the lesson, I want them to get in their groups during DECA time. As Heather begins her instruction, I quietly go into the storeroom where I had Clara wait for me. Clara is a beautiful, bright, second-year Marketing III student who has aspirations to go to college. She is very upset and begins by crying that she is pregnant. As my chest hurts, my stomach feels sick, and I fight the feeling to either yell at her or cry with her, I take a deep breath and hold her while she cries, telling her "everything is going to be O.K.," with a confidence I don't quite feel.

We begin talking, but I know that Sakeena will be on her way down to get me in a few minutes. I encourage Clara to talk to her guidance counselor, her boyfriend, and her parents. I apologize for not being able to spend more time, but I ask her to come back during our lunch—in the meantime, I write a pass for her to see her counselor. (I know she won't be able to concentrate on classwork at present, and I won't be there the entire time to monitor her, so I feel it's best for her to be with her counselor.)

As Clara leaves the room to go to guidance, my attention goes back onto Heather, who is doing a very good job covering the major concepts of the chapter. I had given her suggestions, brief guidelines, and materials for her to use. As Mrs. Forrester arrives, I interupt class to explain that she will be "facilitating" the class, and I will try to be back ASAP! I then wait for Sakeena outside my room.

The Usual Conference—The Parent Defends His Son: No Surprise

The next forty-five minutes are spent in a parent/dean/teacher conference. I support my teacher and am professionally understanding to the father, but disappointed in his stand not to support the teacher or the school with the evidence being provided. Unfortunately, the father is still not happy with his son receiving a one-day in-school suspension for an offense. I tell him his son would in the past have been removed from the class entirely. This would have happened in the present instance, were it not for the gross overcrowding of our school.

Our assistant principal for student affairs, therefore, refers him to her superior, the assistant principal of our school. After learning what the consequences of the incident was, I tell them that Sakeena needs to return to her class, and me to mine. They could contact us there if anything else is needed.

Back to the Classroom

I returned to my room to find mild chaos—but things getting done. Students are working on DECA at the time—Ashley, David, Valerie, and Will are working with Mrs. Forrester on our Civic Consciousness Project, a Golf Fest scheduled for this Saturday for multiple sclerosis. (M.S. was the cause that our DECA Chapter accepted to promote and raise money for this year.) A group of girls are making posters to be used at Saturday's event, and the others are working on their individual competitive areas preparing for District Competition.

Joan, who is working on her Entrepreneurship Manual, is on the computer and Joelle, our DECA secretary, is working on a typing a project for me. Heather, who daily is responsible for calling O.J.T. students' work stations to ensure that they did not work on a day absent from school (state law) is on the phone in my teacher planning office.

I make my way around the room checking on the progress of each group or individual. I thank Mrs. Forrester for covering for me and then quickly call Mrs. Jean (Clara's counselor) to find out if she is O.K. I ask her to let Clara know that I will be in my office during lunch period if she wants to come back.

I take a few deep breaths and return to the classroom to wrap up and discuss what was learned—both positives and negatives—from today. Heather is very upset that after I left three students were not respectful and she was hurt and angry. I remind the class that respect while someone else was talking is a class requirement. I then ask the three girls to pick which chapter for the next week they would like to present. I tell them it is a lot more difficult to teach a lesson than it looks, and I want them to have the firsthand experience of doing so. They pick next Tuesday, and I give out the "guidelines" for presenting lessons.

Afterward I speak to Heather about teaching—the ideals, the realities, and how to do your best while maintaining class interest and control, without losing your temper when faced with individuals not participating. Other students then make their comments about the class period, and we say good-bye until tomorrow!

Again, a bell rings signalling me to stand once again at the door to be present to minimize the chance of problems with students during this changing time, and to greet our Marketing I students. Mrs. Forrester, who is my marketing "partner" while Sally is on leave, shares my room this year because of the shortage of space. My official fourth and fifth periods are O.J.T., so the room is available for her fourth-period class.

The first ten minutes are hectic—students beginning bell work, Mrs. Forrester beginning roll, and my O.J.T. students who leave at 11:00 signing out on a roll sheet I have on the back counter by the door. I am there to talk with them as they leave, and it is the only chance I get to see a great many of them. (With block scheduling, O.J.T. students are only required to take a marketing class at least once each school year— but can be enrolled in O.J.T. the entire year, so for many it is the only time that I can touch base without having to send a pass for them and interupt another class.)

Susan confirms that I received her message yesterday (she had a doctor's appointment and missed school, but wanted permission to go to work). I tell her I did, and praise her for following our procedures. Josh excitedly tells me he got the job at Red's Sporting Goods and starts tomorrow. Others quickly sign out and go and I can't resist saying, "Be careful."

Deanna, who is working very hard leading our Civic Consciousness Project, asks me if I could cover the class and let her keep working on the financial plan of the project. The class was to review for an exam over economics (chapters 1–7) and channels of distribution (chapters 33 and 34). I assure her that I have no problem doing that and compliment her on the hard work she is doing.

Fourth Period: Maslow's Physiology Needs Butt Up Against a New School Rule

Fourth period is a lively group of students—and a very hungry group by this time of the day. In the past I had always allowed this class period to form "social" groups responsible for providing snacks and drinks for the class while we worked. I have found that these groups enjoyed the planning and providing, as well as the participating, in our working lunches.

However, this year the school has strictly forbidden any food in the classrooms. (We still have a monthly "DECA Party" with food and socializing—but we now meet outside under a tent—an idea my students came up with!) Today, however, we provide an "incentive" for the class—a candy bar from our goody bag to all who participate. (It is amazing how food motivates people.)

The Review Game

After discussing the bell work we divide into groups of six to seven students and begin our review game. Deanna has written out about a hundred index cards listing one question per card. I start by outlining the rules: each group/table that correctly answers the card will receive the card. If they answer incorrectly, the next group/table will get a chance to "win" the card.

Ashley, the president of our DECA chapter, stays to work with me during his lunch period, so I have him serve as point taker. Any group or individuals in a group who talk or distract us during the questioning/answering time would *lose* a point/card. We play the game for longer than our instruction time, but I wrap it up in time to give students their candy and have time to spend working on DECA.

Socializing: Maslow's Third Level

This day the students socialized more than prepared for their competitive event, but I believe that socializing is an important part of our program—learning to talk, discuss, and accept all types of people. We spend a great deal of time talking about that *and* practicing this skill during our class. Our school is an excellent example of society—a "melting pot" of all ethnic, religious, and economic groups of people.

Cooperative Learning, Group Work, and Accepting Differences

With the focus on cooperative learning and working together toward group-developed goals, my students have an opportunity to learn about, accept, or tolerate others. These social skills are crucial for them in their lives and their work enviornments. As I tell them all the time, "80 percent of all the people who lose their jobs, do not do so because of lack of technical skill or knowledge, but because of poor human relations skills!"

Lunch—Well, Sort Of

Mrs. Forrester leads today's wrap-up, and I take the opportunity to retrieve my phone messages from the day. I have two employers to call back, one parent, and three miscellaneous calls to return. But as fourth period ends and my thirty-minute lunch begins, I once again return to the door to catch the second group of O.J.T. students leaving. (There are three O.J.T. release times:11:00 A.M./12:36 P.M./1:13 P.M.) As the last are leaving, I see Clara walking down the hall. I greet her with a compassionate smile and hug and we sit in the storeroom to talk privately. At the end of the lunch period, she (with the final group of O.J.T. students) signs out and prepares to leave campus.

The Department Head Meeting

Today, being Monday, means I have about five minutes to eat and prepare my notes to bring to our weekly department head meeting. Today's meeting begins with our principal talking about the state and county changes—focusing now on individual school S.A.T. scores. (We are already evaluated on students' performance on the Florida Comprehensive

Assessment Test, the High School Competencey Test, their attendance, etc.) He ends by asking us to extend his appreciation and thanks to our teachers for their hard work. (We are extremely overcrowded, some teachers have forty-five to fifty students in a classroom, and then we receive word that we did not get a raise. And there is still a hiring freeze on.)

Our assistant principal then takes over and discusses the deadlines for our Professional Development Plan, the dates for testing in October—which include October 1st–5th; exams October 11th and 12th; AGD's and GGD's (grades) for the first quarter (which on block is one-half year) will be due the following week. A list of students' indebtedness is due and a reminder that any student entering the exam with a D or less needs to have a parent contacted. We complete the meeting by going around the room one by one, sharing any information from our department.

The End (of the School Day, Not Mrs. Richards')

The bell rings at the end of the school day at 2:50, and our meeting adjourns. I wait for Marty to meet with him regarding our situation with my teachers and their maternity leaves. I outline the steps I have taken to keep Sloan on, as well as recruiting ideas for next year, so that I can hire Sloan on as the third marketing instructor (and primary DECA advisor). We meet with our principal's secretary for ideas and develop a "plan B." We won't know if it is possible until Marty contacts downtown. Even then, we really won't know until it is done! Some teachers feel that the district office (downtown) sometimes changes plans and rules midstream, as they deal with their complexities and internal and external forces and demands, so I know not to promise Sloan anything.

The "Day" Continues

I then return to my classroom to type the notes from the meeting so I can distribute them to my teachers first thing in the morning. I return my phone calls. One of the two employers who had left a message earlier is very angry with an employee (my student) and wants to fire her. I ask him to please let me talk with her one more time and arrange for the three of us to meet that Thursday at 2:30 to discuss the problems. I record the specifics of our conversation in my O.J.T. Co-op Record

Form for that particular student. I call the student at home to discuss the problem, and inform her of our meeting time/day.

I complete the calls, and then input some of the students' papers I graded from the weekend into the computer—our grading program is all computerized and used by every teacher at our high school.

Visits to Cooperative Learning Sites

At 3:45 I organize my O.J.T. list and student records, and select two coop visits to make before finishing my day. I must visit each O.J.T. training station every nine weeks. When the number of students required to make a unit was forty to forty-five students, this was manageable. Now I carry seventy-two O.J.T. students, and on block scheduling "a new year" begins in January—which means all new paperwork, forms, and so forth must be redone. The required paperwork for each O.J.T. student includes forms they, their parents, and training stations must sign: coop record forms; release cards; monthly timecards; evaluation forms.

I stop by a restaurant and meet with the manager regarding my student. All is fine and it is a welcomed, pleasant meeting. I quickly record our conversation in the student's record form and proceed to the next stop. It is a large retail chain that employs three of my students. I meet with the store manager, and then with each of their respective department managers to see how the three are doing.

Today, Elisa and Brett are working so I observe them dealing with customers, making sales, and working on the register. I can tell they are happy, but nervous to see me there, so I act very casual as I observe them. After spending time with them, I leave and (again) record my conversations and observations in their Coop Record form.

Before calling it a day, I review the few training stations still left to visit before the end of next week. I determine what day I plan to see them and record it on my calendar.

With that, the day has ended.

SUMMARY

The beginning quote sums it up succinctly. The chairperson is, indeed, hurried, harried, and harassed.

QUESTIONS FOR THE CURIOUS

1. The first question that pops into mind is, "How does she stand this pace?"
2. Does everyone in this position maintain this pace?
   A. If so, how can we prevent burnout?
   B. How can we keep enthusiasm and interest high?
3. This role seems far more active than most chairpersons. If so, why is it?
4. What is the role of most department chairs?
5. What is the impact of different personalities on this role?
   A. Ms. Richards identifies herself as an Abstract Random, a people person, who operates a great deal on emotions (using the Gregorc Personality Style Delineator). Are all ARs so heavily engaged?
   B. What about other styles? (Please see chapter 13 "ESOL, Constructivism, and You—Constructivist and ESOL Philosophy and Practice: Another Surprise" for a more elaborate discussion of these personality styles.) How would they play their roles out?
   C. Would a person who is not an Abstract Random people person succeed as well with this chairmanship role in this type of department? Or, this type of organization?
6. In what way is Ms. Richards' role constructivist?
   A. How does she build a culture?
   B. How does she deal with different social systems?
   C. How does she relate to the administrative social system?
   D. How does she relate to the various teachers' social systems, including those of her department?
   E. How important is her flexibility?
   F. How does she organize her classes?
   G. What is the sense of trust and responsibility she generates in her operation?
7. How does she deal with difficult people?
8. Could you do what she does? How would you handle the job?

CHAPTER 13

ESOL, Constructivism, and You—
Constructivist and ESOL Philosophy
and Practice: Another Surprise

> The entire constructivist philosophy and practice fit admirably with
> ESOL philosophy and practice.
>
> —Arthur Shapiro

INTRODUCTION AND ORGANIZATION

The constructivist philosophy is based on the notion that each individual, including siblings from the same family and even twins, constructs his or her perceptual world differently from anyone else based upon his or her unique experiences, personality, and subcultural values, among many other variables. As a consequence, we each have a divergent, highly individualized, constructivistically built world. The highly individualized world for each of us, as perceived through both constructivism and ESOL, are quite similar. The constructivist philosophy mandates decentralizing down to the group (or social system), and to the individual level in each classroom or team.

This chapter first deals with the three major ESOL principles and their relationship to constructivism, with case studies comparing and contrasting a traditional class taught by Ms. Geocaris with that of a constructivist model used by Sue Sharp. A following section deals with developing a culture in a classroom and team deliberately, a somewhat surprising idea for most educators. The case studies are continued to provide realistic examples, followed by analysis of underlying dynamics, with clear application to both ESOL and constructivism. Next, we examine the impact of personality styles on ESOL and constructivism, and on curriculum, and investigate how each style relates to a curriculum governed by other styles. Last, suggestions are provided for constructivist and ESOL teachers and those in leadership positions to deal with the opportunities provided by such divergence.

THE THREE ESOL PRINCIPLES AND CONSTRUCTIVISM

ESOL promulgates three principles:

1. Increase *comprehensibility*
2. Increase *interaction*
3. Increase *higher thinking skills*

The constructivist interactive models that I discussed, developed, teach, and delineated in the book, *Leadership for Constructivist Schools*, utilize as their primary and fundamental instructional vehicle, the small group. Virtually all work is done in the small group, with each group essentially responsible for solving and reporting on their analysis of an article, a problem, or a situation, often one that is chosen by the students.

By comparing and contrasting this model with the classical lecture-style, teacher-dominated model, a real-life case study was utilized in chapters 1 and 3 of that book, which illustrates the differences between the two (Shapiro 2000). Ms. Geocaris, the classical teacher, establishes an instructional system that creates a structure and process in which students work alone, and as such are isolated.

Since no framework of support is established, numbers of individuals often and usually fall through the cracks, this being particularly true of foreign language students, students with difficulties, those who are less mature. Ms. Geocaris literally does not see that her instructional model does not recognize naturally occurring social systems that spring up in every classroom. And then she wonders why so many do so poorly. The culture and system she *inadvertently* creates has no safety nets, no cooperative ethic.

Her system, used commonly throughout American education, treats people as *individuals*, and does not see them as members of social systems.

Ms. Sharp, on the other hand, utilizes the *social system* (that is, the small group, which can be two to seven students) as her primary vehicle, which provides support to everyone in the classroom (including the instructor). She also deliberately creates a culture in which expectations are that people are cooperative and helpful.

The model she uses sets up a problem, or analyzes an article, or any other starting point stimulus. Each group or social system then is free to analyze it using a Great Books format: What are the author's, or the problem's main points? Are they valid? How can I/we use them today in my/our everyday work?

Each group writes its jointly developed perceptions on large newsprint or chart paper and then puts them on the board for comparison and contrast. The person(s) who were the recorders cannot be reporters, whose role is to present and to discuss their group's work with the rest of the class, thus creating roles for more people in each group.

- Note that this model is based on *interaction.*
- Note that this model provides for *active learning.*
- Note that this model provides for repetition of different perceptions of the article, problem, or stimulus by the fact that each group independently creates its own analysis, plan, and evaluation, thereby increasing *comprehension.*
- Note that this model structures analysis through comparing and contrasting different solutions, structures people to develop a plan for their analysis and presentation (synthesis), and finally, evaluates the content and the process, working on developing the *higher cognitive levels* (Bloom 1956) by stimulating questions such as: Are the author's formulations valid? How can they be used today? It also deals with comprehension and application. (How can I/we use it today?)

Thus, the three principles of ESOL are not merely carried out thoroughly, but constitute the basic structure and processes of the operation. That, is, *interaction* is the basic vehicle of instruction, *comprehension* is a major focus since each group presents its own analysis of the material, and *higher levels of thinking* are structured daily.

At the end of the session, students and groups are asked to respond to the following sentence stem: "Today, I learned . . ." (Note the emphasis on reflective comprehension and the higher cognitive levels.)

At the midpoint and end of the semester students and groups are asked to respond to: "My most significant learnings in this class are . . ." (Again, note the higher levels; see chapter 11 "From the Mouths of Students—Interactions with Constructivism.")

Many groups decide on group projects, usually become extremely creative, and have a lot of fun.

CREATING A CULTURE DELIBERATELY, NOT BY ACCIDENT

Virtually all teachers develop three kinds of curriculum:

1. a planned curriculum (what we plan to do)
2. an unplanned curriculum (side comments to a group, admonitions to one or more students about something personal, etc.)
3. a hidden curriculum, about which we are largely unaware. For example, biases favoring one gender or against a racial or an ethnic group emerge in our social interaction but we often are unaware of them.

On a more sophisticated level, most of us in education, like Ms. Geocaris, are completely unaware that we create a culture (one vital aspect of a hidden curriculum), and a system of learning (another hidden curriculum) or that one is created in every classroom and team. Someone like Ms. Sharp is fully aware and sets about creating a subculture that is cooperative, supportive, inclusive, and works for her and for the students.

A culture consists of common understandings, feelings, perceptions, and values that people learn in connection with social living. A shorter definition would be that culture consists of patterns of shared, learned understandings and behavior that a group of people develops; a subculture is generated by a smaller group.

For example, the U.S. Marines develop a different subculture than a nursery school. Retail stores develop different subcultures, as do different classes in schools, and different sections of the country (Southern fried chicken, New England clam bakes). Norms are customs people develop in connection with social living.

The ESOL teacher or team can vastly enhance his or her classroom practice by infusing well-thought-out cooperative, group, and other practices (some of which have been discussed briefly above) to become part of the class subculture and by creating norms or practices that are supportive, cooperative, inclusive, and caring.

CREATING A CULTURE: MS. GEOCARIS COMPARED WITH MS. SHARP AND ESOL

A few lines from case studies involving Ms. Geocaris and Ms. Sharp illustrate these ideas. Ms. Geocaris teaches ninth-grade biology (and note who makes *all* the decisions).

> In the past years *I* [italics mine] took a traditional approach with a complex but vitally important scientific concept: What is DNA and how does it contribute to genetics and the diversity of life? *I* usually presented material to students through lectures and labs. *I* explained key scientific discoveries and told students about the theories that resulted. . . . After presenting the material, *I* expected students to understand the relationship among DNA, RNA, proteins, and genetics. Although many students did, others did not; moreover, my students did not exhibit high levels of student engagement. (Geocaris, 1996–1997, p. 72)

Let's utilize the three key ESOL principles to evaluate this instructional model. Is there any *interaction* among students? Apparently there is little or none, except informal and subterranean, usually negative in nature. Students are passive bystanders. Note that everyone is forced to adhere (or chooses not to, or even sabotages) to the agenda set by Ms. Geocaris.

And who is doing the work? Who is making all the key decisions? Ms. Geocaris appears to be in control, but is she? She certainly was not getting her desired results and ended up so frustrated, so dissatisfied, that she felt forced to change her model. Ms. Geocaris was quite dissatisfied with "her" resulting comprehension, noting that numbers of students did not "get it." As for the higher cognitive levels, she obviously felt she was a failure.

Let's compare and contrast this with Sue Sharp's approach, again keeping in mind the three ESOL principles, plus others featured in ESOL literature (using visuals, manipulatives, demonstrations, etc.).

Sue Sharp bounced from her middle school team meeting with Alana Michelle, Marc Douglas, and Janet Riccardo into the classroom with a full head of steam. Having just left the daily planning meeting she felt loaded for bear and immediately wrote on the overhead in her precise left-handed style:

Today's goals:
Schedule for:

- The Horsemen
- The Magicians
- The Farmers
- The Musicians
- The River Men

Review today's objectives:

- Work
- Dates of presentation

Wrap up, evaluation of the day's activities on the Group Planning or Post-Meeting Reaction (PMR) form [see figure 13.1]

Development of objectives, resources and time needed for tomorrow.

She turned to the first members of each of the five groups filtering in and asked them whether they wanted to alter their plans for today from those handed in yesterday. Four groups indicated that they would stick with their plans, while the Magicians wanted to modify their plan with an additional objective. Chuck would focus on home-building techniques and styles. Sue stated that this would be fine with her if the group was comfortable. Chuck noted that they agreed. As the students came in, they moved immediately into their small groups and began to work with a good deal of intensity.

Sue made the rounds, sitting with each group as they worked on village life in nineteenth-century rural Mexico. She was impressed with the energy of the students, particularly the two from Mexico and Columbia, their energy, their focus, and their creativity. She was pleased with the numbers of visuals developed and brought in, and with the plans for demonstration of cooking patterns and the menu scheduled for the grand finale of the unit.

Well, she thought, her team buddies, Alana Michelle, Marc Douglas, and Janet Riccardo, were on target, as usual. The students were engrossed and were working like beavers on their self-selected tasks (adapted from Shapiro 2000).

A. Date:_____

B. Name of Group: _____

C. Class:_____ D.Pd._____

D. Recorder: _____

E. Long Range Goals   1) _____

2) _____

3) _____

F. Task (s) for Today

1) _____

2) _____

3) _____

G. Amount Accomplished   H. What helped you?

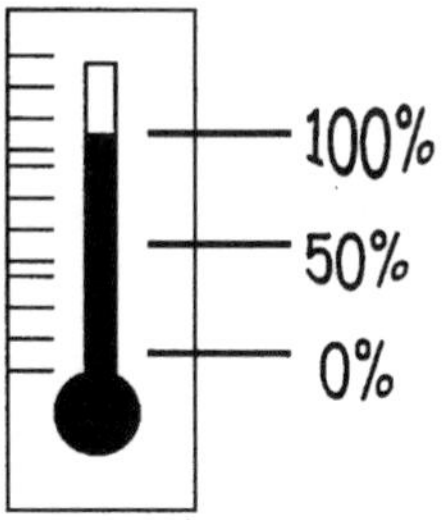

100%

50%

0%

I. What blocked you?

J. Task (s) for Tomorrow

_____

_____

K. What Resources do you need for tomorrow?

Human: _____

Material: _____

Figure 13.1   Post Meeting Reaction (PMR) Form
Group Planning Form

ANALYSIS

What pops out? Acceptance and respect.

Ms. Sharp, in contrast with Ms. Geocaris, accepts and respects the talents, abilities, and good sense of her group of kids. Obviously, she perceives them as self-motivated and trusts them thoroughly, although she is careful to structure the operation with expectations of high productivity so that the social systems (read, teams) work. Note that she checks out the PMR (read, evaluation) forms with the groups as they enter to determine whether they have made any changes.

Compare and contrast this approach with that of Ms. Geocaris, whose whole former approach reeked of mistrust and low levels of respect: "*I* usually presented material. . . . *I* explained scientific discoveries and told students. . . . *I* expected students." (Shapiro 2000)

Social System (Group versus the Individual)

Ms. Geocaris treats her students as *individuals*. She unwittingly creates a structure and system where individuals work alone, and since they can receive only informal help from others, lots of them don't "get it."

What a stark contrast with Ms. Sharp, who establishes a structure and system in social systems that are structured to work cooperatively in order to be supportive of all students. In short, Ms. Sharp constructs a system so that all individuals succeed because they are members of a group organized to succeed. For Ms. Sharp, the ESOL principle of *interaction* underlies her entire operation.

Student: Passive versus *Active* Learner

Again, the contrast is startling. Ms. Geocaris' role is that of *"Captain of the World."* *She* does all the planning; *she* does all the thinking; *she* does all the work. So the roles of the kids are passive. They can either go along, or they can tune out. Or—they can sabotage.

Ms. Sharp? What a difference. The *students* become *actively involved* in planning their own group projects (remember the ESOL principle of *interaction*). Interaction means active learning, which is far more effective than the passive model. Indeed, Davis and Murrell (1993) note:

> The recent research on student learning has concluded . . . that the more actively students are involved in the learning process and personal responsibility for their learning outcomes, the greater are their learning results. . . . The more individuals accept personal responsibility for the outcomes of their actions, the more likely they are to achieve those outcomes. (p. xvi)

A Focus on Motivation—and on Quality

Maslow's (1954) hierarchy of human needs fits admirably into the ESOL philosophy and practice, and, of course, into that of constructivism.

But, although many of us have been taught courses by psychologists, few, if any, will base their classroom practices on anything but the classical model of lecture, which hardly utilizes ESOL's three basic principles.

Maslow's Hierarchy of Needs consists of five levels as follows:

- Physiological Needs (food, shelter, water)
- Safety Needs (safe from physical and social attack, such as criticism)
- Social Needs (acceptance, friends)
- Esteem Needs (recognition, approval, being valued)
- Self-Actualization Needs (achieving one's dreams and aspirations)

In ESOL, all these levels of needs must be met. These constitute one approach toward the fundamental basis of motivating people.

How does Ms. Geocaris fare?

She *hopes* to motivate the kids toward working for quality. But, she leaves many, if not most, behind. She certainly has not met their Safety Needs. By dealing only with individuals, thus avoiding opportunities for interaction, she cannot hope to meet their Social Needs. And, obviously, the students' Esteem and Self-Actualization Needs are hardly blips on her conceptual horizon. Oddly, she perceives the student as a "lone wolf," not remembering Kipling's quote, "The strength of the wolf is in the pack," and not dreaming of meeting any of their Maslow need levels. In short, if she were graded on any of the ESOL principles with this classroom model, she would fail abysmally.

And, Ms. Sharp?

She deliberately structures her operation to generate motivation and quality. As previously noted, her organizing structure consists of using small groups who have a great deal of autonomy in making decisions regarding topics they elect to work on and projects they construct, how they are going to present their work and findings to the other groups, and so forth. Note that Safety Needs are met (with her norm of no destructive criticism), as are Social and Esteem Needs. Students are trusted and respected to produce responsible, quality work and projects. Their productions are creative and well received by both instructors and fellow students. Note that people working on projects are developing plans to analyze and to present their findings, ESOL's third principle of focusing on the *higher cognitive levels*.

In addition, Ms. Sharp's use of the PMR form (figure 13.1) structures the operation to focus on both long- and short-term plans, the former being aims and goals and the latter objectives. Therefore, Ms. Sharp expects the students to develop their own goals as well as their objectives in the unit they are studying. This only can serve to improve the quality because it also conveys to the students that this instructor really trusts and respects them to produce quality work.

ESOL and Cooperative Learning Techniques

Obviously, the instructional approaches utilized in ESOL and cooperative learning, such as carousel, teaching the text backwards, increased use of visuals and manipulatives, demonstrations, careful repetition, creating connections among concepts, moving from the concrete to the abstract, and such cooperative learning techniques as jig-saw, apply here.

Constructive Feedback

Constructive feedback is a major vehicle to improve quality. Let's look at the approach toward feedback in each class.

In Ms. Geocaris' class, students get formal feedback only from the teacher, and only sporadically at that. Students are individuals who sink or swim entirely on their own. Feedback can come from other students, but only informally and sporadically. Reflection is definitely not built into her model. As a consequence, ESOL and minority students usually are left behind.

Ms. Sharp's cooperative enterprise provides for constructive feedback in a variety of ways. Note that students create products in their work, so that they get feedback from within their own group. Next, they present their work to the other groups. Using newsprint to present their findings or any other modality (models, visuals, demonstrations, etc.) provides opportunity for other groups to discuss, to react, to provide constructive feedback. Filling out the PMR form also provides just such an opportunity for self correction (as with the student, Chuck, who indicated that the group wanted to add something to their work that day).

Education as a Social Enterprise: We Inevitably Create a Classroom or Team Culture—and We Cannot Avoid It

This point needs to be made. In Ms. Sharp's class the norm of support for students becomes embedded in the operation. The norm that *everyone is necessary* develops. Groups cannot have people not contributing and fare well.

"Driving Out Fear," Shades of Deming, America's Organizational Guru

Fear is the greatest immobilizer.—Judy Hanson, Vice Principal, Pasco County, FL

Driving out fear is essential to the health and productivity of any organization. Does Ms. Geocaris? Does Ms. Sharp?

PERSONALITY STYLES, ESOL, AND CONSTRUCTIVISM

Personality, too, is destiny.—Eric H. Ericson, *Newsweek*

This analysis is taken from chapter 14 of Shapiro, Benjamin, and Hunt's (1995) *Curriculum and Schooling: A Practitioner's Guide.*

Do different cultures produce different personality styles? According to some sources utilizing the Myers-Briggs instrument (Myers 1962), approximately 75 percent of Americans tend to be extroverts, while 75 percent of people living in Finland tend to be introverts.

How can ESOL (and all teachers-educators) cope with such vast differences successfully in our schools with their relatively large classes. For example, if one personality style is fairly introverted, how can the teacher help this person to interact more effectively? If one or more personalities do not like to deal with ideas and concepts, how is the teacher to proceed?

For the purposes of this brief section, it is useful to utilize Anthony Gregorc's *Personality Style Delineator* (1982a), which proposes four distinct personality styles in contrast with the sixteen personality types characterized in the Myers-Briggs instrument.

Gregorc noted some intriguing patterns in people, which led to his designing his instrument along two continua (see figure 13.2). The vertical axis deals with how people *perceive* the world, from *concrete* to *abstract*. Although most of us can do both, most of us lean toward one or another of these ways of perceiving. People who tend to be concrete like to work with facts, details, physical things. They also tend to be introverted. People who tend to be abstract often are expressive and emotional, or like to deal with ideas and concepts.

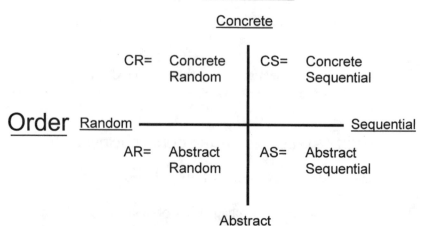

Figure 13.2   The Basis for Gregorc's Personality Style Delineator

The horizontal axis asks how people *order* the world, from *sequential* to *random*. People with strong sequential scores tend to like to do one thing at a time, usually in order. Those who like to do several things simultaneously, have a number of projects on which they are working, many lines of action, read many books at a time, and tend to be random.

Four Personality Styles

Four stereotypical personalities tend to emerge from this framework:

1. CS—Concrete Sequential
2. AR—Abstract Random
3. AS—Abstract Sequential
4. CR—Concrete Random

The Concrete Sequential (CS) Personality Style: The Organizer *(about 25%; Examples: accountants, engineers, draftsmen, pilots)*

- Likes to have things in order (no, loves order)
- Wants to organize things (will volunteer to clean up [read, organize] your files for you)
- Likes to work with details and facts
- Perceives the world very sequentially
- Follows directions literally
- Does not see the big picture
- Is a visual learner
- Often does not like or feel strong emotions, may be somewhat introverted
- Generally not intuitive, nor very creative, unless has a significant random score
- Makes lists for everything, usually in order of priority—and finishes them
- Structured, organized, perfectionist

Issues?
- Power and control (so tries to dominate)
- Things must be done in the right order
- Being on time
- Things need to be "correct," rules should be followed

So, this personality finds it difficult to interact comfortably with others. And, this personality does not like to deal with ideas and concepts, those involved in higher order thinking.

The ESOL teacher needs strategies to deal with this personality consisting of about 25 percent of the American population. What kind of strategies can facilitate utilizing this person's strengths and skills in ESOL classes? One possibility is to assign him or her a role in the small group by asking if he or she would like to make sure that time tables were kept or to facilitate organizing things, such as focusing on tasks and the like. These are roles the CS person likes to take. In these roles, this person can be productive in ESOL classes. Since this person works well with details, *comprehension* (using Bloom's Taxonomy) is a major function on which he can work.

As for the kind of curriculum this person likes and dislikes, the next major section will deal with that.

The Abstract Random (AR) Personality Style: The Feeler *(about 50% of Americans are ARs; 60% of ARs are females; Examples: Auntie Mame, Bette Midler)*

- Swims in a warm ocean of *emotions and feelings*
- Cries at sentimental movies and ads, being highly emotional
- Will drop everything to help a friend
- Is not sequentially or linearly organized—has piles everywhere
- Often dresses thematically, loving color and design
- Loves to work in groups (in Miss America contests is always picked as Miss Congeniality) in which they often stress CS personalities by having a lot of fun
- Highly intuitive and creative

Issues?
- People's feelings
- This is an audio learner, so often is not aware of details, and is usually late, rushing in breathlessly with excuses

How does the ESOL teacher deal with this lively personality? They are a gift, since they love to work in groups, so are the basis for groups developing effective *interaction*. While the CS deals with setting tasks, the AR personality deals with everyone's feelings, maintaining the group's emotional needs and, therefore, health. The AR' s feelings have to be carefully attended to because they can be badly wounded by caustic or sarcastic remarks, and then will withdraw, believing for the rest of their lives that the teacher does not like him or her.

The Abstract Sequential (AS) Personality Style: The Analyzer *(about 3–5% of Americans; Examples: Mr. Spock, Albert Einstein)*

- A "big picture" personality, living in the world of concepts and ideas
- Are great analyzers, coming off often as intellectuals
- Make great "big picture" planners
- Reads, writes, speaks well, with a big vocabulary
- Has high standards for the quality of his performance, and is competitive
- Values expertise, knowledgeable people above all—wants to know about a person's scholarly background

Issues?
- Quality
- Excellence
- Expertise
- Ideas

The ESOL teacher can use the mental firepower of this personality in planning, in being a spokesperson, in researching areas patiently, and becoming an expert in various areas. This person solves problems with a "big picture" conceptual approach, evaluating projects and ideas theoretically, often working on the *higher cognitive levels*, the third principle of ESOL.

The Concrete Random (CR) Personality: The Risk-Taker *(about 15–25% of Americans)*

- This is a risk-taker
- Loves to be divergent, different
- Is a trial-and-error problem-solver, troubleshooter
- Highly intuitive and creative

- Often innovators, inventors (Edison), entrepreneurs (Donald Trump)
- Often fearless, takes great chances (Evel Knievel), independent
- Wants to know how things work, so will take everything apart, but not have the time to put things back together, because has so many projects that he is working on simultaneously, and working on them alone
- Great vigor and energy, but little sense of timeliness
- Marches to his own drummer, so needs autonomy; cannot be controlled

Issues?

- Autonomy
- Independence
- Being divergent (often in personal dress)

The ESOL teacher is blessed with this personality (and with the other three) since working together they can create a synergy, a small group with greater power than one person working alone. This person is stimulated by *challenge* and can develop creative solutions to problems. Paired with other personalities of the same CR ilk, he can develop imaginative solutions to group or class problems. His considerable common sense, but deviant evaluations, can move the group to the *higher cognitive levels.* They are invaluable in groups with their creativity, divergent ideas, and intuitive insights into situations. They see opportunities where others see problems and blocks.

If the ESOL teacher has some CS elements in his or her personality, having a CS on a committee may be very reassuring. Bea Palls, a Spanish teacher, experimented with balanced committees consisting of all four personalities and with two committees consisting of ARs and CRs only. The latter two produced marvelously creative work, but their end-of-the-year projects were late (of course). If deadlines come in second to creativity for the teacher or team, a balanced group may not be that important.

PERSONALITY STYLES, CURRICULUM, AND ESOL

So, what kind of curriculum does each style produce and how does each style react to each other's curriculum style? Table 13.1 describes these.

First, let's portray the kind of curriculum each style will produce. Then, we can find out how each style reacts to the other styles. Next, we can suggest some ways for the ESOL teacher and administrator to deal more effectively and efficiently with the results.

The CS-Designed Curriculum (*Organizers*)

- Practical, no-nonsense, data-based, to-the-point
- Structured, linear, practical, black-and-white
- Product-oriented, nuts-and-bolts in design
- Avoids humanities such as the arts, which are not practical
- Generally, a prescribed curriculum
- Generally, a prescribed set of activities, sequentially organized exercises, drills, ditto sheets, handouts, and workbooks

Reactions by the Other Personality Styles

The other three will find this curriculum too boring and restrictive, with the randoms deviating widely from it. (See table 13.1.)

The Abstract Random Curriculum (*Feelers*)

- Considerable focus on the arts, humanities (they deal with feelings)
- Lots of optional activities
- Freewheeling, not detailed
- Room for creativity and personal decision making
- More process-oriented, than anchored in the here-and-now
- Learning activities are to-the-moment

Reactions

The CS and AS personalities will find it too unstructured, too touchy-feely, with the CS feeling it is too loose, and both turned off by the fun activities. The CR will feel free to deviate, of course.

The Abstract Sequential Curriculum (*Analyzers*)

- Conceptually and theoretically based, big ideas, concepts. One example was a high school curriculum in the social sciences with one year of Liberty, the next Fraternity, the last Equality
- Philosophically based, often essentialist in nature
- *Higher-order thinking* is the key, including comparing and contrasting analyses, synthesis, and evaluation, fitting into ESOL principles like a glove

Reactions

The CS will find this curriculum overwhelming, but will follow it mechanically. The AR will find it too cold, and the CR will play with the pieces of it that he likes.

The Concrete Random Curriculum (*Risk-Takers, Inventors, Innovators*)

- Discovery-oriented, process-oriented
- How things work, therefore, practical, creative, divergent
- Legions of options
- Learning activities will be independent study, games, simulations, problem-solving activities
- Timelines are loose

Reactions

The CS will find it too unfocused, too loose, too unstructured, while the AS will find fault with its lack of a conceptual or theoretical base. The AR will love the options.

ANCHORS

Each personality has different anchors:

- AS and CS personalities will stay with their plan, treating it as their anchor.

- The AR anchor consists of his feelings and emotions, thus activities will be to-the-moment. Thus, they will drift from their own curriculum.
- The CR anchor consists of independence and autonomy, so they will even drift from their own plan to meet those needs and emerging interests.

Table 13.1 summarizes each personality style's reactions to each of the other styles.

SUGGESTIONS TO BE SUCCESSFUL WITH SUCH VARIETY

How does the ESOL (and the regular) teacher deal with such divergence?

Providing faculty and administration with an instrument such as the Gregorc Personality Style Delineator and in-service workshops to make it part of the working operation of his or her organization is a good start. Indeed, in high schools, acquainting students with the Gregorc (older students might take it if their vocabularies are sufficient) might be a successful activity, which would broaden students' insights and interests considerably. Such an approach helps people recognize theirs and others' talents and their considerable potential in contributing to the success of the organization and its enterprise. It certainly broadens people's acceptance, respect, and appreciation for others' skills, strengths, and contributions to the success of their social systems and organizations.

SUMMARY

This chapter points to the (not-so-surprising) similarity between constructivism and the essential ESOL principles of comprehensibility, interaction, and higher thinking skills. The constructivist approaches discussed showcase these principles with their treating the individual also as a member of social systems, utilizing groups as the primary vehicle for instruction, and the absolute primacy of interaction and

Table 13.1 Impact of Curriculum on Each Personality Style

Curric.	CS	AS	AR	CR
CS	Think it is proper. Correct. The "right" way.	Too limiting. Not global enough.	Too restrictive. AR will deviate.	Too restrictive. Too limited. Will ignore and deviate widely.
AS	Too overwhelming. Too global. Will pick a piece and focus, but will not look at total picture. Inadequate for job. Will follow it, but will do it mechanically.	Love it. Challenged.	Too cold. Little interest since it doesn't deal with people and feelings and their experiences. Not experientially based.	Will follow, but will only do pieces of it. Piecemeal approach using parts they like. Couldn't do it and would not care.
AR	Too unstructured. Not enough rules. Too much freedom; too many options; too much use of media, color, experience. Couldn't do the fun activities; would make it a chore, going through it doggedly.	Too emotional. Too frivolous. Lacks conceptual rigor. Feels it is invalid, superficial. Thus, holds it in contempt. Gives it short shrift.	Loves it. Great opportunity.	Fairly compatible. Plays with, treats it as a start. Bends it to own purposes, use.
CR	Too unfocused. Too experimental, intimidated by creativity. Too untraditional in nature, so has trouble handling it.	Not conceptually based. No big ideas. Questions validity and seriousness. Critical of it, since lacks intellectual basis, depth and rigor. Has problems accepting it. Dislikes the fun built in.	Likes it. Finds it fun. Makes it fun. Accepts fully.	At home in the options. Diverges from it at will. Likes the fun.

active learning in developing its instructional systems. The constructivist case studies of Ms. Geocaris and Ms. Sharp fit equally well into the ESOL framework, as does the deliberate creation of a supportive and constructive culture.

In addition, we glanced at the impact of personality styles on curriculum and of curriculum on personality styles, both important for constructivist and ESOL systems. And we suggested approaches to make curriculum more suited to each personality's needs and interests.

QUESTIONS

1. What factors make ESOL programs and philosophy as described here so hospitable to constructivism?
2. And, yet, ESE programs are so behaviorist in following Skinner. What is the difference and why? What are the results?
3. The three ESOL principles of comprehensibility, interaction, and higher thinking skills seem to relate to constructivist approaches to organizing and teaching classes. How would you describe that?
4. How would you utilize the social system as a key to organizing your class?
   A. How did Ms. Geocaris?
   B. How did Sue Sharp?
5. Note that we talk about creating a culture *deliberately* in the classroom? How can you pull this off? And, do you want to?
6. What kind of grade would you give Ms. Geocaris on using constructivist principles? Ms. Sharp? Yourself?
7. This chapter explores two approaches toward motivation, that of the traditionalist, Ms. Geocaris, and the constructivist, Ms. Sharp. Which approach do you lean toward? In your experience, which seems to work best for you?
8. Table 13.1 compares how each personality style reacts toward curriculum designed by each of the four personality styles. How do you react toward each? Which do you like the most?

9. As an exercise, design a curriculum using Ralph Tyler's model. Build it on one of the Gregorc personality styles.
   A. Which one did you select?
   B. Does it fit your personality style?
   C. How do you react toward it?
   D. Why?
10. As an exercise see if you can recognize people who fit into each Gregorc style (Concrete Sequential [your bookkeeper], Abstract Random [Miss Congeniality in the Miss America contests], Abstract Sequential [Mr. Spock], Concrete Random [your local handyman who can fix anything]).
    A. Where does your mother fit? Your father? Siblings?
    B. Principal? Favorite teacher?
    C. Spouse or significant other? Kids?
11. What personalities would seem to be most accommodating to constructivist practices?
    A. Which would find it hardest to adapt to constructivism?
    B. Why?
    C. You?
12. What questions would you ask?

SOURCES

Bloom, B. (Ed.). (1956). *Taxonomy of educational objectives. Handbook I: Cognitive domain.* New York: McKay.

Davis, T. M., & Murrell, P. H. (1993). *Turning teaching into learning: The role of student responsibility in the collegiate experience.* [Abstract]. Washington, DC: George Washington University, 1993 ASHE-ERIC Higher Education Reports; Report 8.

Geocaris, C. (1996–1997). Increasing student engagement: A mystery solved. *Educational Leadership 54*(4), 72–75.

Gregorc, A. F. (1982a). *Gregorc Personality Style Delineator: Development, technical, and administrative manual.* Columbia, CT: Gregorc Associates. (Revised in 1984.)

Maslow, A. H. (1954). *Motivation and personality* (2nd ed.). New York: Harper & Row.

Myers, I. B. (1962). *The Myers-Briggs type indicator*. Palo Alto, CA: Consulting Psychologists.

Shapiro, A. (2000). *Leadership for constructivist schools*. Lanham, MD: Scarecrow.

Shapiro, A., Benjamin, W. F., & Hunt, J. J. (1995). *Curriculum and schooling: A practitioner's guide*. Palm Springs, CA: ETC.

CHAPTER 14

Freedom versus Control—The Scripted Classroom: The High Cost of Control to Everyone (Including Teachers)

Guards and convicts: Who are the prisoners?

—Arthur Shapiro

A SURPRISING REACTION

Jean Kern, an almost ethereally calm and gentle person, and I were talking (before she went to work with VISTA in Florida) about a teacher who ran a very tightly scripted classroom. Every comment he wanted to make was carefully scripted ahead of time. We knew that he was rated by many students as a highly effective, excellent, conscientious instructor.

Jean said, almost angrily, "Yes, but at what cost?"

Jean, a highly gifted, creative, free-wheeling, relaxed soul, stated, "I started out by doing that. I carefully scripted out what I was doing for every class (Jean was an early elementary teacher most of the time). But, I realized after a while that I was robbing myself and my kids of the chance to develop options. In short, by developing a rigid structure, I had curtailed my kids' and my freedom."

I expressed surprise that she had started out so rigidly, inasmuch as her teaching was free-flowing and creative.

Jean continued, "Dr. X's class robbed me of any chance to grow because I had so few options, so few choices to make. Because things were so tightly scripted out, we had few, if any choices available to us. Some people in the class felt that they had only two options: to pay attention or to tune out.

"I actually learned many things, which were useful in my teaching career, but I felt that my freedom was too constructed. I didn't like being placed in such a controlled setting. At least with my personality, I didn't like the heavy structure."

We both noted that some people liked the strictures of the structure, but Jean noted that it was far too constrictive. And because every movement was tightly laid out, she had little opportunity to become creative. She added that most people in education value creativity highly.

MS. KERN'S BEGINNINGS

To my asking (still with surprise) why she started out carefully scripting her classroom, she thoughtfully responded that this occurred at the beginning of her career in teaching, that she wanted to be highly effective, wanted to reach all kids. And, she noted, "I wanted to do it immediately; I thought that that strategy would get me my results immediately. So, I proceeded to plan long and carefully—and tried as hard as I could to control all variables."

Her Reactions

"So, what happened?" I asked.

"It just got too onerous. I had no freedom. The kids had no freedom. And, I couldn't control all the variables.

"In addition, I really didn't develop much creativity—and, of course, saw little being evidenced among the kids. We sure moved along the curriculum at a great rate. But, at what cost? I began to dislike it. I began to see teaching as work—no fun. (And so did the kids.) And I got scared that I would hate teaching.

"It sure wasn't stimulating, as I had imagined it would be in my schoolwork and in choosing it as a career. It was actually a lot, no, a great deal, of work—with little enjoyment (at least, as I first thought, for me)."

The Kids' Reactions

"So, I asked the kids about their feelings about the class. They said that they were learning, but it wasn't very exciting and there was too little fun. And, it was too rigid.

"Yet, about 20 percent liked the structure. They said that they learned. They were told what to do—and they did it. They were able to latch onto the structure, the routine, the expectations—and felt safe and comfortable. These kids never expected school to be much fun in the first place. It was work, but they accepted it and they learned. They were mildly satisfied, but not happy.

"Some of the more creative kids noted that this approach appealed to a worker bee syndrome, that this approach to education appealed to the drones. You can imagine how I felt!

"The rest felt that my class was a lot of drudgery, and provided little or no opportunity to be creative, to develop their own projects, and even to have some fun in learning. You know, I thanked them a lot for letting me know the truth about how they felt and what they perceived (I didn't use that word, though)."

HER REMEDY

"From these conversations, I realized with considerable shock, that my intense and controlling structuring was also robbing *me* of the opportunity to be creative and spontaneous as a person, which I am. I realized that I had felt safe by imposing such a controlling and rigid structure. Safe, but not happy—nor effective. I felt safe (shades of Maslow) as a result of my super-careful planning, but my higher levels of needs (social, esteem, self-actualization) were conspicuously absent.

"And, so were the students' higher cognitive and emotional needs. My structure was robbing them of these levels. It was a sort of a personal and professional epiphany I experienced.

"So, I began changing my organization and structure into projects, into problem-based learning approaches, group projects, lots and lots of hands-on activities. I embraced active learning with a vengeance."

ONE PROJECT

"My friends even began kidding me about my rather considerable shift. For example, in my second-grade class, for St. Patrick's Day in March, the kids studied stories about leprechauns, rainbows, pots of gold, and other Irish myths. We decided to build leprechaun traps, which generated immense levels of motivation and excitement, to their parents' great amusement and satisfaction. (I had sent home a newsletter informing the parents of the unit.) Teams of kids designed different traps, and compared and contrasted their creative products.

"On St. Patrick's Day, when the kids rushed into the classroom, they found that the traps had been kicked over, and little green footprints were visible going across the floor, up the walls, and across the ceiling. The kids had a wonderful time—and the shamrock-shaped green cookies, punch, and Irish soda bread baked by parents were wonderfully wolfed down.

"That was merely one constructivist project we developed."

SOME ANALYTIC COMMENTS—AND TOUGH QUESTIONS

One analyst (Matthews 2000) recently noted:

> This ethical dimension is manifest in the frequency with which notions
> of *emancipation and empowerment* [my emphasis] occur in constructivist writing; constructivism is thought to be a morally superior position
> to its rivals in learning theory and in pedagogy.

1. Obviously, one issue here is freedom vs. control. Many of us want to have more control. Indeed, some of us need to have more control, while others want less.
   A. What is the impact of this not only on the kids, but also on us?
   B. Jean's answer is that it has a great deal of impact both on the kids and on ourselves.
   C. After all, we are the models for our own kids and for those in our schools.
   D. If we're administrators, we are models for a lot more people.
2. Do some of us equate control with safety? Jean did, at least until the kids disclosed their perceptions and feelings.
3. Additionally, what are we modeling for the kids?
   A. If kids see us fearing freedom and independence, what will they do?

    B. If kids see us not trusting kids and other people, what is the hidden message to them?

    C. Will they, too, learn to fear these basic qualities of a good life?

4. When I attended the University of Chicago some time ago, one of the major questions being asked in the humanities survey courses was "What is the good life?"

    A. Some of these questions relate directly to that question, which each of us has to decide for ourselves.

    B. Is freedom, in enhancing our creativity, worth the risks it may generate?

    C. A major question facing us after the September 11, 2001, terrorist attacks is, can we have safety with freedom, with autonomy? This is a serious question for our total society, let alone for us as individuals and for our institutions, including schools, colleges, and universities.

5. What other questions would you generate in this area?

SOURCE

Matthews, M. R. (2000). Appraising constructivism in science and mathematics education. In D. C. Phillips, (Ed.). *Constructivism in education: Opinions and second opinions on controversial issues*, pp. 161–192. Ninety-ninth yearbook of the National Society for the Study of Education, Part I. Chicago, IL: University of Chicago Press.

Part II

CASE STUDIES IN CONSTRUCTIVIST LEADERSHIP

The final test of a leader is that he leaves behind him in other men the conviction and the will to carry on.

—Walter Lippman
"Roosevelt Has Gone"
New York Herald Tribune

Constructivist theory provides an impetus for many current educational reform efforts.

—J. A. Rainer & E. M. Guyton
Action in Teacher Education

CHAPTER 15

A Constructivist Sports Program:
The Case of Principal Marc Douglas's
Unusual Basketball Team

It ain't over 'til it's over.

—Yogi Berra

THE SIZE—AND THE CHALLENGE

The first thing Asher Sharp, the high school principal, noticed about the initial middle school basketball practice was that a lot of boys were milling around. He estimated that about thirty were there already, and more kept straggling in. He knew that Marc Douglas, the recently appointed middle school principal, had sent out a notice to all boys interested in playing basketball to meet at the gym right after classes were over. Strangely, to Asher's and to everyone else's eyes, the notice had said that all students who wanted to join the team would play! But thirty-five! Asher knew that most teams would be winnowed down immediately to about twelve of the best players, so he wondered how Marc would reduce the large excited group to a manageable size.

Marc, he realized, was a quiet and thoughtful mavericky man for the principalship. Asher early on had realized that Marc was a conceptually based administrator, somewhat rare for the field, but which Asher valued highly. At last, he thought, he had found a colleague with whom he could converse about ideas. In their relatively small but growing schools, which shared a number of facilities and even a handful of teachers who were flexible enough to work with both middle and high school kids, their positive personal relationships were essential for effective function.

No Cutting

So, he went over to Marc, and asked if he needed any help. Laugh-ingly, the taller Marc asked if red-headed Asher, all of 5′6″, could dunk a basketball. Asher responded by saying that he'd join in the fun, but that he might need a boost once in a while. Marc's response to cutting the team down to a baker's dozen at the most was surprising.

He told Asher that he wouldn't cut anyone. Nor did he want the cheerleader sponsor, upbeat, outgoing Madeline Linkin, to cut anyone who tried out, either. And, he said that Madeline not only took the job with that proviso, but also was positively enthusiastic about the idea.

Opportunity

Madeline bubbled over the endless possibilities of creative forma-tions that she and the girls could develop with such a large squad. In addition, she thought that the girls could develop real leadership skills in the process, because with so many girls, she'd need sub-leaders to take on an assortment of responsibilities, such as coordinating forma-tions, props, and many others. She told Marc that where others might see problems and constraints, she saw opportunity!

Both men were extremely impressed with Madeline's reaction, and Marc remarked to Asher that he'd had the same thoughts. The idea had enormous possibilities, great potential. With so many boys, they would have to pitch in and assume an assortment of leadership roles over a variety of functions, adding considerably to their educa-tion and social and emotional development. And, as with sharing playing time, the boys could share and rotate their various leadership roles that emerged from the size of the squad and the needs for co-ordination.

Marc added that he felt anyone who had the guts to try out should be honored in his or her effort. Asher, who at first rolled his eyes at this unconventional model, thought it had great potential and an unusual richness of possible outcomes, and said he'd see Marc after the prac-tice. He was going off to mediate another situation in which a parent with bared teeth was defending his child from a teacher's assertion that his precious child had skipped a class.

Managing the Horde

Before going home for dinner, the two friends met. Asher said that he'd take Marc at his word, but how was he going to manage thirty-five highly energetic, squirmy middle school boys? Marc affirmed that that was precisely what he was prepared to do.

"Look," Marc asked, "aren't these young kids? We're a relatively new school, just starting this program. I really believe that we should go intramural with middle school kids, and so do all the middle school associations. But the Board and the superintendent want to go interscholastic to compete with other districts, despite the widely shared middle school philosophy of avoiding such competition for kids that age."

Consequently, he had to go along with this policy decision.

Determining Who Has Talent

But, he told the Board and the superintendent that he would do it his way. He asked Asher, "How do we know who has talent and who doesn't? How do we know which boys will mature into good players at this time of growth and development? If we play everyone, we will get to see who develops and who has talent, but it takes a long time for some kids just to develop."

He noted that Asher had described his younger brother, Norman, as only a small 5'2", even as a sophomore. Now, he's a 5'11" star sprinter and swimmer, beating even Johnny Weissmuller's records (an Olympic champion and one of the earliest Tarzans). "How can you predict such development and deny kids a chance?"

He then pointed out to Asher that every coach in the universe knows that Michael Jordan was actually cut from the basketball team when he was in high school, a coach's action that made a lasting impression on Michael—and every coach, as well. But Marc pointed out that the ritual of cutting kids still persists, and persists, and persists—despite what we know. He asked Asher, "Who am I to predict whether a boy (or girl) will mature enough physically, emotionally, and mentally to play well enough in the future from first impressions? Would you have ever predicted that Norman would have become such a whale of an athlete when he was a little kid?"

ANOTHER ISSUE: WINNING—AND LOSING

Asher asked Marc about winning games, since his course of action looked like it would lead to a losing season. Marc's response was, "Our team will lose at least all of the first third of our games. But by the second third of the season, we'll win a couple. By that time, our boys will have gotten their feet under them, you'll see quite a difference, and, with some luck, we should win most of the rest."

Asher then noted that Marc was following the same course of action with the cheerleaders, who totaled about forty-four middle school girls so far on the squad. Marc noted that his own sister and her friends had tried out for the cheerleading squad in junior high, but only five girls were selected, and she was one of the majority who were cut, a heartbreaking experience for her and for her friends.

Like the boys who were cut, they all felt rejected—and humiliated.

Marc remembered that his sister and her friends had screwed up their courage to try again in high school, but the girls who won in junior high were so polished by that time that they easily won again. Marc also pointed out that a social class factor had played a role in his sister's situation. Only the elite girls won. And, these were the girls whose stay-at-home mothers (several themselves former high school and college cheerleaders) arranged to get them lessons even in middle school, so that they would win handily. The playing field was tilted!

Marc indicated that he would finesse that social-class advantage by giving everyone who wanted to participate an equal chance—all boys would get a chance to play. All girls would participate equally on the cheerleading squad. No one would be cut! Everyone would be urged to hang in. Over the long haul, it would pay off handsomely in lots of ways.

POSTSCRIPT

Outcomes—The Basketball Squad

To Asher's surprise, Marc's predictions were right on target, as Asher noted to his wife, Sue. The team lost every game in the first third of the season (much to the rather open amusement and delight of the other coaches, who were somewhat loud in their putdowns of Marc), won a couple in the second third, and surprised everyone by winning all relatively handily in the last third.

But the boys took on various leadership roles, such as coordinating and secretarial roles, and even participated in designing different plays against various opponents, which made them the talk of the athletic conference. This led to other coaches in the conference informally (and very casually, to be sure) visiting Marc, claiming they just happened to be in the vicinity, and just dropped by to visit, and see how things were. But, it was pretty clear that they wanted to figure out how Marc had pulled this supposed miracle off.

The Cheerleaders

As for the cheerleaders, forty-four girls were quite a gaggle (even a giggle) to deal with, but they hung in, even the most awkward persisted (since they began forming a close supportive and bonding social system), despite some early ridicule from other squads. The outgoing and cheerful Madeline made sure that norms (read, rules) were established that supported the girls, that cutting comments were out of line in the group. After a short while the girls realized that they all fared better when they all performed at the top of their ability, and that effort was a major index for respect.

More Outcomes

Both Madeline and Marc recognized that they had a potential gold mine in their hands—and so did a number of astute students. With such a premium on developing leadership skills, they began to consider expanding this in a more formal manner. For example, a number of their players and cheerleaders began to run for office and impact the Student Council.

Leadership Skills Workshops

Students and the two Ms decided to run a leadership skills workshop, which was so successful that they began to design and run a series of leadership workshops. These were opened to all students, who attended in larger numbers than predicted. This, in turn, led to the Student Council becoming much more active because they not only saw value to the Council, but also realized that they would learn a lot about leadership in the process.

They began considering summer workshops for the kids, including experiences in a camping setting. To their surprise, this was over-enrolled virtually immediately.

A New Course: Leadership

The two Ms, along with a top-notch teacher, Melissa Sohng, and several students, began to consider developing a course called "Leadership," which would be a regular for-credit course in the program and scheduled during the day. Utilizing the Curriculum Steering Committee (see chapter 25), which Asher, Marc, and the teachers' association had established for the district, they proposed such a workshop-focused course for the high school, which was readily adopted.

As a consequence, students interested in leadership flocked into the course, with most of the Student Council taking it. Madeline, Melissa, and Marc designed the course, largely consisting of workshop and active learning experiences.

Students on the Council argued for making the course mandatory for all members, but all finally agreed that that would change the dynamics. The course became widely publicized, resulting in Madeline, Melissa, and Marc being asked to do state and national workshops during the year and all summers. Madeline and Melissa even ran two-week workshops in Alaska, and were able to wangle scholarships for some of their kids, as word spread about the program.

The Local University—An Undergraduate Leadership Minor

The local university had begun to consider developing an undergraduate leadership minor, and asked the three sponsors if they would consider participating and providing input. They worked with the faculty, often providing a measure of reality and suggestions for workshops that they found effective. This fed into the perception by the community and schools that they were doing quite a job.

The Parents Become an Asset

In the beginning of the first year the parents constituted quite a crowd by themselves, since virtually all of them came to all the games to cheer their kids on. The parents even started chartering special buses to go to the games out of town. By the middle of the first year, the parents had formed close and bonded social systems and support groups for both basketball and cheerleader teams, to the extent that both the basketball boys and cheerleader girls sponsored several school events. The parents' groups then picked up the idea and began to want to do the same, and communicated with the two principals asking how they could assist the schools. They began to participate more and to sponsor events in the middle school that everyone thought important.

The large parent groups rapidly became a force in the community, eagerly becoming more involved in the other schools in the district (they had kids in elementary and high schools, as well). The superintendent and board of education, realizing the value of this resource, established relationships with the parent groups, perceiving their value as informal advisory boards.

Some members of the parents' groups also formed a support group for the bands the schools were trying to form and develop. Later, the base groups volunteered to support tax and bond issues needed for construction and expenses, as the district grew and needs surfaced.

Community Impact

By the second year of the large basketball and cheerleader program, the teams, parents, teachers, and administrators began to notice that they were drawing crowds of parents from other schools in the district and from schools in other districts, as well. Surprised, they tried to figure out why this was occurring. They found a range of responses, from curiosity to see the formations and exercises the groups had developed, and wanting their cheerleader squads to imitate the action, to those wishing that their schools would consider the idea.

A number of parents and students from the these schools were interested in the possibility of transferring to the school, recognizing the value of the leadership skills the boys and girls were learning—and wanting to become involved in the expanding quality leadership development programs the teams and schools were developing.

Asher noted that his high school coaches were beginning to see value in expanding membership and improving leadership skills. "Well," he thought, "miracles do happen."

THE MORAL?

You draw your own.

QUESTIONS

> Good decision making comes from experience.
> And, experience comes from making bad decisions.—Anon

1. What do you perceive to be the relationship between constructivism and authoritarianism?
   A. If democratic decision making differs significantly from that of authoritarian models or approaches, where does constructivism fit in?
2. Have you ever heard of a coach who involves students in decision making?
   A. How do we teach students (teachers, people) to make wise decisions without experience in making decisions, where they can make mistakes and learn from the experience?
   B. Similarly, how do we teach kids/people to be *responsible* without providing experiences for them to take responsibility?
   C. Similarly, how do people learn *good judgment* without having experiences in which they learn to make judgments, some of which may be poor?
   D. How about *leadership*? How do we learn to become good leaders without appropriate experiences, hopefully, constructed by our mentors and teachers?
3. Could you or I go against the grain and contemplate, let alone forge ahead and pull off, what Marc did? What Madeline did?

4. This question applies to any other major divergence from established orthodoxy.
   A. Can you think of something so far out of the box that you can do?
   B. Is your environment safe enough so that you can try some sort of initiative or idea—and, still make mistakes?
   C. What kinds of experiences could we design so that people, including students, could have a condition of being and feeling safe, and yet can make mistakes in learning leadership skills and concepts?
   D. Decision-making skills and concepts?
   E. Trust?
   F. Any others you might suggest?

CHAPTER 16

Beliefs, Myths, and Realities: A Case Study of a Rogue Junior High: Transformation into a Model Middle School

There is nothing more difficult to take in hand, more perilous to conduct, or more uncertain in its success, than to take the lead in the introduction of a new order of things.

—Niccolo Machiavelli, *The Prince*

BEGINNINGS

So, what do you do when a colleague you like, essentially a very gentle and dedicated man, asks if you would like to work with a school that seemed to be having some problems?

Intrigued, you respond by saying "sure."

So, off Wade Burley and I went to chat with an assistant superintendent who had his head on straight and a supervisor who had taught in the school. After the normal shmoozing, the pair seemed to accept me (I hoped), and started to describe the school, a junior high that seemed alienated from the district, and quite distrustful of the central office.

All too often the administrators didn't bother to show up for key meetings for principals, and about as frequently ignored central office policies that all the other schools followed, such as suspending and then sending a junior high student home, entailing that he had to cross four miles of major thoroughfares and railroad tracks. They also made numerous derogatory comments about the central office administration rather publicly, and the school's teachers, and even in interviews for promotions, made disparaging comments about central office personnel to their faces, which the latter found quite disquieting.

CALLING IN THE CAVALRY

Rather than punishing the school, they were concerned enough to call us.

Wade and I agreed on the rudiments of a change strategy in our conversations. The first step was to have lunch with the principal, who turned out to be an easy-going man committed to his kids and faculty. Our hope was he would accept us. If he did, we would urge him to establish a planning committee of high-prestige teachers, at least one counselor, the assistant principal, and other key people to deal with some of the issues and concerns the teachers and administration perceived they faced. He agreed. We set up a date for the committee to meet right after school.

CHANGE STRATEGIES USED COMMONLY VERSUS THOSE THAT ARE EFFECTIVE

The Favorite Myth—The Quick Fix

Now for a few not-so-random thoughts about making effective changes in organizations.

We Americans go for the quick fix. What is the best way to eliminate gangs? Or, how do we help the Russians reform their economy? Or what is the best and quickest way to make sure that all the schools in a district or districts in a state or districts in the country become reformed fast, real fast?

Use an overall strategy from the top, usually with coercion.

Does it work?

Of course not.

About dealing with gangs effectively, first we have to find out why people join and stay in them. They have very good reasons for their action. And then, we have to grasp the essential nature of any organization (and gangs are organizations). That's why we're generally quite ineffective in dealing with them.

About the Russian economy—it takes enormous effort, time, resources, commitment, and so forth, to reform just one company, let alone an entire nation's economy. (For example, look how long it is going to take Daimler to reform Chrysler.) So far, we and they are not too successful in the Russian reform enterprise.

And Now, *Reality*

As for schools, each school, each district (in fact, any organization), is an exceedingly complex entity that *resists change*. Sarason's (1971) book title, *The Culture of the School and the Problem of Change*, states it all. His recently reissued book, *Revisiting the Culture of the School and the Problem of Social Change* (1996) (note the addition of the word, *Social*) certifies his original thesis.

All organizations develop a *culture*, that is a set of patterns of common understandings, customs and practices (norms), feelings, and beliefs that gradually develop as people live with each other. Another quick description is that a culture consists of patterns of shared, learned behavior. Your family develops a culture, so does your school, so does any store and every organization.

Most school reform attempts become top-down strategies, since people design them based on often somewhat simplistic beliefs on how to change complex organizations. Generally these methods consist of a one-size-fits-all strategy. The Annie E. Casey Foundation (Wehlage, Smith & Lipman 1992, Spring) approaches schools with this model, as does the Coalition of Essential Schools (Muncey & McQuillan 1993, February), and so do virtually all states (while talking from the other side of their mouths about site-based management or decision making). The shelf life of most reform efforts, as a result, is usually relatively short—and then the next panacea arrives to bring back those wonderful (and mythical) years of yore.

Fortunately, I have been able to work with a lot of schools and districts to develop effective changes. In the course of these efforts, a change strategy developed. That is, a pattern or a model emerged from my work (Burley & Shapiro 1994; Shapiro 1995). Wade and I talked about this model and how to apply it to the junior high.

THE CHANGE STRATEGY IN ACTION

The model is essentially a highly individualized diagnostic, analytic, and implementation change strategy. That is, it diagnoses each organization on its own merits, assuming little, if anything. As a result, since each organization is quite different from others (although they all have

commonalities) each reform or change effort must take these differences into account and then develop different courses or lines of action
to make effective changes. A one-size-fits-all strategy not only doesn't
cut it, it misleads reform efforts significantly.

Obviously, first we had to make certain that the central office, including the superintendent, supported these intentions. He did. So did
they. We also consulted with the Teachers' Association. They were
highly supportive, and wondered at first whether a university professor
could relate effectively to hard-pressed teachers on the firing line.

Let's see how the change strategy was applied to this junior high.
(See table 16.1.)

Concerns/Issues

What *Concerns/Issues* did the people perceive? Note we didn't say
"problems." Mention problems—and people freeze up.

For our first meeting we brought some refreshments (grapes, apples,
cantaloupe, cookies), so that people, tired from a full day, could relax,
grab a bite, socialize a bit, and watch us surreptitiously, and then look
at some of their concerns and issues. First, of course, people sized us
up, and the principal made introductions, accepting us.

Fortunately, Wade had been working with the district for fifteen
years with their Teacher Education Center Planning Council, so was
well known and accepted. He dragged me along on his coattails. But
trust and acceptance take time.

I put up 24″ × 36″ chart paper on the wall and asked folks what their
major concerns were, and wrote them down with colored markers.
About two sessions (every other week) after school were used to get
these perceptions and feelings out.

Here's a summary:

- The teachers were most concerned about *socioeconomic* changes
  in the community, which were causing their students to *value education* less.
- Working mothers were less able to take their kids home from the
  intramurals, which the faculty really valued, so that program collapsed.

Table 16.1 Analysis of Dynamics of Change

Concerns/Issues		Summary/Conclusions		Underlying Themes
Socioeconomic changes in community: From single home to duplexes. From parents to single parent. Reduced intramural participation. Reduced parents' participation.	—————>	Changing students' values, attitudes: Value of education. Not doing homework. Impact on teachers: Reduced standards.	--->	Changing community changes———> students' attitudes. Decreasing respect for teachers, education. Teachers increasingly alienated from parents, students each other, administration, guidance, central office.
Impact on Teachers:— Feelings of high stress. High frustration. Morale collapsing. "Family" feeling collapsing. Considering leaving school.	—————>	Social organization——— holding school together, but fraying. Key teacher social systems upset, publicly considering leaving.	--->	Teachers' control over———> professional life decreased: Feel powerless. School sliding downhill.
Hopelessness.———————	—————>	Need sense of hope.———	--->	Loss of morale, hope,———> positive attitude toward work, purpose.
Passive, laissez-faire administration——— not functioning:	—————>	Administration, deans,——— guidance dysfunctional:	--->	Passive, laissez-faire———> administration functioning poorly. No accountability.

continued

Table 16.1 (continued)

Concerns/Issues	Summary/Conclusions	Underlying Themes
One of two deans not functioning. Guidance dysfunctional. Administrative clock-watching spreading to teachers, students.	Not cooperating. Not proactive. Limited work ethic affecting teachers, students. Teachers angry at students for this.	
Junior high school departmental organization dysfunctional. Teachers disorganized.	Formal organization blocks effective action: Isolates teachers. Teachers with same students do not see each other.	Relationship between form and function: Organization dysfunctional prohibits teachers with same students from working together. Centralized/decentralized. Central office indifferent.
Departmental organization.	Little accountability.	Administrators, deans, guidance not accountable.
Norms (attitudes, practices, behavior).	Culture dysfunctional: Norms must change.	Norms need to support changes, work ethic, cooperation, responsible professional behavior. Self-esteem, recognition for all, repersonalizing to a family.

Table 16.1 *(continued)*

Potential Lines of Action/Initiatives	Rationale for Actions	Major Outcomes
Major intramural program. Major recognition program. Major involvement of parents: Volunteers in school. Fund-raisers. Administration, faculty involved. In-service programs to understand students.	Develop sense of belonging for all: ——————→ Sense that teachers care, that parents care, sense of pride. Teach parenting skills. Faculty, administration understand, accept students. Involve community.	Major intramural programs. Major recognition program for all. Major parent involvement program, with staff development. In-service program on nature of students.
Develop grade-level administrative teams. Develop teacher teams.	Decentralize: ——————→ Work/cooperate in small units. Make all visible/accountable. Personalize. Increase ownership, morale. Increase sense of belonging.	Grade-level administrative teams in place. Teacher teams in operation.
Develop plan with purpose: Form three committees to reorganize. Planning. Guidance. Classroom management support team.	Teachers involved in ——————→ reorganization: Increased ownership. Empowerment. Support groups.	Long-range plan developed. Reorganization Support Team functioning: Sense of hope. Strong teacher ownership of plan and support of Reorganization Support Team.
Pro-active leadership to form and support.	Develop support by all reference groups ——————→ (administration, deans, guidance, faculty, students, community central office)	Administration strongly supports plan, Reorganization Support Team, process. Accountability clear, visible.

continued

Table 16.1 *(continued)*

Potential Lines of Action/Initiatives	Rationale for Actions	Major Outcomes
Planning and guidance committees.		
Formal organization must change to facilitate cooperation: Form teacher teams, work in small decentralized units with same students. Form grade-level administrative teams.	Decentralizing facilitates: ⟶ Personalizing. Empowerment. Greater responsibility. Accountability—all visible. Cooperation. Interdependent operation.	Formal organization changed from a junior high school to a middle grade-level administrative teams. Teacher teams with block of students. Implementing Teacher as Advisor Program.
Grade-level teams for administrators, teachers.	All organizational components ⟶ become visible—thus, accountable.	Accountability.
Establish new norms with above changes.	Decentralization increases ⟶ students', teachers' cooperation, responsibility.	Cultural norms, beliefs, practices changed.

- Teachers, as a consequence, felt highly stressed and perceived their *morale* declining.
- Indeed, people talked about transferring—and one high-status person did transfer, to the great shock of the faculty, most of whom had been there almost two decades.
- Their *work ethic* suffered, as people left school as early as they could.
- Their sense of *hopelessness* zoomed up.
- The administration and guidance counselors were really *not functioning.*
- The *junior high school organization* was preventing faculty from communicating with each other and dealing effectively with the kids.

See the first column in table 16.1, *Concerns/Issues,* which displays this information.

It should be noted that all these points were then printed on paper with copies being given to everyone including office staff and custodians to make sure that we set up a system of communication with and for everyone. That way you get buy-in.

Summary/Conclusions

We next summarized these perceptions on the paper, which are the basis for the second column in table 16.1, *Summary/Conclusions.*

- Since students' *valuation of education* was reduced, homework was not being done.
- Teachers did not want to reduce their *standards,* and mourned the loss of their *intramural program.* As a result they became annoyed and angry with the kids.
- The *social organization* holding the school together was fraying, leading to key teacher social systems becoming very upset, and publicly contemplating leaving.
- *Hope* is the gasoline of any social system—and it was evaporating.
- The *administration and guidance were dysfunctional,* too passive.

- The formal *departmental organization* was blocking effective action, isolating teachers.
- The *culture was dysfunctional*; norms had to change.

After this, a faculty meeting was called, at which we went thoroughly through the findings and conclusions. One faculty member noted that all the indicators were downhill, which I corroborated. The assistant principal then noted that we had better do something. (Note that Lewin's first step of organizational change was accomplished: unfreezing.)

Underlying Themes

The next stage was to analyze the *Themes* that underlay the *Concerns/Issues*.

- A *changing community* leads to *changed student attitudes and values*.
- These are reflected in reduced *value for education*.
- In turn the teachers become increasingly *alienated* from the community, parents, kids, each other, the administration—and angry with the kids.
- Teachers' control over their professional life is reduced, so they feel *powerless*.
- The organization's sense of *hope* slips, as does *morale* and *esprit de corps*.
- The *passive, laissez-faire administration* and *guidance* were functioning poorly.
- The *departmental organization* is dysfunctional, prohibiting teachers with the same kids from working together—leading to the kids being organized and teachers not.
- The administration and deans are *not accountable* with this departmental organization.
- *Norms* need to support work changes, cooperation, work ethic, *recognition* for everyone from the custodians to the students to the teachers to the administration.

Table 16.1 reveals the progression from *Concerns/Issues,* to *Summary/Conclusions,* to the third column, *Underlying Themes.*

Potential Lines of Action/Initiatives

In order to get maximum feedback and communication with the entire staff, we drew up an eighteen-item questionnaire and asked teachers to list their five greatest concerns.

The four highest were:

1. The present operational role of *guidance and counseling*
2. *Unified, consistent procedures* for handling student *discipline* by faculty
3. *Student attitude toward education*
4. Total staff *morale* (faculty, administration, others)

The next step in this individualized change strategy was to look at *Potential Lines of Action/Initiatives* to change norms, practices, structure, and processes. This we did.

- Since the faculty highly valued their *intramural program, resuscitate it.*
- Since everyone needs recognition, institute a major *recognition* program. To do this, place photos of everyone doing something significant on the glass by the front office, an area that everyone passes into, around, and out of the school.
- Develop major programs to *involve parents and involve teachers and administrators.*
- Institute *in-service programs* to understand kids and community better.
- *Reorganize* the school *into grade-level administrative teams and teacher teams.*
- Develop a *plan* with a purpose.
- Form *three committees* to reorganize the school.
  1. *Planning* Committee.
  2. *Guidance* Committee.

3. *Classroom Management Support Team* to help new teachers
   with discipline problems, for utilization by the principal at his
   discretion.
- Leadership has to become more *proactive* and *support* these initiatives.
- The formal junior high departmental organization must change to
  facilitate cooperation among teachers by forming *grade level administrative teams* and by beginning to form *teacher teams,* thus
  decentralizing the school.
- Establish *new norms* in line with the above changes.

You will note that table 16.1 presents these and their relationships to
Concerns/Issues, next a *Summary/Conclusions* of these *Concerns/
Issues,* then *Underlying Themes*, and then in column four, *Potential
Lines of Action/Initiatives.*

Rationale for Actions

Each of these changes obviously is based on theoretical and pragmatic grounds. The following provide a rationale for the changes:

- Develop a sense of *belonging* for all—humans are social animals
  and need this. Maslow is a basis for this. This demonstrates to kids
  that parents and teachers care.
- Teach *parenting* skills.
- *Involve* community. Demonstrate that teachers and administration
  understand and accept kids and community.
- *Decentralize*
  - Increases sense of belonging, ownership, morale, personalizes
    (you know everyone on your team).
  - All organizational components become visible, thereby making
    everyone visible and accountable.
  - Empowers, fosters cooperation, interdependence.
  - Involve teachers, administration, guidance, community, central
    office in reorganization, which increases ownership and empow-
    erment.
  - Establish support groups.

In table 16.1 the *Rationale for Actions*, in column five, is presented for *Potential Lines of Action/Initiatives*.

Major Outcomes

The last column in table 16.1 presents *Outcomes*. While this may appear a bit mechanical, it was anything but that. As the above were shared with faculty, a planning and decision-making workshop was held before the close of school. At that time, the following was decided upon for implementation. Note that Lewin's second step in his granddaddy of change models was achieved, namely, moving to a new level, that is, implementing changes.

Note also that expectations, norms, and roles changed:

- A major *intramural* program was instituted.
- A major *recognition* program was developed and instituted, placing color photos of anyone who did anything significant on the office glass wall. People crowded around it.
- A major *parent involvement* program, with staff development, and an *in-service* program on the nature of the students was implemented. Teachers gave up their evening basketball session to staff this, since earlier teacher attendance at parent meetings was erratic (a euphemism, to be sure). A fund-raiser was implemented and $14,000 was raised to everyone's astonishment and delight. Parents were welcomed as a volunteer program surfaced.
- The school was *reorganized into three houses* consisting each of a different grade level with its own *administrative team* (dean/administrator, counselor, secretary/clerk).
- Two volunteer *teacher teams* at the sixth-grade level were agreed-upon and implemented, leaving people not ready to move into that model to teach traditionally.
- A *long-range plan* was developed, including: a *Reorganization Support Team* from the Planning and Guidance Teams; a *Classroom Management Support Team* of status teachers to help anyone needing it, as assigned by the principal.
- The survey used the preceding year was given again. It indicated: a sense of *hope* had developed; teachers felt strong *ownership* of

the plan and supported the Reorganization Support Team; amazingly, all questions regarding satisfaction showed improvement, some indicating considerable improvement; and for the two following years, we were astonished to find that satisfaction increased on all eighteen questions.

The administration, both of the school and the district strongly supported the plan, the Reorganization Support Team, and the process. The central administration added a counselor to the school to facilitate the plan.

- *Accountability*, murky before, was clear; everyone was very visible. The following year the sixth-grade team increased its teams from two to three, involving all teachers. The seventh and eighth grades each developed a volunteer team. By the succeeding year, all teachers in these three grades worked on teams. Much to our surprise, the special teachers (art, physical education, industrial arts, special education) also joined these teams.
- Key *social systems* of the school served on the Reorganization Support Team, indicating intense support. Regular meetings of this team saw virtually 100 percent attendance at all times. One member refused coaching assignments to retain membership on this team.
- *In-service* training was provided to teams and to grade-level administrative teams to function better, the latter group to supervise more effectively.
- Clerks/secretaries contributed considerably by meeting regularly to improve their function. Their minutes, as well as the minutes of every meeting of the Reorganization Support Team, were provided to everyone, making sure that the system of communication worked.

MORE RESULTS—REALLY, AN EPILOGUE

The administrator who initiated our work called the school "one of the most improved schools in the county."

Three of the four highest priorities for the faculty changed radically by the end of the second year. Here are the pre- and post-change priorities:

#1 to #15: The present operational role of guidance and counseling.

#2 to #5: Unified, consistent procedures for handling student discipline.

#3 to #3: Student attitude toward education.

#4 to #1: Staff morale.

- Now they could work on morale and student attitudes. The others had been cleaned up.
- Attitudes toward students changed. With decentralization and teaming, fewer kids were sent to the office, and less anger was being expressed toward children or their parents.
- With the implementation of teams, everyone gets to know each other, a family feeling develops, people get to care for each other, and teams "take care of our own." So, teachers become advocates for "their" kids.
- Student surveys indicated more positive attitudes, also.
- An ineffective junior high became an effective middle school.
- At an annual party celebrating the end of the second year of implementation, at least seventeen people told us that it was the most successful year in education they had ever had professionally.[1]

Here are anonymous comments at the end of the second year of implementation, when we asked, "How have things changed at the school over the past three years?"

- "The office is working beautifully and people seem to know what their roles are and generally are comfortable with them. Because of more effective in-service, there is less negativism and more willingness to try new ideas. Most of us feel we are having a positive effect on our students. Teaming is working well so far."
- "There has been a positive attitude at (the) top . . . accountability . . . visibility of all staff [members] have changed."
- "I think the front office alignment has worked out beautifully. Grade level adms. [administrators], counselors, and staff have worked well."

- "We have been exposed to new ideas and ways of doing things. Staff has had more opportunities to interact in a variety of settings and in some cases 'forced' to work together. I think this has been beneficial in sharing needs, concerns, and frustrations among staff members rather than in just departments. We have all been looking for an easy 'fix' for other problems; but, we are learning that with assistance and input of other experts, we have the answers to the future of our kids if we will patiently and cooperatively put it all together. We are not there yet; but, we have made some huge strides."[2]

NOTES

1. By the end of the third year all junior high schools in the district had used this model to become middle schools. When I mentioned in passing that the central administration considered this school the district's model middle school, the faculty were amazed. Several thought for some time that I was making a joke.

2. Based on a case study, Burley, W. W. & Shapiro, A. S. (1994). "Beliefs, symbols, and realities: A case study of a school in transition." In K. M. Borman & N. P. Greenman (Eds.). *Changing American education: Recapturing the past or inventing the future?* Albany: State University of New York Press. Also reported in "The dynamics of organizational change: Organizational Mapping, a construct to diagnose, plan, and implement organizational change." In J. L. Burdin & J. R. Hoyle (Eds.). *Leadership and diversity in education: The second yearbook of the National Council of Professors of Educational Administration.* Lancaster, PA: Technomic.

QUESTIONS

1. Is there another change strategy you might think about using to deal with these complex issues?
   A. Lewin's Force Field Analysis approach? If so, how would you proceed?
2. What do you think of the change strategy we used, which we called *Analysis of Dynamics of Change*?
   A. What are its strengths? Its focus?

    B. Its weaknesses? What does it miss?

    C. How could it be improved? [If you can figure out a way to do this, please contact me.]

3. What alternative strategies would you use to get into the school?

    A. To become established/accepted?

    B. What other underlying themes do you perceive?

    C. What alternative lines of action could you develop to improve the school?

    D. And, what are the rationales underlying these lines of action?

    E. What other outcomes might you predict might occur?

4. Why do you think that the other junior highs changed without any help into middle schools, essentially using the same model we developed?

    A. What advantages do you see over the old junior high model?

    B. What advantages do you think they perceived?

5. What other questions would you ask?

SOURCES

Burley, W. W. & Shapiro, A. S. (1994). Beliefs, symbols, and realities: A case study of a school in transition. In K. M. Borman & N. P. Greenman (Eds.). *Changing American education: Recapturing the past or inventing the future?* Albany: State University of New York Press.

Lewin, R. (1952). Group decision and social change. In G. E. Swanson, T. E. Newcomb, & E. L. Hartley (Eds.). *Readings in social psychology* (rev. ed.). New York: Holt, Rinehart & Winston.

Linton, R. (1955). *The tree of culture.* New York: Vintage.

Mizruchi, E. H. (Ed.). (1967). *The substance of sociology.* New York: Appleton-Century-Crofts.

Muncey, D. E. & McQuillan, P. J. (1993, February). Preliminary findings from a five-year study of the Coalition of Essential Schools. *Phi Delta Kappan,* 486–89.

Sarason, S. B. (1971). *The culture of the school and the problem of change.* Boston: Allyn & Bacon.

Sarason, S. B. (1996). *Revisiting the culture of the school and the problem of social change.* New York: Teachers College Press.

Shapiro, A. (1995). The dynamics of organizational change: Organizational Mapping, a construct to diagnose, plan, and implement organizational change.

In J. L. Burdin & J. R. Hoyle (Eds.). *Leadership and diversity in education: The second yearbook of the National Council of Professors of Educational Administration.* Lancaster, PA: Technomic.

Wehlage, G., Smith, G., & Lipman, P. (1992, Spring). Restructuring urban schools: The New Futures experience. *American Educational Research Journal 29*(1), 51–93.

Wilson, L. C., Byars, T. M., Shapiro, A. S., & Schell, S. H. (1969). *Sociology of supervision.* Boston: Allyn & Bacon.

Also, literature on size of school is relevant, such as:

Barker, R. G. & Gump, P. V. (1964). *Big school, small school.* Stanford, CA: Stanford University Press.

Hampel, R. L. (2002, January). Historical perspectives on small schools. *Phi Delta Kappan 83*(5), 357–63.

Oxley, D. (1989). Smaller is better. *American Educator 13*(1), 28–31, 51–42.

Raywid, M. (1997, December–1998, January). Small schools: A reform that works. *Educational Leadership 55*(4), 34–39.

Schoenlein, J. (2001, March) Making a huge high school feel smaller. *Educational Leadership 58*(6), 28–31.

Shapiro, A. S., Benjamin, W. F., & Hunt, J. J. (1995). *Curriculum and schooling: A practitioner's guide.* Palm Springs, CA: ETC.

Wasley, P. A. & Lear, R. J. (2001, March). Small schools, real gains. *Educational Leadership 58*(6), 22–27.

CHAPTER 17

Looking Up the Wrong End of the Horse

Our Testing Mania—Viewoints of Politicians and Practitioners (and Maybe Kids): A Cheap, Fast Way to Weaken Education (but It Sure Looks Tough)

There is always an easy solution to every human problem—neat, plausible, and wrong.

—H. L. Mencken, "The Divine Afflatus"
The Mencken Chrestomathy

To provide an objective viewpoint on assessment, let's quote W. Edwards Deming, America's organizational guru:

Evaluation of performance, merit rating, or annual review . . . nourishes short-term performance, annihilates long-term planning, builds fear, demolishes teamwork, nourishes rivalry and politics. It leaves people bitter, crushed, bruised, battered, desolate, despondent, dejected, feeling inferior, even depressed . . . unable to comprehend why they are inferior. It is unfair, it ascribes to the people in a group differences that may be caused by the system that they work in.

—W. E. Deming, *Out of the Crisis:
Productivity and Competitive Position*

This year's report begins with a brief chronicle of the testing madness that seems to have gripped us.

—Gerald W. Bracey, *Phi Delta Kappan* (1999), who authors a
monthly journal column called "Research" and writes
an annual report on education, starts his Ninth Annual
Report on Education with this statement

. . . every grade from third to eighth must be tested.

—George W. Bush

By now, we have a craze. Why? Is it because "high-stakes testing" has become the symbol of the bottom-line accountability movement ushered in by that world-renowned educator, Ross Perot? Does it symbolize a popular approach to control education and educators?

CONSTRUCTIVIST AND "NORMAL" TESTING COMPARED

It would seem useful now to compare and contrast a constructivist approach to assessment with the so-called high-stakes testing movement that has swept our educational landscape.

Authentic Assessment: Some Examples

Constructivist assessment tries to determine what students learned as a result of the activities in which they engaged. These activities were driven by their interests, needs, and abilities, as well as by various local and state curriculum mandates and standards. Constructivist assessment rests on students' *products* of their learnings, such as portfolios of their work over the year, "exhibitions of 'mastery'" as identified by the Coalition of Essential Schools, or other "authentic evaluative" results of student work and self-assessment.

Merrow (May, 2001) notes that Sizer's Coalition and other schools

> require [their] students to demonstrate their mastery by standing up in front of a group of adults or their own peers to "exhibit" what they have learned. That's a far better basis for evaluating, describing, and diagnosing, but it's also time-consuming and expensive, which means that it's unlikely ever to be more important than machine-scored, multiple-choice tests. (p. 655)

The May 2001 "Education Update" [Willis] published by The Association for Supervision and Curriculum Development (ASCD), suggests several other constructivist authentic evaluation models, such as:

Students in reading groups, for instance, can discuss common themes from different books and determine how various authors examined those themes in their writing. Students also can glean an understanding of the time in which authors and characters lived through the examination of primary sources, such as photographs and diaries, to help deepen their understanding of what life was like in different times. The rights of people, for example, could be examined from the time of the Revolutionary War in the 18th century through the Civil War in the 19th century and up through the Civil Rights movement of the 20th century.

Authentic assessment really is based on *authentic learning*, thus focusing on the tough issue of *inquiry*, where teachers have to structure their operation in such a way that kids have to work to discover knowledge new to them and where they have to construct new meaning from their grappling with the issues or problems on which they are working. This is the essence of constructivist teaching and learning—and it focuses on Bloom's higher levels of his Taxonomy. It certainly is not memorizing for a test.

This, of course, does not mean that testing is thrown out the window. The preceding suggestions fuse teaching approaches with assessment integrally. It also simply means that we have to individualize assessment processes to discover what students have actually learned as they work daily in the schools.

HIGH-STAKES TESTING: ITS ASSUMPTIONS—AND, WHAT IT DOES

Obviously, this movement assumes that high-stakes testing will improve teaching and learning. Otherwise, why go to such effort?

Let's look at the research:

NAEP Reading Scores Show Testing Mania Fails to Improve Learning; Education Quality Undermined for Low-Income, Minority Children; Bush Annual Testing Scheme Would Make Situation Worse

"The Reading Report Card . . . provides further evidence that the testing mania sweeping the nation fails to improve school quality and, in fact damages the education of our most vulnerable children," said FairTest Executive Director Dr. Monty Neill. "These data should bolster reformers working to stop President Bush's ill-conceived plan to force states to administer tests to every student grades three through eight."

Among the facts from the National Assessment of Educational Progress (NAEP) Fourth Grade Reading Report Card cited by FairTest:

There has been no gain in NAEP grade four reading performance nationally since 1992 despite a huge increase in state-mandated testing. NAEP scores in southern states, which test the most and have the highest stakes attached to state testing programs, have declined.

The NAEP score gap between white children and those from African American and Hispanic families has increased, even though schools serving low-income and minority-group children put the most emphasis on testing; and test scores of children eligible for free lunch programs have dropped since 1996.

"The emphasis on high-stakes standardized tests is a proven failure," Dr. Neill continued. "It continues to undermine educational opportunity for low-income and minority students. More testing, as proposed by President Bush, will only reinforce the racism of low expectations and leave many more children behind."—Monty Neill, Executive Director, *FairTest*

High-stakes testing essentially judges academic progress "by a single indicator and when high stakes—such as when a student is promoted from one grade to the next or is eligible for a diploma—are attached to that single indicator, the common effect is to narrow curriculum and reduce instruction to test 'prepping'" (Thompson 2001). High-stakes testing also is being utilized in several states and many school districts as a basis for salary increases or bonuses (or none) for teachers and administrators, and in several states to grade schools from A (terrific) to F (failing).

The fantastic outcome for this latter use is that people *actually believe* that the grade assigned from A to F is a statement of the quality of the school. In Florida not a single school with predominately upper-middle-class students received a D or an F; and none of the schools with children from the very lowest socioeconomic levels received an A or a B on the first two administrations of the test.

Is this surprising? People (and even teachers and administrators in schools) actually treat this myth as a reality.

Textbooks and high-stakes tests are like hot dogs: If only people knew how they were made, they would never allow their children near them again.—Susan Ohanian, *Goals 2000, Phi Delta Kappan,* Jan. 2000, 350

James Popham, one of educational testing's gurus, is extremely critical of the poor quality of high-stakes testing, as the following points out. He does support properly constructed and administered tests that can have a positive effect on educational quality—and makes a number of cogent recommendations for their improvement.

> Now, in 2001, there's no question that a score-boosting sweepstakes has enveloped the nation. Who has been tasked with boosting students' test scores? Teachers and administrators, and of course . . . U.S. educators have been thrown into a score-boosting game they cannot win.
>
> The vast majority of high-stakes tests are bad—that is, their use hurts the quality of children's schooling.
>
> The critical question of "How do we teach Tracey the things she needs to know?" is forced aside by this far less important one: "How do we improve Tracey's scores on the high-stakes test she will be taking?"—W. James Popham, *The Truth about Testing* (2001)

THE CREDENTIALING PROCESS CARRIED OUT— BUT, PROFESSIONALLY

When a school is up for professional credentialing by a state or a regional accrediting agency (Southern Association of Colleges and Schools, for example), a sizeable team of experts is assembled and examines every aspect of the school in terms of meeting its purposes. Program, organization, staffing, physical conditions, administration, support staff, and so forth are carefully examined, a process taking about three days. Of course, the school never ends up with a grade.

Rather, a series of recommendations and suggestions are made to assist the school to meet its purposes. Grading is a recent political process for ulterior purposes, such as degrading the public schools to promote private education, or convincing the public that one is an "education governor," or to demonstrate to the public that the public schools are "failing."

AND NOW FOR HIGH-STAKES TESTING—RAISING THE BAR

That politicians and business leaders who strongly favor high-stakes testing are so strongly opposed by most educators is extremely significant.

Again, it is significant that the bar has been raised so high by politicians eager to make a quick fix or to denigrate the schools in several states (New York, Virginia) that most kids cannot pass. Ohanian notes, "New York's Commissioner of Education, Richard Mills, is insisting that subjecting fourth-graders to a test they can't pass is a 'good strategy.' What can we say about an era that coins the term 'raising the bar' to describe the way it thinks young children should be treated?" (*Phi Delta Kappan,* Jan. 2001, 345).

> In the same spirit, when 97 percent of the schools in Virginia flunked that state's new high stakes test, Kirk Schroder, president of the state school board, announced that he was confident that the state's testing program would become "a national model for excellence in measuring student achievement." If 97 percent of my students failed a test I'd devised, I'd figure that something was wrong with the test—not that teachers nation-wide would be beating a path to my door for copies.—Susan Ohanian, *Goals 2000, Phi Delta Kappan,* Jan. 2000, 345–55

And now for a few quotes on the impact of high-stakes testing:

> Don't let anyone tell you that standardized tests are not accurate measures. The truth of the matter is that they offer a remarkably precise method for gauging the size of the houses near the school where the test was administered. Every empirical investigation of this question has found that socioeconomic status (SES) in all its particulars accounts for an overwhelming proportion of the variance in test scores when different schools, towns, or states are compared.—Alfie Kohn, *Phi Delta Kappan,* Jan. 2001, 349–57

One wag commented that Governor Jeb Bush of Florida had found an extremely expensive way to assess the socioeconomic status of a school with the Florida Comprehensive Assessment Test (FCAT, for short). But, when the *St. Petersburg Times* challenged Florida's political leaders to take the high-stakes test, all declined.

> But here's the problem: even results corrected for SES are not very useful because the tests themselves are inherently flawed. This assessment is borne out by research that finds a statistical association between high

scores on standardized tests and relatively shallow thinking.—Alfie Kohn, *Phi Delta Kappan*, May 2001, 349

The longer students take the same tests, the better they do. Texas, California, Florida and other states may certainly claim that the test scores show that their students are learning more. However, introduce a new test in any of these states, and Sisyphus' rock crashes back to the bottom of the hill.— Ann C. Lewis, *Washington Commentary, Phi Delta Kappan*, April 2001

THE LAW OF UNINTENDED CONSEQUENCES (LUC) RAISES ITS UNPREDICTABLE HEAD

And now for a series of new and unexpected twists on the Law of Unexpected Consequences.

Headline:

Students get paid for FCAT (Florida Comprehensive Assessment Test) success. Two middle schools in Hernando County (Florida) are rewarding those who do well on the state test with payouts up to $150.—*St. Petersburg Times*, St. Petersburg, FL, May 19, 2001

I thought it was pretty good. It's a little bribe. That way it's not just a pain-in-the-butt test, you actually have something.—Jeannie Mounger, student, *St. Petersburg Times*, St. Petersburg, FL, May 19, 2001

I want to know where they got the money. I think it's sad because I don't think they should have to pay us to do good on the tests.—Ryan Armstrong, eighth-grade student, *St. Petersburg Times*, St. Petersburg, FL, May 19, 2001

The issue even came before Gov. Jeb Bush during a visit to Tampa (FL) on Wednesday. Asked by reporters for his thoughts on the student payouts, Bush said it was "the wrong approach" to test incentives.—Gov. Jeb Bush, governor of Florida, sponsor of the FCAT, *St. Petersburg Times*, St. Petersburg, FL, May 19, 2001

So why not pay the students for it? There is an answer to the question. The answer is that it crosses a line that we ought not cross—a line of crassness, a line of surrender of something important. I saw in the paper that the governor (Jeb Bush) is uncomfortable with the idea. He should be; it is his doing.—Howard Troxler, columnist, *St. Petersburg Times*, St. Petersburg, FL, May 18, 2001

There is a lot of research to show rewards have a detrimental effect. The incentive becomes the goal, not learning. And interest in school eventually wanes. . . . Giving cash to students is "unbelievable." I guess because there is no authentic reason for kids to be concerned about this awful test, it's necessary to resort to shameless bribery so they'll become more concerned about test scores than learning.—Alfie Kohn, educator and author, *Punished by Rewards*, "The Trouble with Gold Stars, Incentive Plans, A's, Praise, and Other Rewards," *St. Petersburg Times*, May 19, 2001

MORE UNINTENDED CONSEQUENCES

Creating a Generation of Scientific and Social Science Illiterates

In Florida, the pressure of the FCAT has led many elementary teachers to drop science and social studies in order to study for English, writing, and mathematics tests. Consequently, until the states start to test science, we are presently producing a generation of children who haven't a clue about science or its object, nature. Susan Ohanian (*Phi Delta Kappan*, Jan. 2001, 365–66) notes that Carol Holst "points out that her son's school had no science or social studies, because they aren't covered on the TAAS (Texas Assessment of Academic Skills)."

Others note that numbers of fourth-grade teachers are pulling out of the grade because of the stress they and their students feel in facing such tests.

Headline:

In New York, Putting Down Their Pencils: Parent Rebellion Against Standardized Testing Strikes at Heart of Bush Plan (*Washington Post*, May 18, 2001, pp. A1, A12)

The headline speaks about Scarsdale, New York, a very tony suburb with top-ranking schools, but also Rochester and Ithaca, New York, are mentioned, as well as communities in Massachusetts, Michigan, Maryland, Virginia, and California. The New York commissioner's response?

State Educational Commissioner Says Test Boycotts Won't Fly in New
York (ASCD's Eye on Curriculum, October, 31, 2001).

New York State Education Commissioner Richard P. Mills has ordered
school districts to punish students who boycott states tests next spring.
Mills' crackdown comes in response to a nationally publicized boycott of
exams this year by Scarsdale, NY. (*The New York Times* [10/31])

What is he going to do? To paraphrase Calvin Trilling writing for
The Nation, take away their lunches? Or their shoes?

THE VALUE OF TESTS

In the long run, test scores don't predict much of anything.—Gerald W.
Bracey, "Research," *Phi Delta Kappan,* April 2001

Is it on the test?—Student

High-stakes tests create intense pressure on teachers and administrators
(and kids), and unfortunate decisions are being made as pressure for "accountability" overwhelms common sense. Here's an example from my
daughter's teaching experience in a New York City middle school. As the
mandated state exams drew near in the spring of 2000, her principal directed her to spend 15 minutes of each class period giving students practice in answering multiple-choice questions, particularly in math. "But,
sir," she said, "I teach Italian and English, not math." That did not matter to her school leader, who simply repeated his directive. She did what
she was told. It did not work, of course, although her students did learn
several (unintended) lessons from the experience.

The *first lesson* they learned was that neither Italian or English mattered. The *second lesson*, learned after seeing how their teacher had
been treated by her boss, was that Ms. Merrow was not in control of her
own life and therefore probably not deserving of their *respect.* The *third
lesson* was that the state test, and only the state test, mattered. That *last
lesson* her eighth graders learned well—so well that, immediately after
the test, about one third of them simply stopped attending school, even
though the school year had five weeks to go. Although most of these
students did not expect to do well on the state exam, they recognized
that the test meant everything and therefore that nothing else mattered,

including coming to school. In the end, most eighth graders in New York City (including my daughter's students) did poorly.—John Merrow, *Phi Delta Kappan,* May 2001, 655

Donna King talks about the FCAT a fair bit in class. Probably too much, the way she figures it. I had a poor little kindergartner all stressed out. He asked his mom, "When am I going to have to take the FCAT?"—Donna King, kindergarten teacher, Duette School, Manatee County, Florida, *St. Petersburg Times,* May 13, 2001

There is pressure all the way down into the second grade.—Linda Caldwell, sixth-grade teacher, LeCanto Middle School, Citrus County, FL, *St. Petersburg Times,* May 13, 2001

In December we pulled our son (a first grader) out of public school and put him into private school. He was so stressed out from the FCAT practice drills he had been doing. Even though he was an above-average student and doing well, he had lost all interest in school. (In Florida, private schools are exempted from the FCAT.)—Ashley Newhaller, parent, Palm Harbor, FL, quoted in Howard Troxler's column, *St. Petersburg Times,* May 23, 2001

I have no space left for comments from the teacher of exceptional education, who sees the shame in her students' faces when they "fail." Neither can I quote the teaching aide whose job is being eliminated because her school's students didn't score well enough (now *there's* common sense). If you begin with contempt for the public schools, this is the kind of public policy you produce. How long before the pendulum starts to swing back the other way? Maybe it has started already.—Howard Troxler, columnist, *St. Petersburg Times,* May 23, 2001

PULLING IT TOGETHER—AND SOME HARD QUESTIONS

In the face of all this evidence, why do we allow our legislators to run the schools?

Most politicians have been a product of the public schools, and yet by now most conservative politicians seem to have joined the litany of anger and hatred focused toward the public schools. Why? Would our legislators have any compunction about invading our dentists' offices, or our physician's office, taking control, and mandating tests and procedures to make sure that they are functioning properly? In Florida, the legislature actually had the chutzpah to mandate number grades for test scores.

A LAST COMMENT

Donald Orlosky, a highly respected and well-published professor emeritus at the University of South Florida and a former president of the National Council of Professors of Educational Administration (NCPEA), went to the 2000 conference of the organization, where a Midwestern governor, widely known as an "education governor," was a keynoter, and spoke of reforming education.

Dr. Orlosky's succinct evaluation?

He doesn't have a clue.

QUESTIONS AND IDEAS

1. What are your beliefs about the testing movement in this country?
   A. Its assumptions?
   B. Its value?
   C. Its limitations?
   D. Its impact on kids? On instruction?
   E. Its impact on teachers? On schools?
   F. Its impact on administrators? On supervisors? On curriculum?
2. Why is there so much pressure behind it?
3. Why does the business model (parents as customers, children as chattel, etc.) appeal to some? A bottom-line mentality seems to be involved. What are its advantages and disadvantages? What's your view on it?
4. Can everything be measured? Can what's truly important, (such as empathy, freedom, independence, a good heart, love, caring, intuitive insight, and much more) be measured?
   A. Can the things you value most be measured? What are they?

5. What procedures do you utilize to evaluate your teaching, your administration?
   A. How measurable are the most important factors (instilling a love for learning in your kids, appreciation of autonomy in your staff, respect for education [what else?])?
6. What unintended consequences have you seen in this testing mania sweeping over the nation?
   A. In your state? Community?
7. Do you know any highly regarded educators who think this approach to testing is advisable?

SOURCES

Bloom, B. S. (Ed.). (1956). *Taxonomy of educational objectives: The classification of educational goals. Handbook I: Cognitive domain.* New York: David McKay.

Deming, W. E. (2000). *Out of the crisis: Productivity and competitive position.* Cambridge, MA: The MIT Press.

Kohn, A. (2001, January). Fighting the tests: A practical guide to rescuing our schools. *Phi Delta Kappan 82*(5), 349–57.

Merrow, J. (2001, May). Undermining standards. *Phi Delta Kappan 82*(9), 652–59.

Ohanian, S. (1999). *One size fits few.* Portsmith, NH: Heinemann.

Ohanian, S. (2000, January). Goals 2000. *Phi Delta Kappan 81*(5), 345–55.

Popham, W. J. (1999). Where large-scale assessment is heading and why it shouldn't. *Educational Measurement: Issues and Practice 18*(3), 13–17.

Popham, W. J. (2001). *The truth about testing.* Alexandria, VA: Association for Supervision and Curriculum Development.

Thompson, S (2001, January). The authentic standards movement and its evil twin. *Phi Delta Kappan 82*(5), 358–62.

Willis, Scott. (2001, May). "Trying too hard? How accountability and testing are affecting constructivist teaching." *Education Update 43*(3), 1, 4–5, 8. Alexandria, VA: Association for Supervision and Curriculum Development.

CHAPTER 18

How to Make Your School (and Your Classroom) Work Better—Decentralize into a Constructivist Approach

In a small school, everyone is needed.

—Stanton Leggett, Educational Consultant

You can get lost in a big system. I did.
But it was deliberate.

—Sue Shapiro, Counselor, Teacher

IS IGNORANCE BLISS?

The idea that small is beautiful, that smallness of size generates major advantages was a concept about which I was blissfully ignorant until I experienced the difference firsthand.

Like most Americans, I worshiped large size. The bigger, the better. Isn't that the way we respond to the advertising about cruise ships? The bigger they are, the more amenities they provide.

The bigger, the better! Isn't that the approach the airlines take? The bigger the planes are, the more powerful they can be—and fly us farther. But, the bigger ships and planes take a lot longer to unload. And, are they confusing! Which deck am I on now? How do I find my room? How long will it take to load the plane? To get my luggage?

I worked as a substitute in a boys' vocational-technical high school. It had six thousand boys. But, I never saw a vice principal. It ran well because the students wanted to be there, and because they gave faculty and administration little or no trouble.

As a newly hired director of secondary education, a major task of mine was to make a new high school building work. It was designed by the educational consultant, Stanton Leggett, and featured a decentralized house plan. I had never really thought about the importance of small size in operating schools and other organizations.

THE NEW SETTING—A TRULY DECENTRALIZED HIGH SCHOOL

Apprehensions

I arrived with two years in advance to plan the program and organization of the school before it occupied this new building, about which the small community was becoming nervous as expressed in the local newspaper. In the first place, it was publicized as having no windows (although it did). Second, the very conservative community was anxious about this newfangled and experimental hall- or house-plan school. Would it work? they wondered. We had to reassure them that Evanston Township High School in Evanston, Illinois, had house plans in the 1920s. Wasn't Evanston Township High School one of the premier schools in North America?

Still the apprehension didn't fade.

We spent the two years planning the administrative structure and function—and the curriculum for the school.

THE ORGANIZATION AND STRUCTURE—AND PROGRAM

The new structure provided three separate halls or houses, each of which was to hold about four hundred high school students, grades nine through twelve. Students in each house were to take social studies, language arts, and mathematics for all four years in their house, unless specialized courses were developed. In that case students from more than one house could take a course together to avoid very small enrollments. Also, the students from one house were to dine together in one lunch period. This meant that the teachers in the three departments in each house taught the students in their house for all four years. The kids were *their* kids.

Programs requiring specialized facilities were to be shared by all three houses. These included foreign languages, science, physical education, vocational and business programs, and the fine arts. The assembly areas also had to be shared.

We spent a great deal of time focusing on trying to make the operation work well. For example, each hall had a separate color for its flooring, so it could build its own identity. Each house was designed to have faculty work spaces in common, so that the faculty members could communicate with each other, even though they were divided into departments (which normally operate exceptionally well as impermeable membranes, effectively separating teachers from each other—so they cannot work together. After a short time, they will not work together, because it becomes "them" vs. "us." "They" become the "other," to be watched suspiciously, not as cooperating and valued partners).

The Administrative Structure—Operating as a Team

In each house, Leggett designed office space for a hall principal, a guidance counselor, and a clerk—to work as a team. Additionally, each hall's design included space for student activities, such as a student council and newspaper. Each hall, thus, could produce its own paper, specialty journals, and its own individual program of student activities. It could, for example, develop its own sizeable intramural and student activities program. Each hall did, with our support.

Curriculum

One of the two reasons the school consolidation movement was so powerful in the first two-thirds of the last century was the belief that a large high school could offer a much richer program. Conant (1959) contributed to this by insisting that a high school should have at least one hundred kids in each grade to offer a respectable program. The second reason was thought to be financial savings. Neither are valid, as we will see.

The first year I was there, we worked on developing a curriculum, and started generating courses that combined language arts and social studies programs into humanities programs. These included a Western world studies one year, and a non-Western world studies the next year for all freshmen and sophomores. Essentially, we ungraded the first two years of high school in social studies and language arts, in a very conservative community.

Next, virtually all states require American history in the junior year of high school. So, we fused American history and language arts into an interdisciplinary program. The rationale was clear. American history teachers teach American literature when they teach history. And language arts teachers teaching American literature have to teach history to clarify much of the literature. But, they often are out of synch with each other. So, we fused these two heretofore separate courses and developed considerable economy in doing so. Teachers and students could dig deeper and more widely with this arrangement. They loved it.

You might expect this highly conservative community to erupt in an uproar with this newfangled approach, but we involved the community from the beginning in developing the program, which the community leaders supported. The upshot? The community loved it! The conclusion? You can generate a huge program in a small high school (Leggett & Shapiro 1983).

How? Cut yearlong courses into *semester* and *quarter courses* (nine week) in length.

You don't have to offer small enrollment courses, such as physics, every year. Get rid of grades (freshman, sophomore, junior, senior), so that kids who are ready can take courses when they are ready. You now have an *ungraded* high school. With this structure, *uncommitted time* can be built in, so that everyone (students and teachers) can have the luxury of reflecting.

The Smallways school, referred to above, was designed with these in mind (Leggett & Shapiro 1983).

HOW THE OPERATION CHANGED

While we changed the program in the year before moving into the new building, the school still operated as a normal, traditional high school in its old building. That is, it had twelve hundred kids traveling through the corridors to go to each class. It still was not decentralized into the house-plan model. It still had the normal atmosphere of a large, impersonal high school. The departments still had trouble communicating with each other. I left for another district when the school moved into the new building. But, I was anxious to visit the new school about a month after it opened.

SIGNIFICANT CHANGES

Administrative Roles—Huge Differences

The normal large American high school operates very impersonally. In this model the administrators generally operate as firemen, frantically rushing about to head off impending and actual disasters. They race about putting out fires, never able to get on top of them. Life is very stressful. My visit to my old (but new) high school was shocking.

No one was racing about madly putting out fires. People had time to talk to me and to each other. The atmosphere was calm, almost serene (to me, almost surreal). I almost felt that I was in a time or a space warp.

What was the difference? They *knew all* their kids. They were on top of things before anything could happen. One hall principal mentioned that if a kid came to school with problem behavior, the faculty members could spot it, could warn their teammates. The key structural reason for this was that both teachers and administrators had started working in teams. Teachers changed their roles—they often became advocates. They could let the administrative team know that a student was having trouble in order to head off problems. And they did.

Changes for Teachers and for Kids

Similarly, as I talked to the teaming teachers, they had the same feelings. They knew all their kids, knew them well. They could spot problems as their kids came into school. Or, other kids could let them know that someone was upset and needed help or looking after.

Kids liked the smallness, liked the intimacy. They felt much more comfortable. Kids could take advantage of the opportunities open to generate a wide variety of programs for student activities—and they did. Each hall developed its own newspaper, its own journals. One hall developed a literary journal, another a science journal (that hall principal had been the state science coordinator). Teachers felt they could become considerably more professional in their teaching and behavior involving each other and the kids.

CONCLUSIONS AND CONSTRUCTIVIST IMPLICATIONS

Size

Stanton Leggett once observed that it's a lot harder to develop a good, big school than a good, small one. We realized that he was right. Size is *absolutely* crucial in schooling—but normally overlooked.

Three Indispensable Elements of an Organization

Clear Sense of Mission

Chester Barnard (1938), the father of administration, pointed to three indispensable elements of an organization, the first being to develop a clear sense of mission. Diana Oxley (1989, p. 29) notes that people in a large school interact primarily with their departments, so the shared sense of school purpose is lost. In the small school, faculty and students can develop a shared sense of purpose (as in the school discussed above). Since people feel that they belong, they can buy into the shared goals, developing a greater sense of participating and belonging. No one falls through the cracks.

A System of Cooperation

The second of Barnard's indispensable elements is that an organization must have a system of cooperation to achieve a common purpose. It was easy to see that the smaller school was quite successful in this essential component, while the larger school had considerably more difficulty in pulling this off—if they could pull it off at all. People in the smaller school felt that everyone was needed and valued, so they cooperated much more readily.

A System of Communication

Barnard's third indispensable element is that a system of communication must be established to develop the common purpose and to achieve the system of cooperation. Note in the smaller school the clear evidence of highly effective communication.

Social Climate/Social Distance/Trust

The social climate of the small school was much more intimate; people felt closer to each other. Social distance was closer. People felt greater trust. How many large schools can produce that?

Governance and Control

How Is Consent Obtained?

In a large school the authority structure is imposed; decision making is often top-down. In a small school, it can emerge from interaction within the community in the school. Social controls operate very effectively, as I saw upon entering the new building. "Small schools are more orderly and have more social controls operating. In part this is due to everyone knowing everyone, something that is impossible in a large school" (Leggett & Shapiro 1983). With less sense of shared community, greater social distance, it is not difficult to realize that destructive student subcultures often develop in larger schools (Oxley 1989, p. 28; Gregory & Smith 1987).

Sense of Community

A genuine sense of community develops. This enables kids to identify with teachers, and, consequently, to develop deeper intellectual interests. The healthy mutual respect can generate a healthy self-concept, a greater sense of confidence among both groups. Greater emotional support becomes provided.

Beyond five hundred or six hundred students, teachers and administrators do not know all students by name. In a school of one thousand kids you cannot tell an intruder from a student (Oxley 1989, p. 28).

Beyond eight hundred, marginal students become alienated. In a small school no "outsiders" can develop.

Role of the Principal

In the smaller school, the principal is closer, takes the role of head teacher, is more approachable. The authority barrier tends to be removed, as I witnessed immediately.

Role of Teacher and Student

In large schools, cliques often form to protect both teacher and student from the organization because they feel helpless. In small schools, people in both the teacher and student social systems can take more proactive roles, get to know each other, and become more supportive. In small schools, the kids are really needed to make the school operate. Both groups can develop greater autonomy, and yet greater interdependence. Students can become primary control agents (as I discovered on my first visit).

Responsibility and Wise Decision Making

Both can develop greater sense of responsibility because of the greater latitude allowable in small enterprises. Similarly, student decision making can be enhanced because of wider provision for student participation and action in the smaller school. Two students in one of my high schools who experienced such a school's model were asked separately about eight years later (at a cocktail party) what they learned. Pam said, "I learned to take responsibility for my time." Gregg later thoughtfully noted, "I learned to make wise decisions."

Dropout Production

A high school of two thousand kids generates *twice* as many dropouts as a school of six hundred (Shapiro 1995). "Research indicates that large school size adversely affects attendance, school climate, and student involvement in school activities and contributes to higher rates of dropping out, vandalism, and violence" (Oxley 1989).

Participation in Extracurricular Activities

Small schools offer three to twenty times more opportunities to participate in extracurricular activities (Barker and Gump 1964). Extracurricular activities are often a key element in student satisfaction, retention, engagement, and so forth.

Diversity

In small schools one can generate greater support for diversity, although as noted above, in larger organizations one can be more anonymous, can become lost. However, adolescents' growth needs of independence and identity can be met more easily in a small school because they can develop greater autonomy (Shapiro 1995).

Cost

Cost savings were the second reason for building large schools. What does the research say? The facts kick us into reality.

> Empirical evidence for cost savings only applies to very small schools: (Walberg & Fowler 1987), and "only if achievement and other positive school outcomes are not considered" (Fowler & Walberg 1990). With regard to the supposed economy of scale, much of it results from providing proportionately fewer support staff and extracurricular activities, and providing less space for these items. However, these savings also represent costs in terms of dropout rates, poor attendance, vandalism, etc. If the financial costs associated with the negative effects of large schools were accounted for, any economy of scale probably would not be evident. (Oxley 1989, p. 28)

SUMMARY

Our American predilection for hugeness runs counter to any sensible analysis, which compares and contrasts the large and the small school, whether it be on any level—primary, elementary, middle, or high school. The benefits of smallness outweigh any perceived or imagined limitations of small schools. Students and teachers learn to value each other since everyone is needed. People simply participate more—they have to.

And the social costs of large scale are prohibitive. Dropping out ruins lives. William Raspberry (1994, March 3), the columnist, reported on the Annie E. Casey study that if a student drops out, marries, and has a child before twenty years of age, he or she has a 79 percent probability of living in poverty, in comparison with those who do stay in school and neither marry nor have a child before age twenty. That student has only a 9 percent probability of living in poverty.

THE LAST WORD?

Today, the alienating effect of large schools is more profound than ever. High schools in the United States often enroll as many as 3,000 students. Yet schools this large are difficult to defend on educational grounds. . . Further, the social and psychological support formerly provided by families and communities appears to have declined, especially among the urban poor, which suggests that today's students may be even less able to cope with large schools. (Oxley 1989)

QUESTIONS FOR REFLECTION

1. Have you ever worked in a decentralized school or organization?
   A. If so, how did it work? How did people working in it feel about it? The kids? The community?
   B. What were its advantages and disadvantages over a centralized model?
2. Have you ever seen or heard about ungrading a school (sometimes called continuous progress, nongraded)?
   A. How did that work?
   B. How did teachers feel about it? Parents? Kids?
3. Have you ever thought about the size of your (or others') schools?
   A. After reading this, what do you now think and feel about smaller schools, or about decentralized schools?
   B. Would you consider visiting a school organized into smaller units?

    C. Note all the advantages of small schools, and the negative disadvantages of much larger schools. Why, then, do we keep building large schools when the research evidence contradicts their effectiveness, and even their efficiency?

    D. Does it surprise you that even the supposed cost savings of larger schools turn out to be illusory, especially when you take into account the social costs (dropouts, lack of involvement, participation)?

4. The upshot—if you were superintendent or a board of education member, would you argue for or against decentralized schools?

    A. How would you coach your arguments?

    B. With which key social systems would you first think about discussing your ideas?

    C. Which tier of social systems would you approach next?

5. Why do we Americans have this love affair with large-sized organizations?

    A. Do you?

    B. Does your administration and school board?

    C. How can you get them information to question that (without, of course, creating problems for yourself)?

6. Do have any questions you can add to this array?

SOURCES

Barker, R. G. & Gump, P. V. (1964). *Big school, small school.* Stanford, CA: Stanford University Press.

Barnard, C. I. (1938). *The functions of the executive.* Cambridge, MA: Harvard University Press.

Conant, J. B. (1959). *The American high school today: A first report to interested citizens.* New York: McGraw-Hill.

Fowler, W. J., Jr. & Walberg, H. J. (1990). School size, characteristics, and outcomes. Unpublished paper.

French, T. (1993). *South of heaven: Welcome to high school at the end of the twentieth century.* New York: Doubleday.

Gregory, T. B. & Smith, G. R. (1987) *High schools as communities: The small school reconsidered.* Bloomington, IN: Phi Delta Kappa Foundation.

Hampel, R. L. (2002, January). Historical perspectives on small schools. *Phi Delta Kappan 83*(5), 357–63.

Johnson, J. (2002, January). Will parents and teachers get on the bandwagon to reduce school size? *Phi Delta Kappan 83*(5), 353–56.

Leggett, S. & Shapiro, A. S. (1983). *An analysis and commentary on policy and rules #5000 as amended August 18, 1983 by the School Board of Broward County: Subject: Adequate educational facilities, designation of schools and attendance areas, elimination and consolidation of schools.* Martha's Vineyard, MA: Stanton Leggett and Associates. (An analysis undertaken for the City of Fort Lauderdale.)

Leggett, S., Brubaker, C. W., Cohodes, A., & Shapiro, A. S. (1977) *Planning flexible learning places.* New York: McGraw-Hill.

Meier, D. W. (2000, June 5). Smaller is better. *The Nation 270*(22), 21.

Muir, E. (2000–01, Winter). Smaller schools: How much more than a fad? *American Educator,* 40–46.

Oxley, D. (1989). Smaller is better. *American Educator 13*(1), 28–31, 42–51.

Oxley, D. (1994). Organizing schools into small units: Alternatives to homogeneous grouping. *Phi Delta Kappan 75*(7), 521–26.

Raspberry, W. (1994, March 3). How to predict a life of poverty. *Sarasota Herald Tribune.*

Shapiro, A. (1995). Size of school and the effective school. In *Curriculum and schooling: A practitioner's guide.* Palm Springs, CA: ETC.

Walberg, H. J. & Fowler, W. J., Jr. (1987). Expenditure and size efficiencies of public school districts. *Educational Researcher 16*(7), 5–13.

Wasley, P. (2000). *Small schools, great strides.* New York: Bank Street College of Education.

CHAPTER 19

A Day in the Life of a Contructivist Principal

Leanna Isaacson

Three simple steps will lead you to success:
One, prepare. Two, prepare some more. Three, prepare even more.

—General Norman Schwartzkoff

FRIDAY, AUGUST 31, 2001: PRE-DAWN

As I traveled the fifteen-minute trip to school, the agenda for the day went through my mind. I mentally prioritized the things I needed to accomplish. It was a beautiful morning, the stars were twinkling and the moon was shining as they prepared to disappear and let the sunrise take over. I pushed open the gates and drove to my familiar parking place. Principal parking only, I laughed to myself as I thought how funny it would be if the words were reversed and it said principal, only parking.

As I moved toward the door I had to stop. The magnolia tree at the front of the school contains the most fragrant blossoms. I chose the latest blossom as the one to capture my attention today. The smell was wonderful. Each blossom's cycle of beginning and ending reminds me of the cycle of our children as they move from one grade to the next, beginning a new journey into their learning each year. The time seems to go so fast, and the children change as quickly as the blossoms.

THE DAY STARTS

Opening the door, I began the all-too-familiar routine of the morning. Turn off the alarm, turn on the lights, deposit my homework on my desk, turn on the computer, and start my coffee. The first of many multitasking skills begins. I listen to my voice messages while reading my e-mail messages while writing down any notes from the many messages that require my response or action and unpack my homework from the night before.

Since I cleared out the messages yesterday evening before I went home, I have twenty-five e-mail messages from the staff. I consider every one of them important and respond immediately. Of fifteen additional messages from the county level, only one is important to me; I can forward five others to members of the leadership team. A voice mail from a crabby parent requires a return phone call. I add this to my mental "To Do" list. I'm not very conscientious about creating written lists.

Financial Problems to Solve

The sun begins to rise; the rest of the world is about to come alive. My secretary arrives, and we begin our day together collaborating on how to respond to the many needs of a school of 935 students and 100 staff members. Today we tackle three issues of major concern. First, we will now have to find $13,000 in the budget to cover the cost of yearly maintenance on our copy machine. As a literature-based progressive school we use the copy machine a lot. The machine will need replacing in a year or two. Where will we find the money? What can we do without? Should we share this information with the teachers? Of course we will. They need to be a part of the decisions that must be made in their behalf.

Decision Making on Distribution of Bonus Monies— Or, Avoiding Disaster

Second, we received $90,000 additional money for improved test scores. My personal opinion about the procedure, process, and incentive for standardized testing performance becomes a nonissue when money is attached to the "carrot and stick" approach to teaching and learning. Teachers will decide among several possibilities about how the money must be distributed.

The options include any combination of the following: teacher bonuses, hiring teachers or paraprofessionals, and purchasing materials and supplies. Other schools that faced the same decision in the past had mixed results in working with teachers to build consensus. Often teachers and staff became angry with decisions. Feelings were hurt and that set a negative tone for the whole school for a long time. How could we avoid that? Who would imagine that utilizing a constructivist approach in a school would include such issues?

The Leadership and Support Team

We decided to think of all of the problems that other schools faced when handling the same issue. Then, when teachers faced the same decisions, they would at least have all of the facts to examine.

We thought of a process to use, information to develop, and a timeline. Once this was created I would take it to the Leadership and Support Team (the assistant principal, secretary, curriculum resource teacher, and technology coordinator) for additional ideas before presenting a process to the staff. The decision must be theirs.

The criteria for decision under these circumstances entail that when making decisions that involve others, the process requires a representative group who clearly present the information to all the identified stakeholders with well-thought-out rationale, who remain fair, and who don't leave anyone out. I would present the information later on in the day to the team. The secretary would develop the fact sheet, which would include the exact amount of money that each person would receive, given a variety of possible scenarios. She will work with the bookkeeper to make sure the facts are accurate. We'll present the information to the staff next week, and have a representative group meet to decide how they want the money divided. We are working so hard to build a collegial environment. I hope this won't get in the way.

More Budgetary Decisions

Next on our early morning agenda is another budget item. The budget is built on the county projection of the number of students we would enroll by the tenth day of school. We are under about forty children from projection. The budget department will remove $131,000 from our existing budget by the end of next week. We anticipated that we would not meet the full projection figures and withheld $90,000 already.

However, we now had a serious problem. What are the options? What is our goal? The goal will be to do everything we can so that we do not lose existing classroom teachers. Our class sizes are reasonable at each grade level and any other combination would greatly impact a grade level's numbers. How many staff members are not yet hired?

Since the county defines the salary as an average of everyone in the school district, we have specific cost figures for every position. We then calculated the money that the unfilled positions would generate. We asked more questions. If our numbers increase, will we recoup the money and add the positions later after the recalculation count in October? We are still short of the money required. After the secretary dug around into other line item accounts, she could see that we could squeak by through creatively drawing from the acceptable accounts and come up with enough money to give the required amount back. We agreed that it would work.

The paperwork was completed and the numbers given to the county finance department. I kept pouring my coffee to get through this part of our morning discussion. Whenever we have to decide about people's jobs, something will have to give. In this case, we'll make sure the teachers understand the decision and the potential impact that the decision will have.

Interaction with Staff

The staff began trickling in as everyone else's day was beginning; it is 7:15 A.M. In the next ten minutes, one could observe the technique of not multitasking but "multi-conversationaling" (my word). In rapid-fire succession the A.P. came in and we started to discuss the traffic problems, and two teachers came in together, each with a different concern over a couple of their students.

As I began responding to them, the PTA president pushed her head through the teachers to explain all the details of a petition to get another traffic signal light at a busy intersection. The trick is to respond in sound bites to each person. Since women are especially good at talking over one another during conversations, they did not think anything of my strategy to make sure everyone knows that I am paying attention to each one, while never completing any conversation at one time. After several rounds of responding, the entire discussion is eventually completed to everyone's satisfaction.

The other part of the strategy—I cannot lose track of what I am saying and to whom. I believe there must be a specific part of constructivist strategies that address this often-needed technique.

After all the women left, thanking me for my time and information, my A.P, who remained seated, just rolled her eyes and shook her head. I just shrugged my shoulders and prepared for the next onslaught, which would come about three minutes later (long enough for me to reheat my coffee).

More Interactions

This time, however, there were only two teachers each with different needs concerning their students. In the midst of those conversations, a third teacher stopped by to share a funny anecdote about one of her children. We all laughed and immediately returned to where we left off.

I must now acknowledge yet another unnamed skill. It is required of principals when staff members have very little time. When they see me, they need me immediately. So, it is common that they interrupt whatever I am doing or saying to ask or tell me something. This requires the skill of never forgetting where I am in a conversation so that for whatever period of time I am interrupted, I can resume my previous conversation at the sentence where I left off. I think this may be called "multi-remembering." The A.P. left. I think she felt it was easier to go outside and handle the morning school traffic.

As soon as they left, four more came by, one after the other with different needs and questions. Would I proofread a newsletter, so that it could be copied right away? When could the P.E. department talk to me regarding a fund-raising idea they had? The nurse needed to talk to me as soon possible regarding a parent phone call and one of our students. The clerk needed me to place one of the newly enrolled students in a classroom.

Meeting Parents and Students

I immediately answered each request and went into the lobby to greet the parents and the new students. They had arrived from Argentina and spoke some English. They are beautiful children. They did not have any school records with them, and we had to determine the last grade they were in and when they were last in school. They needed a couple more documents before we could enroll them, so they left to return the next day. The clerk and I carefully reviewed the existing paperwork. The calendar year for school is different in most South American countries and it is very confusing when they enter American schools to figure out the grade that is appropriate. We sorted it out and placed the children.

I quickly drank another couple of gulps of coffee and raced to a kindergarten room where I am scheduled to assist the teacher every morning. In this room is a five-year-old child who is absolutely adorable for the minute or two that he can remain calm and focused.

The teacher and I spent hours analyzing this child and determining how best to handle him. He is so active that in order for him to let the teacher teach, I go into the room and hold him in my lap for the first forty minutes of class. He is on medication for hyperactivity but he is more involved than that. He has some cognitive skills, but functions at the level of a beginning three-year-old. He does not make any connection with other children, and does not engage in any of the classroom activities. The parents are Haitian, and cooperative. I am part of a large school team that meets to determine the best course of action for this child.

Our first intervention is for him to stay in school for only a portion of the day until we can complete the evaluation for him and determine if a regular classroom environment is the best placement. My next task will include getting the kindergarten team together and get their assistance in placing a paraprofessional, assigned to the team, to help their teammate with the child. We started the paperwork to have him evaluated in case the psychologist can unearth more definitive explanations for his behavior. It will be three more weeks before the process will be completed.

Next, the Psychologist—and, a New Role for the Leadership and Support Team: Guidance Counselor

After I returned from the kindergarten room, I spent time with the psychologist to review yet another role of the Leadership and Support Team, that of guidance counselor. Our counselor is on maternity leave until the end of October, so we are taking on her tasks until she returns. We agreed to structure the guidance jobs with each of us on the team assuming responsibility for five teachers and the students in their rooms. In this way we keep better track of the individual students and maintain the support the teacher needs.

We meet once a week with the psychologist and review the current testing and staffing needs of the students. We may also sit in on a staffing with the parents as part of the team determining the best way to serve the needs of a child. There were no staffings today.

The Nurse

I then found the nurse to discuss the concerns she had. We talked at length about the special needs of another five-year-old in kindergarten that must go to the bathroom several times a day and change his own "Pull-ups." The teacher, team, and I had concerns regarding the sanitation for the other children and the independent skills of the child.

The kindergarten teacher arrived, and we continued the discussion with her. The end result was that the nurse wants to meet with the parents, teacher, and me to develop a documented plan. The parents do not want the child singled out for any reason. They are only as cooperative as the accommodations we make for their child. We arranged a time to meet. I followed the teacher back to her class and helped calm her frustration with the time this child's needs were requiring of her. We arranged a time to get together so that I could provide the support she needs.

I found the nurse again. We sat down with another teacher who has a child with hemophilia. We met with the father to clarify the child's restrictions. The mother was not able to attend the meeting. As we discussed the concerns of the father, it became obvious that both parents did not agree about their child's limitations. We will need to meet again, when we can have the two of them together to figure out what we are expected to do.

More Troubleshooting

As soon as I returned to my office area another kindergarten teacher approached me with a concern about a child in her room. The child is identified by a local child evaluation center with emotionally handicapped behaviors. He is an acting-out child and hits other children. This is a new teacher who needs a lot of support. I found the curriculum resource teacher and together we developed strategies that would support the teacher.

I thought, "How hard this is on teachers, with children this young, who are not ready for school. Parents insist that the children begin formal schooling when they have so many other needs. Special-needs children are becoming more prevalent. They are placed into regular education classes when budgets do not allow for any additional assistance for the teacher. Our children with medical needs are very difficult. The pressure on our teachers to maintain an academic environment for a five-year-old with problems is just not appropriate. Yet, where should these children go?" I will have to worry more about this at a later time.

Another teacher called for me. She needed someone to help her. James had his head stuck in the sink of the play kitchen. A little coaching, a small adjustment of James's head within the opening under the sink, and he was freed. Since the child was fine, the teacher and I had a good laugh. We could imagine James's interpretation of what happened when he got home.

As I returned to the office I received word that one of the first-grade students bit another one. Both children came to the clinic where we could see that the "biter" needed a good scolding even though Phoenix, the "bitee," seemed fine. The teacher will call both parents. I needed to spend time with the "biter." In the meantime, I received a phone call from one of my colleagues who asked my advice concerning her budget. By the time I returned to Phoenix, he was sound asleep. Maybe sleep is what he needed. I decided to let him stay in my office until he woke up. It was thirty minutes later before he was awake enough to return to class.

NOON

Meeting with the Leadership Team

The morning disappeared as usual, and the Leadership and Support Team attempted to sit down and eat together. It is a great time to discuss common issues.

As usual, that lasted for less than ten minutes when I was interrupted. A teacher who is taking educational leadership classes wanted help with a college assignment. The teacher did a thorough job of analyzing student test scores on the standardized test and compared them with the running records that teachers use for each child. There is an enormous gap between many students' classroom performance and the test.

We discussed her perception of why this happens and arranged for her to facilitate a brainstorming session with third-, fourth-, and fifth-grade teachers. This is a time when we will study carefully the standards, expectations, and instructional strategies for test taking and reading performance. We determined that if there seems a need, we will provide a planning day for the teams, so that we can analyze the scores more thoroughly and draw sound conclusions about ways we can better narrow the gap between classroom and test performance. She left with a plan she developed.

More Interaction

Two other teachers followed immediately. They came into the office to discuss ways in which we might develop projects for the identified gifted students who are in their classrooms.

We have a classroom-based model taught by one of many of our teachers who are certified to teach the gifted. It is up to those teachers to provide a service-learning project for the students as part of the student's Individualized Educational Plan. We discussed ways that we could incorporate projects into their existing curriculum.

We then ran out of time, and it was necessary to arrange to meet again. Once more I believe that we will need to provide at least one planning day for the teachers of the gifted to meet and discuss the more in-depth projects and strategies for their students.

Forget lunch. I then met with the Leadership and Support Team to review each of the cases we assigned ourselves. We reviewed each case and determined the next step in assisting the teachers and students.

Communicating with Faculty

Afterward, we discussed the weekly newsletter that each teacher receives on Friday. We reviewed the events coming up and determined how we would facilitate the meetings or assign a key teacher leader to chair the meeting. We know how important it is for teachers to meet; yet we need to be sensitive to their time. Teachers are more willing than ever to both lead and organize various groups to solve problems and identify strategies to meet the needs of their students. This is a very positive position for teachers to take.

AFTER SCHOOL

Developing Monthly Social Functions—and Its Impact

The afternoon evaporated as well. It was Friday; teachers go home earlier than usual. However, a meeting was arranged with a small group of teacher representatives. It was their job to determine how to organize and develop monthly social functions for the staff. Instead of hurrying up the process so they could go home, they continued to stay and brainstorm ideas.

Teachers showed how far they have come in their understanding of the need for the staff to know each other better. Until now grade-level teams rarely spent time with other grade-level team members. Even within teams, there were divisions.

Today, a new attitude became obvious. As the teachers began discussing who would host each month's social, several teachers expressed their ideas about how the staff could become more integrated. They said that since we might look at vertical teaming models next year we needed to spend more time in vertical team arrangements. Each member of the social committee recognized that planning the social of the month was a time to informally get together. Time to plan together and exchange ideas seemed more important to them than the actual event. They then created ways to mix teachers among the grade levels in a vertical model as opposed to always having a horizontal grade level team. (I was nervous that they were taking so long. The contract says they can leave with the students before a holiday.) But, the ideas kept coming, and the teachers stayed as long as it took to plan, develop, and organize vertical teams.

I was so excited to see the process unfold among staff members, who one year ago would never conceive such an idea. They added a new level to our group norms in a constructivist way.

EVENING

The Leadership Team—Debriefing

On Friday, at 5:00 P.M., my assistant, curriculum resource teacher, and I go to a local restaurant to unwind and regroup for the coming week. After we laugh at all of the unbelievable moments of the week, we discuss the important issues.

Today, our discussion turned primarily to the need for providing a full day of planning for each of the teacher groups who will develop specific projects. We then determined the priority for each of the areas, identified the source of money and agreed upon a timeline. The curriculum resource teacher and I would facilitate the first round of pull-out days, with the understanding that we would turn over that responsibility to one of the group members for future meetings.

Each area is important, yet we easily agreed on the order of importance. First, we decided to create a vertical team that would review the county-developed vertical alignment document, identify the conditions under which the skills and concepts would be taught, and then determine which concept-based thematic units would support the skills. We decided this would require two consecutive days.

Second, we need to pull our planning team together with our consultant. If we are to develop alternative delivery models for next year, we need to begin discussions and planning. Our deadline for the decision is December, so we need to get going.

Third, we identified an additional need to bring grades three, four, and five individual planning time in order to create strategies for the standardized testing. We will need time to identify individual student test scores, compared to student's classroom assessments, determine if disparities exist, and decide how best to approach the instruction and delivery models currently in use. Alternative ideas may surface during those meetings.

During preplanning time teachers identified their individual needs for problems to solve and their own desire to receive additional training in a variety of areas. The rest of the conversation focused on deciding on the committees that must meet, and the dates we can agree upon for all of the remaining issues we need to address.

We talked briefly about how hard it is to facilitate the pull-out days, especially when we may have as many as two in one week. But we agreed that even when teachers take over the groups we must be present. We all knew the research about the importance for teachers to know they are supported and that when the principal is present, the task becomes validated.

We finally decided that we could not think any more. It was late and my twelve-hour day at the end of the week creates a mental wall at some point. My brain shuts down to allow it to process all of the important information I have received. I did return to school to pick up some homework and place my remaining papers in an unclassified pile and return the phone call from the crabby parent. By that time neither one of us wanted to make a big deal out of his concern over the length of time it took him to work his way through the morning traffic.

ENDINGS—AND BEGINNINGS

As I walked out the door I stopped at the magnolia tree. The blossom that was at its peak of beauty this morning was fading. But I could see many other buds that would be in full bloom by Monday morning. I look forward to arriving at school to smell the fragrance of the newly formed flowers as the cycle goes on.

The metaphor continues.

QUESTIONS—AND THOUGHTS

1. Do you detect a similarity between Janet Richards's day in chapter 12 (as a high school teacher and department chairperson) and that of Ms. Isaacson?
   A. Any differences?
   B. What seem to be the causes of the similarities?
      1. Their personalities?
      2. The demands swirling around them?
      3. Which social systems/groups seem to be taking up the bulk of their time? Is it the same for both women?
2. How does Ms. Isaacson handle this emotionally? Could you?
3. How about Ms. Richards? What accounts for their capacity to handle their complex jobs?
4. Ms. Isaacson has developed a Leadership Team. How does it work?
   A. Is this an idea you would use? Why?
   B. Whom would you include in this group? How often would you meet?
   C. What appears to be its major functions? Would you add others, or subtract some? Why?
   D. Why does it seem to work? Do people need support systems? Do you? (I certainly do.)
5. Ms. Isaacson has developed a weekly newsletter to communicate with the faculty. Is this something you would do? Why? Is there any support in the literature for this idea?
6. What does the principal mean in her last sentence: "The metaphor continues"?
7. If you could meet Ms. Isaacson, what questions would you like to ask her?

CHAPTER 20

Moving Orange Blossom Trail Elementary School toward Constructivism

To accomplish great things,
we must not only act,
but also dream,
not only plan,
but also believe.

—Anatole France

What do you do when a high-energy elementary principal, who has just started her doctorate, asks if you would help her resolve conflict between a group of excellent teachers who had come this year from a widely known and celebrated school with some equally competent faculty who had been at the school? And, she also wanted to move the entire school toward constructivist models of instruction.

Both of these comments got my attention. Better have a good change strategy in your hand (or, your head).

ORGANIZING FOR CHANGE

An Outside Facilitator

Sitting down and talking about the situation in the school with the principal was a first step, particularly focusing on concerns and issues people felt. First, of course, we chatted about each other.

The Principal

She had been one of a rarified and declining number of female principals in a Western state, had come to this state for a change of scenery, had had to serve several years as a teacher, had done it willingly and with a sense of humor, had become a principal, and when the district decided to build a new school was chosen to serve as its principal.

One reason for that was her experience, and another was the confidence the district personnel had in her. Teachers joked about the fact that the district pretty well left her alone, because she was obviously so competent and highly regarded. Being unassuming, she thought that that was amusing. One of everyone's conclusions about her was that she was not afraid to take risks (for example, moving in mid-career to a new state where she had to become a teacher for several years and take beginning teacher's training to become qualified for a principalship to get established).

A Major (and Unintended) Source of Conflict

One of the sources of conflict was that the group of new people, all excellent teachers, had suffered huge disappointments in their former school as its widely heralded mission for which they were recruited nationally, and to which they were totally and deeply committed, had changed rapidly and radically into a traditional school.

The end result was they felt betrayed and were suffering emotionally. So they came into the new school and, feeling defensive, "had come in with their guns blazing." As a result, issues of trust/distrust, we/they (acceptance/rejection), defensiveness, and other perfectly normal organizational processes immediately surfaced.

When "new members" enter an organization, conflict might occur based upon perceived differences between the "old and new" people for a variety of rather predictable reasons. First, experienced people are often hired because they are perceived as being able to enrich the existing organization with their ideas. However, with that experience comes their own set of ways to do things. New ideas in this school were perceived as a threat to the already existing "ways of doing things." Because the people from the outside entered as a distinct group rather than as individuals, who could be more easily assimilated, the impact appeared, and was, considerably greater.

Resolving This

In this case, it took an additional year of reflection and dialogue among everyone to determine that the apparent conflict in beliefs really did not exist. The problem came as a result of semantics and the original distrust by the established faculty of the newcomers. The semantics lay in the fact that the teachers referred to methods of instruction by labels familiar to them, a situation that can generate problems (which it did).

The new group, however, had different labels for the same procedures, which was perceived as doing things in a different way. This led to a build-up of resentment since the newbies were perceived as trying to take over. Once, however, the horizontal teams began to discuss specific reading strategies, rather than a specific label, all the resistance regarding instructional differences vanished. What occurred was an agreement to abandon the use of labels.

THE SCHOOL—BRIEFLY

The elementary school was large, with over nine hundred students, but not packed. Fortunately, people had room to function, as the district and principal had done quite well in planning for adequate space and equipment. It was also new, in its third year, with a growing community mostly of people living in homes, some of whom were immigrants from a variety of cultures and nations. The parents were mainly middle and working class.

A DIAGNOSTIC, ANALYTIC, PLANNING, AND IMPLEMENTATION PROCESS MODEL: *ORGANIZATIONAL MAPPING*

This planning model and process flowed out of my work with several schools and a hospital. Actually, as I was working with faculty and administration in each school, trying to grasp the complexities of two schools, the model fell out. I stepped back from the chart paper sheets on the wall, and thought, "Holy smoke, I've come up with a change model!"

An *Individualized* Change Model

But, it's considerably beyond a simple change strategy, inasmuch as it enables one to *diagnose and analyze* any organization's *Concerns/Issues*, then to develop a *plan* to deal with them, and then to *analyze the consequences and outcomes* of implementing the plan as it evolves.

In short, it is a highly *individualized* change strategy, in stark contrast to most attempts, which try to change organizations top-down. Examples are Goals 2000, and many state change strategies, such as Florida's Competency Assessment Test (FCAT).

All, of course, are fatally flawed, since they use one change strategy to try to force very complex organizations to move in a direction they've decided the organization ought to take. And the inhabitants resist.

States, which use tests to force districts to move in the directions they unilaterally and politically decide upon, generally find the teaching profession vigorously opposed to such coercion. And the change strategy is usually implemented by only a few true believers, who generally leave the school after a short while because they get sick and tired of the slings and arrows aimed their way by the rest of the faculty. The Annie E. Casey Foundation's attempt reveals this (Wehlage, Smith & Lipman 1992, Spring), as does the Coalition of Essential Schools (Muncey & McQuillan 1993, February).

This diagnostic, analytic, implementation, and change strategy is essentially a process of "Organizational Mapping," since it uncovers the processes organizations generate in their functioning daily. The resultant chart I titled "The Dynamics of Organizational Change," which has been published and utilized more than once (Burley & Shapiro 1994; Shapiro, Benjamin & Hunt 1995; Shapiro 2000). In addition, modeling constructivist thinking requires focusing on higher level cognitive thinking, such as dealing with *Concerns/Issues*, analyzing underlying *Themes*, constructing a *Plan* to deal with the *Concerns/Issues*, analyzing *Outcomes*, and finally evaluating them.

HOW THE ORGANIZATIONAL MAPPING
MODEL WORKS—A SUMMARY

The *Organizational Mapping* model works like this:

- The first stage, informal in nature, of course, is to get the confidence of the people in the organization, particularly those who are able to make decisions. Otherwise, you're out on your ear.
- The next step, still informal, is to get a representative *Planning Committee* of key people who are trusted and who represent all shades of opinion and feeling in the school/organization. (If you stack the deck by making it unrepresentative, you will destroy its and your own credibility.)
- Next, we have to get at the underlying *Concerns/Issues* people perceive. This takes time, and cannot be rushed. Otherwise we will miss something crucial. And these *Concerns/Issues* have to be written down on the large sheets of chart paper for all members of the Planning Committee to see. Then, they must be reduced to 8 ½″ × 11″ and sent to *everyone* (and, I mean everyone—or the uninformed will get upset, suspicious, and harm the effort), teachers, PTA, office staff, ensuring immediate effective *communication* to one and all. No one can be left out—or, they will feel, and be, left out. So, when it comes time to need their support—they won't be there!
- The succeeding step is to *Summarize* those *Concerns/Issues.*
- Next, we try to analyze the *Underlying Themes*, which unify the inquiry, and which also winnow down the insights into a few unities or factors that can be handled. We will see how that works.
- Next, we try to figure out *Potential Lines of Action/Initiatives* to take action to resolve the *Concerns/Issues* and the *Themes.*
- We then work at figuring out the underlying *Rationale* for each *Potential Line of Action/Initiative.*
- The last step is to evaluate the *Outcomes, or Consequences* of each *Line of Action.*

This is really much more simple than one might think (if people develop confidence in you). It just takes time. It is useful, however, to listen very carefully to everything said in order to pull off an accurate and thoughtful diagnosis. I always check to see if I understand comments made, especially side comments. Now, onto the process of organizational mapping in the school.

FIRST, A PLANNING COMMITTEE

After a very short while, it became clear that a planning committee would be crucial to the process. Participants had to be selected from all K–5 grade levels, and they had to be substantial, respected people who were trusted. And the group also had to have representatives from the newer teachers recruited from the other school. Fortunately, the curriculum specialist, there a year, had come from that school, had been active in recruiting those teachers, and was trusted and perceived as a highly competent, caring, woman of integrity, committed to the school and the staff. So, she and one other teacher from the "contributing" school served.

When I walked into the planning committee in a room off the main office area, people were already there, and the principal had arranged for sandwiches from the cafeteria, as well as potato chips, fruit, some candy, and lots of markers all over the place. I had lugged in my 24″ × 36″ inch chart paper, along with tape and markers. People were very friendly, while covertly sizing each other and me up.

Introductions

The principal introduced me, mostly stressing very briefly my work as a teacher and administrator who had worked with a variety of schools. We had a representative from every grade, one or two grades had two; the principal; the curriculum assistant; and a technology/ graphics specialist who took notes and was highly competent with her computer.

The graphics expert was able to transfer my printing on the long, taped-up sheets of chart paper into legible characters. Also, she was able to construct graphic figures from the discussions, a terrific help in visualizing the issues being discussed, as can be seen in figure 20.1 (and all the figures in this study).

PURPOSES

The principal explained the purposes, one of which was to deal with conflict. Another was to think about moving toward vertical teaming to improve what was going on, and anything else to improve the school and learning for the kids. This was a pretty wide-open agenda, so people were being told that their input was crucial.

We then moved to using the "Organizational Mapping" model, which is also called "The Dynamics of Organizational Change" to develop insights.

CONCERNS AND ISSUES

Many people working with organizations tend to ask people what *problems* they are facing. Note that we did *not* talk about problems, but rather *Concerns/Issues*. Talking about problems often tends to block discussion, since people may start to complain, rather than analyze their issues and concerns.

The first *Concerns/Issues* raised was that of *team trust/distrust/ rumors*. People felt that distrust was a major issue. The group from the other school was quite taken aback by this perception of them/us and by the perceptions of *schisms* in the school. So, there I was, up on a step stool, marking these *Concerns/Issues* down on my long sheets of chart paper, all taped together. As figure 20.1 indicates, a number of issues surfaced:

- *Team trust/distrust* rumors swirling about
- *Schisms* in the school creating *distrust, them/us* feelings
- *Team building* was needed to improve team functioning
- *Curriculum* was a concern of many: in terms of aligning; differing views about what curriculum to use; some ignoring curriculum alignments
- *Communication* was a major concern: communication with the administration; among teams, within, across, and among grade levels; some speaking up more; and some chosen/volunteering more
- The school seemed to have a lot of bickering, struggling for *control*, differences of opinion being *personalized*

Analysis of Dynamics of Change

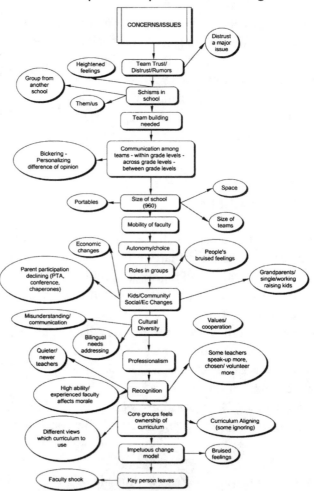

Figure 20.1   Concerns/Issues Expressed by Teachers

- The *size* of the school was discussed, scale being an important issue in the functioning of organizations. They had a number of portable classrooms
- *Size of teams* was mentioned, some being eight teachers (to which I responded that that was probably a bit too large to communicate and to work together adequately, since as Thelen [1954] had noted, the maximum number of roles available in work groups appeared to be seven. Once you had more than seven in work

groups, the quieter persons will be squeezed out and will participate less)
- In the first three years of operation, the school grew, which meant
that faculty had to be increased, and people moved out, which led
to a good deal of *staff mobility*
- Faculty felt that their *autonomy* was crucial to them, and that that was
being honored, autonomy being synonymous with *professionalism*
- Faculty reported that some felt that their *feelings* were bruised, and
that people's roles in their grade levels were sometimes not as satisfying as they wanted
- *Social and economic changes* were occurring in the community:
parent participation declining; PTA conferences weren't as well
attended; fewer chaperones were available for field trips; more
grandparents were raising kids; more single parents were working
and simultaneously raising their kids
- The community was experiencing more influx of immigrants,
some of them doubling and tripling in houses: greater *cultural diversity* was occurring leading to misunderstanding, difficulties in
communication; more *bilingual* needs for students, nineteen languages being spoken; some of these kids not motivated
- *Professionalism* a concern
- How satisfied people felt with the *recognition* they and others were
getting: high ability, experienced faculty, but with *morale* problems; some teachers speak more than others, chosen/volunteer
more; quieter/newer people getting lost; faculty morale problems;
core group feels ownership; core group feels ownership of curriculum; impetuous change models sometimes raised, which
bruises feelings
- A *key person* left (the charismatic second-in-command) in the previous midyear: causing great sense of loss; hurt feelings; loss of
purpose; faculty shook
- The group from the other relatively highly publicized school coming on board, as a group: some people being very cautious, no or
little *trust*; *them/us* feelings; heightened feelings occurring
- *Gifted* program needs addressing: "It doesn't appear that there has
been much going on this year with this program"; "We have to take
our time and be cool about it."

SUMMARIZING CONCERNS AND ISSUES

This may seem pretty complex, since we elicited so many *Concerns/Issues*. It becomes necessary to summarize them, or we become overloaded and lost with too many details and are unable to see the overall picture. Figure 20.2 summarizes the issues and concerns. Since summarizing consolidates similar items (note that there are fewer items than in *Concerns/Issues*), it helps point up overall

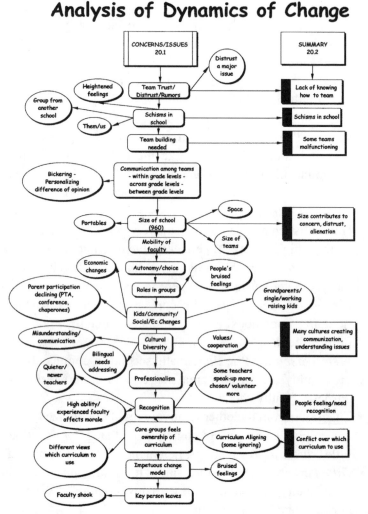

Figure 20.2   Concerns/Issues Summarized

patterns and decreases the amount of data with which we have to contend.

- Distrust hampers effective team functioning
- Faculty lacks knowing and applying the skills to *team* properly
- *Team building* is necessary
- *Schisms* in the school: faculty apparently *not accepting differences* among each other—presently
- Some *teams malfunctioning*: people do not know *how to resolve conflict*; we have to break down the *them/us* mentality; some teams half functioning
- *Size of teams* is a contributing factor; teams generating problems
- *Size of the school* is a contributing factor to *concerns, distrust, alienation*
- *Communication* with administration, across and among teams and grade levels not sufficient
- *Community* experiencing *socioeconomic changes*: community seeing more *immigrants* move in; greater *cultural diversity* arising, creating communications, understanding, acceptance issues; community participation declining
- *Heightened feelings* creating problems with interpreting, *accepting others, generating distrust*
- People have strong needs for *recognition, acceptance, autonomy*
- Conflict over *which curriculum* to use

UNDERLYING THEMES

Note that analyzing for *Underlying Themes* makes the potential for action easier, since there are far fewer *Underlying Themes* than *Concerns/Issues* and *Summary* items. And, it helps point up the big picture more clearly. Figure 20.3 presents these themes.

- *Trust/mistrust. Trust* is essential for an organization to thrive
- Unification and consistency are necessary, *interpersonal strife* causing *tension/mistrust*
- *Teams developing problems, need support* to improve, such as *team building, conflict resolution* exercises: excessive *bickering,* struggle for *control*

Analysis of Dynamics of Change

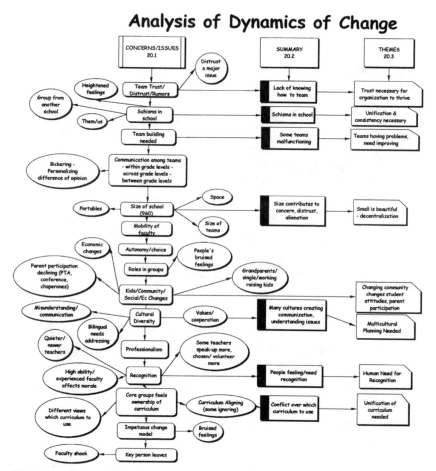

Figure 20.3   Themes Underlying Summary of Concerns/Issues

- *Size of teams and school* are generating problems. Need to *decentralize*
- *Changing community* changes *student attitudes toward school, parent participation* declining
- *Multicultural planning* needed
- Humans need to be *recognized*
- *Curriculum* needs to develop in a *unified* direction

The themes also help us to discern underlying unities in our quest for practical action. These underlying unities are essential for focusing efforts.

POTENTIAL LINES OF ACTION/INITIATIVES

Now that we've been able to analyze the *Concerns/Issues* that people express, and then summarized them, we have a flow of analysis. Note that this next flow of analysis, developing *Potential Lines of Action* in this Organizational Mapping change strategy, is based on the preceding analysis of *Underlying Themes*. These potential lines of action are represented in figure 20.4.

The following comprise some *Potential Lines of Action/Initiatives:*

- Develop *trust-building* exercises
- Develop *team-building and conflict-resolution* exercises
- Implement an exercise to help people *understand and accept* each other, such as using the *Gregorc Personality Style Delineator*

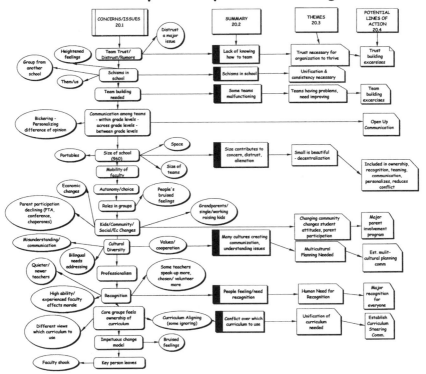

Figure 20.4   Potential Lines of Action to Resolve Concerns/Issues

- Open up lines of *communications*; make communication a top, riveting priority
- Develop *Lines of Action to decentralize:* this will produce more people who will be included in *ownership, recognition, teaming, communication*
- *Reduce size of teams from eight to four*
- *Decentralization personalizes*, since we deal with fewer people, units are smaller, so we get to know each other better, reduces *conflict*
- Develop major *parent involvement* effort
- Establish a *Multicultural Planning Committee*
- Develop a major *recognition* program for everyone
- Establish a *curriculum steering committee*

UNDERLYING RATIONALE FOR EACH
POTENTIAL LINE OF ACTION

Why develop a rationale? John Dewey (1938) and a host of others all point to the fact that theory usually underlies successful action, that theory is highly practical. So, I believe it is necessary to develop a rationale to support each *Potential Line of Action*. Figure 20.5 shows this *Underlying Rationale*.

- Developing Trust
     The first underlying *Rationale* for developing *trust* is that *cooperation rests on trust*. If you distrust someone or an organization, you really cannot work effectively with that person or organization, which you feel you must watch very carefully at all times.
- Team Building
     Team building is essential for teams to function more effectively and efficiently, as are *conflict resolution techniques*. Burying anger and other emotions, which elementary faculties frequently use, only serves to impede constructing healthy relationships and organizational processes. That is why we opened them up, although people at first felt that they were very painful.
- Using a Personality Style Instrument for team building and improving understanding, acceptance, and communication, among other goals
     Implementing a *personality style* instrument exercise has never failed to help most people become more aware of themselves, others,

Analysis of Dynamics of Change

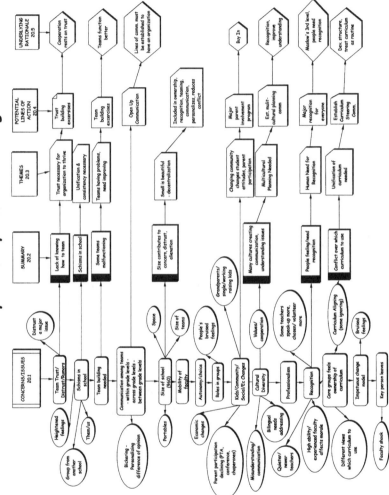

Figure 20.5   Underlying Rationale for Potential Lines of Action

parents, students, brothers and sisters, administrators, authority figures, and virtually everyone else. Administering the *Gregorc Personality Style Delineator* proved very helpful in facilitating faculty to understand and to accept each other. People realized that the other person was not doing something to spite them or to challenge them, but that that was their way of reacting as a personality to situations.

- Using the Gregorc Delineator, which has four personality styles
  1. *concrete sequential (CS)*, illustrated by such occupations as a bookkeeper or an engineer, who is concerned with details and facts, is highly organized, always on time, likes things to be in order,
  2. *abstract random (AR)*, who are people people, highly concerned with people's feelings, who are wonderful friends, attracted to the helping professions, people who are outgoing, emotional, love color (like Bette Midler),
  3. *abstract sequential (AS)*, often lawyers, professors, who are "big picture" people, who live in the world of concepts and ideas, are excellent "big picture" analyzers (much like Mr. Spock and Albert Einstein),
  4. *concrete random (CR)*, big-time risk-takers, innovators, trouble-shooters, entrepreneurs, often love to take things apart to see how they work, like Evel Knievel, Donald Trump.

Results

Analyzing the Gregorc provided an outlet for humor as we became more familiar with the idiosyncrasies that individual personalities generate. We were able to laugh at ourselves, a behavior that has continued. For example, asking a strongly concrete sequential person how he or she shops at a grocery store might elicit the response that his or her shopping list is organized by the aisles of the store. He or she is a perfectionist, and a loner.

Whenever a party is to be organized, whom do you expect will volunteer? Of course the abstract random personality will love to do it, and will have lots of food, loud music, and hordes of people. This person loves to work with others. The concrete sequential? He will not want to come, but will come on time, will hide in a corner hating the loud music, and will want to leave first. Who will love to fix some equipment? The concrete random, who will take it apart to see how it works, but will often bandwagon to another of his many projects, and will not want to bother putting it back together again (it's too boring). The abstract sequential is a reader, thinks deeply, is a great analyst—and, a loner.

We overheard the teachers teasing the principal (a very strong abstract sequential personality) with, "I can tell it's your abstract sequential personality kicking in again. I know, you need to think about it, and then we can talk about it tomorrow." Her district superintendent approaches every conference with, "Please don't talk to me about what you've been thinking. It just makes my brain hurt."

- Using Chester Barnard's (the father of administration) Three Indispensable Elements to All Organizations—to improve the school (and any organization), Barnard (1938) noted that there are *three interacting, indispensable elements* to an organization:
  1. It must have a *common mission or purpose* (otherwise it goes nowhere).
  2. It must have a *system of cooperation* to facilitate achieving the common mission.
  3. It must have a *system of communication* to facilitate achieving the common purpose.
     - The Gregorc helped considerably in establishing a *system of cooperation*, since it increased trust and eliminated much suspicion.
     - We established *lines of communication* that must be developed to facilitate achieving a *common purpose*, and for organizations to achieve their goals. Sending our minutes after each meeting with graphics that illustrated all these processes to *everyone* was helpful to achieve this goal. Providing everyone in the organization with the same information at the same time with full details allows for clarification of the issues by those who did not attend. Without a common frame of reference, attempts to recall the specifics of a meeting are usually misquoted, reinterpreted, or misunderstood. Using a small portion of a ream of paper seems well worth it. Interestingly, we were able to meet Barnard's three indispensable

elements of an organization. The underlying rationale for developing a *major parent involvement program* is that it promotes *buy-in* by all involved.

- Using Maslow's Hierarchy of Needs

    Maslow's (1954) *Hierarchy of Needs* stresses that the third level of needs is *social* in nature: people *need recognition and acceptance* (without it they become unfulfilled, and will begin going after it, sometimes in unacceptable ways).

- Developing a Curriculum Structure

    Developing a *curriculum structure* enables a faculty to generate curriculum on a *routine* basis, and leads to avoiding needing a supreme effort to make one change in any curriculum. If people feel that curriculum can be changed as a *routine* of everyday life, such change can become a routine, normal part of the everyday functioning of the school or school system. You've essentially destroyed the barriers resisting instituting any change in the program, a rather remarkable outcome.

CONSEQUENCES/OUTCOMES (SO FAR)

It is pretty clear that the Organizational Mapping process did, indeed, do exactly that, as revealed in figure 20.6:

- It uncovered the dynamics the organization was generating so that we could diagnose, analyze, and implement changes to achieve goals we decided upon.

    For example, implementing the Gregorc Personality Style Delineator was effective in facilitating considerably *improved faculty understanding and acceptance, of themselves and of each other.* Additionally, the main styles of each staff member were listed.

- The *trust-building* exercises helped improve *trust*—and the open discussion reduced distrust so that it faded.
- The *team-building exercises* fulfilled their goal to improve the *functioning of the teams.*
- The *relationships* among the teachers who came from the other school and those from Orange Blossom Trail had improved so

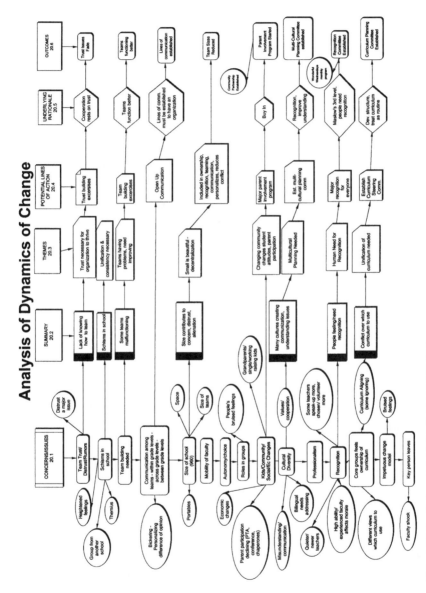

Analysis of Dynamics of Change

Figure 20.6 Outcomes of the Process (So Far)

much by the beginning of the fall semester that the *distrust had completely disappeared.*

One of the teachers from that group, who served on the planning committee, said, "All we wanted was to be happy," which struck quite a chord with all of us. Focusing intently on making sure that we *communicated* the discoveries of the Planning Committee to everyone paid off handsomely, since no one could possibly feel left out. By the end of each meeting of the committee or of the entire faculty, everyone had duplicated minutes in his or her hand.

- *Lines of communication* were established.
- *Decentralization* was moving ahead: *team sizes were reduced.* However, we decided that it was premature to decentralize the entire school at the present time, since we weren't ready yet. Rather, the Planning Committee unanimously agreed that people should work with each other in directions that they decided upon, which were shared and agreed upon at the meeting. Teaming was thus supported for those who were interested, and those who chose not to team were also supported.
- A major *parent involvement program* began to be developed, which included a *Multicultural Planning Committee,* and a *Community Partnership Committee.*
- A major *recognition program* was developed, implemented by a huge "Orange Blossom Trail Spotlight Bulletin Board" located in an area of heavy traffic, and run by a *Recognition Committee.*
- In addition, the school promoted a better sense of community among staff with a "Wonderful Wednesday" program monthly, in which each of these Wednesdays was sponsored by a different team of teachers who devised clever names for themselves, and designed different activities for each session.
- A *curriculum structure* was devised to generate curriculum as a routine.

SUMMARY

The Organizational Mapping process performed its functions admirably. Its diagnostic function uncovered key *Concerns/Issues,* which were then summarized. It then analyzed *Themes* underlying these *Concerns/Issues,* and pointed up *Potential Lines of Action/Initiatives* to take. It facilitated analysis of *Rationales* to evaluate these potential lines of action, and it is useful in evaluating *Outcomes* of action in terms of these rationales.

The school has moved significantly in meeting its goals. But, it is only part way there. More remains to be accomplished.

QUESTIONS

1. What is your first impression after reading this chapter (which, at the time of this writing, is still ongoing)?
2. Do you admire the courage of the principal in forging ahead in moving the school toward a constructivist approach? Note how she involved everyone in the school.
    A. What approach would you have considered before reading what her lines of action were?
3. How do you analyze the change model? Do you see any similarities with the model used in chapter 16 "Beliefs, Myths, and Realities: A Case Study of a Rogue Junior High"?
    A. What additional elements would you add to it to make it more effective?
    B. It is interesting that people were willing to confront issues head on, rather than dodging them, as often occurs in many organizations (witness the Enron debacle). Why is this?
        1. What role did the principal play in this forthrightness?
        2. Did the Planning Committee play a role?
        3. Was the membership of this committee selected to be representative? How?
    C. Why did the conflict between the two groups essentially disappear so rapidly? What contributed to it?
    D. What patterns did this Organizational Mapping change model uncover? What patterns did it seem to miss? How could it be improved?
    E. How would you use it with your own organization? What patterns would it uncover that could be understood, and, perhaps, improved?
    F. Do you like the idea of looking for themes underlying a lot of issues and concerns? What is the advantage of this approach?
    G. What do you think of avoiding using the word "problems" and using "issues and concerns" instead? Does it make sense to you?

H. How about looking for a rationale underlying potential lines of action or initiatives? What advantages and disadvantages does that provide?
4. What do you think of the idea of moving an entire elementary school toward a constructivist approach? What advantages does it seem to generate? Disadvantages?
  A. How is the staff reacting to it? Why has no opposition arisen? Is it because of the heavy involvement?
5. What next steps would you take?

SOURCES

Barnard, C. I. (1938). *The functions of the executive.* Cambridge, MA: Harvard University Press.

Beckhard, R. (1969) *Organization development: Strategies and models.* Reading, MA: Addison-Wesley.

Burley, W. W. & Shapiro, A. S. (1994). Beliefs, symbols, and realities: A case study of a school in transition. In K. M. Borman and N. P. Greenman (Eds.). *Changing American education: Recapturing the past or inventing the future?* Albany: State University of New York Press, 325–50.

Dewey, J. (1938). *Experience and education.* New York: Macmillan.

Maslow, A. H. (1954). *Motivation and personality* (2nd ed). New York: Harper & Row.

Mintzberg, H. (1994). *The rise and fall of strategic planning: Reconceiving roles for planning, plans, and planners.* New York: Free Press.

Muncey, D. E. & McQuillan, P. J. (1993, February). Preliminary findings from a five-year study of the Coalition of Essential Schools. *Phi Delta Kappan,* 486–89.

Shapiro, A. (2000). *Leadership for constructivist schools.* Lanham, MD: Scarecrow.

Shapiro, A., Benjamin, W. F., & Hunt, J. J. (1995). *Curriculum and schooling: A practitioner's guide.* Palm Springs, CA: ETC.

Thelen, H. A. (1954). *Dynamics of groups at work.* Chicago: University of Chicago Press, 63–65.

Wehlage, G., Smith, G., & Lipman, P. (1992, Spring). Restructuring urban schools: The New Futures experience. *American Educational Research Journal 29*(1), 51–93.

CHAPTER 21

Outside the Box: Three Team Leaders as Co-Principals

This is an interesting school system.

—Stanton Leggett, Educational Consultant

What do you do when you have three really talented team leaders in a new, small elementary school, who have loads of experience working in teams and are leading teams that also have a goodly number of experienced and highly competent teachers?

The challenge was to figure out an approach that would utilize this array of talents.

BREAKING THE BOX

As we talked about the organization and structure of this new school, it became clear that we had been able to draw a number of talented people to the school. And we had done it without gutting the rest of the elementary schools in this moderately small district of about forty-eight hundred students. That is, we did not rob everyone else of their most highly talented people to build a showplace.

We also had tapped an experienced principal, who was both popular and good with parents and teachers, and who was respected as a quality person and educator in the schools and in the community.

We were shorthanded in the central office with an extremely thin staffing of top administrators (four, with a grantsperson). We felt we needed to build our school-community relationships districtwide, but never felt we had the resources to pull this off systematically, with a

carefully designed conceptual and operational plan, as we had in virtually all other task areas. We were operating piecemeal and didn't like
the somewhat spotty (we thought) results.

TURNING A CHANGE INTO OPPORTUNITY

Was this an opportunity?

Could we chat with the team leaders, all of whom were warm, experienced, and talented educators, and see what their reaction would be to
include some administrative functions along with their instructional
roles? We first talked with the principal who was thinking about heading up the school. What were his insights and interests?

We knew he was talented in working with the community, he liked
and respected people, he was a longtime and well-respected community
leader, his wife was a professor in the university, and he had established
a good community-relations program in his elementary school. We
thought that could be a function of his with the central office, on a part-
time basis, while simultaneously he could carry on key, selected roles
and tasks as principal of the school, with some functions and tasks being delegated to the three team leaders. We wondered what his reaction
would be to a split school-based and central office–based role.

The individual endorsed the idea, which had strong possibilities of
contributing significantly to this missing piece of our operation.

With his positive interest, we then met as a group with the three team
leaders and the principal. When the idea of a partial team principalship
was broached at this meeting, people were quite interested. Of course, the
major concerns consisted of trying to figure out what roles the appointed
principal would take and what roles would the three would share with the
principal. The team members made clear that while they thought the idea
was a good one, they did not want to be overburdened with administrative
functions to the detriment of their team leader functions—nor did we.

COMMUNITY INTEREST IN THE NEW SCHOOL

The district had a large university with a laboratory school in its
midst, as well as a private and internationally famous agricultural re-

search corporation in its environs. Also prominent were feed lots where cattle ranchers would send their cattle to fatten up prior to sending them off to market. Many of these families and others in the university community had been sending their kids to the laboratory school for years.

A Pleasant Surprise

Much to our surprise, we began to get calls from some of these folks asking for appointments to talk about the boundaries of this new elementary school. They began coming in to ask if their homes would be included within the new school zones. We had publicized the school as a team-taught operation, with a pod-based structure as its building design, before going to the community for a bond issue to raise the revenue necessary for construction. Our schools had begun developing a reputation as quite good, but we thought that we were better than our reputation. (This was one reason we wanted to develop a more effective school-community relations program.) But, we were quite unprepared for this interest. We knew that the lab school had lost a lot of its experimental purpose over the years, and had become somewhat less than on the leading edge (read, stodgy), and we were clearly on the upswing, but we did not think the community was fully aware of our quality.

BREAKING THE BOX ON ADMINISTRATIVE ROLES

We started to think about administrative and supervisory roles in relationship to task areas in education (Campbell & Gregg 1957). These task areas follow.

School-Community Relations

Typically, this function or task area is centralized, that is, it is located in the office of the superintendent because the total district needs to communicate with parents and with the community. So, thinking about improving this function means staffing it centrally. This certainly does not mean that each school should ignore developing a highly effective program of relating to, communicating with, and involving its parents and community.

George, the principal, was effective in communicating and relating to kids and to their parents and the community. As we thought about designing this model, it seemed a natural to have him as the spokesperson for this new school. Of course, this did not mean that the teams and team leaders would not deal with parents and the community. Obviously, they would have to do so, but the chief person in this function would be the principal. Yet, in a small school of about 350 kids with three teams, this could hardly be a full-time responsibility. And the team leaders and teachers obviously had a major role in communicating about instruction and other vital matters with parents and the community. So, it looked as if George could take major responsibility for this function centrally.

Organization and Structure

Usually, decisions about the structure and organization of a school system (or any organization) reside in the central administration, and not with each suborganization. The subunits, such as schools, or branch offices, usually find it difficult to grasp the big picture, so that this function is reserved for the central unit. As for the new school being built, its organization had been established with teacher and administrative input, together with working with one of the outstanding educational consultants in the country. They had emerged with a solution early on in planning for the building. The school was designed as a team-taught model of three pods, each housing a team, with a team leader.

What became different was seizing the opportunity to look "outside the box" in structuring divergent roles for the team leaders by their assuming some carefully selected administrative roles normally performed by the principal. The small size of the school was a factor in our thinking about this critical task area. Did we need a full-time principal?

As we (including the principal, team leaders, and teachers) thought about the other task areas, we had to factor that question into our thinking.

Curriculum and Program

See chapter 25 "Designing Our Structures to Do Our Heavy Work: What a Curriculum Structure Can Do to Make Our Professional Lives *a Lot* Easier." In some districts, the local school and classroom teacher have strong input in decisions in such areas as curriculum, although in recent years, state control has zoomed, particularly in the Southern states.

The Curriculum Steering Committee: A Key to Effecting Change with Heavy Involvement

In this system, curriculum and program design decision making were centralized through a Curriculum Steering Committee structure in which the teachers had primacy. Teachers, thus, had major input into the decision making, but such decision making had been developed to become more systemic, that is, systemwide, over the whole district, rather than by each school, grade level, or each classroom teacher making decisions independently.

The route for teacher input into major decisions was via a teacher or a group of teachers coming up with an idea, formulating it with help from the assistant superintendent, presenting it to the relevant curriculum area committee (natural sciences, humanities [language arts, social studies, arts], practical arts, and special areas), and after thorough consideration, to the district Curriculum Steering Committee for recommendation to the assistant superintendent for implementation.

Obviously, teachers had a great deal of autonomy in selection of teaching methodology, in the selection of materials and the like. In the area of curriculum and program, teachers had considerable power and influence in the determining the decision making. I must say, we also tried with some success to have a principal on each of the subcommittees, since some of them were knowledgeable in some areas. But administrators were clearly outnumbered on both the area committees and the entire Curriculum Steering Committee.

However, this meant that the role of the principal in instruction was important, but shared with the faculty and team leaders. Evaluation of teacher competence in instruction obviously had to be shared between team leaders and the principal in the new school. In schools that valued their teachers, they were involved in such activities.

The Pupil Personnel Programs

Pupil Personnel Services Structure: A Second Key to Effecting Change

See chapter 26 "Developing and Running a Pupil Personnel Services Council: Making Our Structures Work for Us." Needless to say, some aspects of pupil personnel procedures, functions, and structure need to be districtwide (reporting to parents via report cards, bus schedules), while others can be local school (in the high school, tardy policies), grade level, or even left to the decision-making prerogative of the classroom team and/or teacher (grading decisions, student evaluative procedures, some disciplinary decisions).

The Value of Teams

Thus, this area was also shared among teachers, team leaders, and principal. However, in establishing a structure of teams and team leaders, the very nature of discipline changes fundamentally, considerably for the better. For example, if one teacher is unable to cope effectively with a student, another team member who might have a different relationship with the student, can step in. Teachers can spot a kid who is having problems when they enter school, can communicate with their teams, and the teacher who has a relationship can take appropriate action to work with the kid. In effect, teachers' roles can change with a team structure.

A Little Research and Examples of the Value of Teams—On Discipline

As an example, a junior high school was changed into a middle school with teams. After the change was implemented, I came back early one day about the middle of September to work with the principal who was quite concerned about the impact of the move to a middle school model on his roles, met a key teacher in the hall, stopped to say hello and shmooze, only to be told, "Can't talk. I'm heading to meet with my team to advocate for a student."

That says a great deal.

So, the normal load of discipline on the principal becomes diminished since the teams and teachers tend to handle most disciplinary problems. As a matter of fact, in developing data to work with the faculty and administration of that junior high school, I sat unobtrusively in the corner of the office for a couple of hours to watch the goings on (mostly disciplinary problems and frequency).

They were out of hand, with about twenty-five kids coming in for each of the last two periods of the day. This data proved a gold mine in discussing with the faculty and administration the benefits of moving into a middle school structure based on teams.

More Results

The middle school team structure virtually eliminated this administrative disciplinary function. So, we knew that in a small team-taught elementary school, George's disciplinary functions would be diminished. You can be sure, however, that we worked to assure George that he would have some functions in this new and intriguing school model. By this time, all of us knew that he could afford to be away for some time focusing on his central office school-community-relations responsibilities.

Staff Personnel Programs

Since we had a teachers' union, we had a contract with a four-step grievance procedure. Thus, decisions about staff personnel programs were largely made centrally. In terms of being carried out, the principals had the primary responsibility in the schools. But, they needed to operate with knowledge, requiring us to run an in-service program to help the administrators avoid errors. This did take a chunk of time to work out.

Budget and Finance

Again, obviously, the overall budget is done centrally. But, different school districts and organizations develop different philosophies regarding how much authority and autonomy are delegated to the local unit, in this case, the school. We felt that if schools were expected to carry out their missions, they should have as much autonomy as possible, consistent with the decisions of the Curriculum Steering Committee and of the Pupil Personnel Services Committee.

Particularly in the case of schools whose organizational structure is based on teams, did we feel that this autonomy should be extensive. So, while the typical, nonteam-based school would generally see the principal having a good deal of input into decision making (depending upon her personality style and needs), this team-based school had to work out delegating much of this decision making to the team. In this case, and, realistically, the team leaders had considerable influence. Again, this reduced somewhat the function of the principal. And, as we told George, he might not have to visit the school too often since he might gum up the works (which he and team leaders thought was pretty humorous).

Building and Facilities

This is primarily a local, school function, although some central responsibilities exist. These would include developing districtwide emergency procedures, with each school responsible for developing its own plan. Team leaders could help with this function, although scheduling central facilities has to be done by the principal or team leaders operating as a team themselves.

RESULTS

After considerable thinking, and actually building several models, we and George agreed that he could fulfill his local school functions in about half time. We agreed, however, that in opening the school, he would need to set his own schedule, probably being there about 75 percent of the time at first, but he should not get locked into routine. For example, being there when the buses came early in the school year would be important—and symbolic. As the first month continued, team leaders and teachers could provide the necessary symbolic and real presence in this function.

George gave a considerable kick to the school-community relations program, stimulating it into a much better program (developing a realistic newsletter that went to all parents monthly at first, better organized parent nights for each school, a focus on informing parents about some of the interesting things and successes happening in the schools and with the kids). And the team-taught school with its three top-notch team leaders and teams prospered exceedingly well, becoming another model school in the district.

QUESTIONS AND INSIGHTS

1. What factors made this unusual organizational arrangement work?
2. How could it have gone awry? Why didn't it?
3. Why was George the right person? The three team leaders? What professional and personal attitudes and skills did they have to pull it off?
4. We broke the task areas into six categories. On which did George largely focus, and on which did the three team leaders?
5. Did breaking the organization into three teams help with problems of discipline, relieving the principal of a lot of time-consuming effort? Why did this work?
   A. Are there some commonalities with chapter 18, which deals with decentralizing schools?
6. What other positive results occur from decentralizing this school? Any negative?
7. What would you do in a situation such as this?
8. Could you take some of the elements discussed here and apply them to your own operation?

SOURCE

Campbell, R. F. & Gregg, R. T. (Eds.). (1957). *Administrative behavior in education*. New York: Harper & Row.

CHAPTER 22

Our Evaluation Ritual Trap:
And How to Spring It

This year's (annual) report begins with a brief chronicle of the testing madness that seems to have gripped us.

—Gerald W. Bracey, *Phi Delta Kappan,* October 1999

If 2000 was the year that testing went crazy, 2001 was the year it went stark, raving mad.

—Gerald W. Bracey, *Phi Delta Kappan,* October 2001

All that exists can be measured.

—Lord Kelvin, Nineteenth-century Physicist

Can love?

INTRODUCTION (ACTUALLY, HOW WE ORGANIZED THIS CHAPTER)

For this chapter, let's peer first at our national evaluation ritual in education (which has *become* literally our standard operating procedure) but from the divergent perspective of the sociologist and anthropologist. Why has this evaluation ritual become so pervasive in the culture of American education? Next, we illustrate a sample of rituals in everyday life, and then in schools. Following that, we tie our present "testing madness" to our quest for certainty in an increasingly insecure (and now, violent) world. We'll take a quick glance at how two quite

different kinds of kids (structured and unstructured) react to our testing ritual, and then we'll dig away, uncovering the assumptions underlying our testing ritual, with a brief critique based on constructivist
principles. Last, we'll provide several dynamite illustrations of an authentic alternative approach to testing, namely asking adults and children what were their most significant learnings in school classes. We
might be surprised.

SOME MIND-TICKLING QUESTIONS

Why do we test children, but not most adults? For example, we would
not consider testing our physicians, dentists, or attorneys yearly to determine their competency. (It is true that some of these groups do require continuing education credits, but this is distinct from sit-down
testing.)

Why don't we have an annual test for our presidents, our legislators?
(As a matter of fact, Florida's governor, commissioner of education,
and legislators, when asked to take the high school level Florida Comprehensive Academic Test [FCAT] that they have mandated the schools
to give to students yearly, refused to take the high school test, providing lots of humor with their hilariously lame excuses.)

Why just our children?

Some key questions about educational testing remain: How do we
discover what each student has learned? (And, maybe, how he or she
has learned?) And, more importantly, how can we approach evaluation
from a scientifically valid approach that is constructivist in nature?

BUT, FIRST OUR NATIONAL EVALUATION RITUAL AS S.O.P.

Our national Standard Operating Procedure (S.O.P.) in evaluating student learning is relatively simple, virtually universal, and some would
say, time tested: we teachers construct a test (usually either at the end
of a unit, or on Friday); the students respond (they have to take the
test); we grade the test; and students get their grades.

Onto the next teaching-testing cycle—and the next—and the next—
until the schooling semester or year ends. All teachers expect it. All stu-

dents expect it. Virtually all administrators expect it. All policymakers (having endured it in their own educational experience) have bought into it and set laws and rules based on it. (In Florida the state has set numerical scores for letter grades [A is 100–94, etc.].) This is a ritual. But, it has little to do with knowledge, with comprehension.

This has become a major component of our national educational culture, culture being defined as patterns of shared, learned behavior that people learn in connection with social living (Kroeber & Kluckholm 1952; Linton 1955). As is true of many rituals, a culture develops in its life cycle, it is a way of dancing, often meaninglessly, through the motions.

Illustrations of Rituals in Everyday Life

If someone asks us how we feel, and we feel lousy, do we say, "Simply awful"? Usually not. The ritualistic response is "Fine." If a newborn arrives to friends or family, and is patently a rather ugly child, do we say, "Boy, what an ugly kid"? We say, "What a good-looking boy," for a boy, and "What a pretty child" for a girl. Christmas gift-giving has become a hugely important ritual. So has the Thanksgiving turkey dinner with all the trimmings. These are rituals.

Illustrations of a Handful of Rituals in Schools

High schools usually have homecoming celebrations, which are loaded with rituals, such as the custom of choosing a king and queen (normally of opposite sexes), and then parading them between the first and second halves of the football game (often in an open, upscale convertible). They often are trailed by a court of runners-up, trying hard to smile and look happy.

Secondary schools (and some middle schools) often schedule a pep rally before football or basketball games. Note that these cultural customs are peculiar to middle and secondary schools, not to elementary schools. The next illustration of a cultural ritual can relate to any level school, including preschools and kindergartens.

Selecting a speaker at graduation (in fact, the entire ceremony of graduation [robes, music, speakers, diplomas, walking down the center aisle]) is a ritual. In some respects graduating is similar to a marriage ceremony. Sociologists and anthropologists would call this a "rite of passage."

So is the ritual of teaching/testing, that is, going through the motions often without anything significant really happening. Actually, final exams are a rite of passage in a twofold sense (in that if you do not pass the examinations you will not be passed to the next grade).

(Thankfully, however, in recent years some alternative evaluative approaches, such as portfolios, have gained considerable use, particularly in the elementary and colleges of education ranks.)

THE TESTING RITUAL—AND OUR QUEST FOR SECURITY

In a world loaded with uncertainty (and, now, violence), seeking and believing we have found security looks increasingly appealing. Wasserman (2001, September) digs into this sense of our insecurity. "There is little doubt that we live in times of turbulence—when things all around us seem to be accelerating beyond our control. . . . Our lives are full of dissonance and upheaval, and it seems that we no longer can count on anything to be stable and enduring. . . . We want to combat this instability with a new sense of order."

The precise-appearing numbers we get from tests definitely create an illusion of certainty in our quest for a sense of order and for certainty. Wasserman (p. 32) continues, "In the area of human judgment, which is at the heart of qualitative assessment, the risks of uncertainty are very great. 'Judgment and belief regarding actions to be performed can never attain more than a precarious probability,' Dewey reminded us. And this 'creates a desire to escape from the vicissitudes of existence by means of measures which do not demand an active coping with conditions.'"

Does the testing ritual actually produce the opposite of what it intends? Called "Education's Different Drummer" by the *Washington Post* (January 9, 2001), the paper notes, "Alfie Kohn and his many allies cite research showing that children who learn because teachers stimulate their natural curiosity tend to retain and understand more than those who learn to get good grades or high test scores. Adding on more tests, they say, will only encourage more bad teaching."

Kohn states, "Surveys of elementary school students reveal that they have learned they are supposed to finish the assignment, do it quickly, and if possible, get the right answer. Much more rarely does a child think he is supposed to try to understand what he is working on. . . . And the more emphasis teachers and parents place on performance, the more students are set back by failure."

Wasserman (2001, September, p. 32) notes that Edward Fiske, then education editor of the *New York Times*, criticized standardized tests for the following reasons:

- "They assume a single, correct answer to problems. They don't allow for complex answers or multiple ways of arriving at them."
- "They measure how good students are at recognizing information, not generating it. We don't ask whether students can synthesize information, solve problems or think independently. We measure what they can recognize."
- "Since tests are timed, even most writing tests, they place more value on thinking quickly than on thinking profoundly."
- "Most standardized tests focus on basic skills, such as calculating in math or the literal translation of a reading passage. They don't say much about higher-order thinking skills like inferential reasoning or problem solving."
- "They emphasize isolated learning, not the integration of facts and ideas."

It is self-evident that these constitute fairly profound criticisms.

Another Widely Held Ritual—And Some Comments Destroying It

Brooks and Brooks (1999, November, p. 19) note:

Many state education departments have placed even greater weight on the same managerial equation that has failed repeatedly in the past:

- State Standards—State Tests;
- State Test Results—Student Achievement;
- Student Achievements—Rewards and Punishments.

As we have learned from years of National Assessment of Educational Progress research, equating lasting student learning with test results is folly.

The authors further state that

despite rising test scores in subsequent years, there is little or no evidence of rising student learning. A recent study by Kentucky's Office of Educational Accountability (Hambleton et al. 1995) suggests that test score gains in that state are a function of students' increasing skills as test takers rather than evidence of increased learning. . . . Inevitably, schools reduce the curriculum to only that which is covered on tests, and this constriction limits student learning. So, too, does the undeviating, one-size-fits-all approach to teaching and assessment in many state that have crowned accountability king. Requiring all students to take the same courses and pass the same tests may hold political capital for legislators and state educational policy-makers, but it contravenes what years of painstaking research tells us about student learning. (p. 20)

HOW STRUCTURED AND UNSTRUCTURED STUDENTS RESPOND TO TESTING

The Structured Student

This student is sequential, likes to do one thing at a time. He often does well in algebra because he is linear, follows rules, and generally is considered by teachers to be a good soldier.

This person typically is a visual learner—and a loner.

The test ritual fits him or her to a "T." This student is quite good at looking up facts and details in the text. And, for the most part, since they are good soldiers, they tend to read and follow the directions and the rules. They will prepare daily, do their homework in plenty of time—no last-minute rush for them. And although they are good with details, we find that they generally are not as able to see the "big picture." So, they will do quite well—if the test is detail-focused. If it deals with the big picture, with ideas, if it is an essay, then they will not do so well.

The Unstructured Person

This student is a last-minute learner. There are two kinds of unstructured learners: either quite social, or a loner and risk-taker. The first, the social person is not very visual, so not at all good with details, and messy in his or her organization. His desk and room is usually cluttered, but he can always find things. He is more of an audio learner, since he usually learns by listening. These are people-people, highly empathetic, very intuitive, and tuned into others' feelings—often are very emotional, reacting to things emotionally. That's why they like to work in groups. Not sequential or linear, so they usually are not good with algebra, but better often at geometry. Because they are not visual, they often do not spell well. (This has nothing to do with intelligence.) They do not memorize well, except for plays. Many of the more strongly sequential, structured learners tend to criticize them as flakes. Jokes about "ditzy blondes" typify this stereotyped put-down, intolerant reaction. So, these unstructured learners do not do well with tests given by a structured teacher whose idea of a good test is one loaded with details. They will do well with discussions, with essays, but not too well if detail and exactness are demanded, which, obviously, runs contrary to their free-wheeling personalities and life-styles.

The second kind of unstructured person often may be a risk-taker (even physically), usually is an innovator, often quite good mechanically, but a loner, also will not bother to prepare for an exam or a paper until the last minute. This person is highly intuitive and often lives on the edge. They can handle details, but not the "big picture." He or she often will balk at doing more than two problems of mathematics homework, since the person will do one or two problems successfully, and then will say, "Well, I know how to do these, why bother to do the rest? I've got other and much more important things to do."

They have lots of unfinished projects going on, much to the dismay of their more sequential friends/spouses/significant others/parents. So, they have little patience for routine and repetition. This person also tends to march to his or her own drummer.

Often this person likes to fix things, but is a jury rigger, only reading the directions as a very last resort, and fixing things only when absolutely necessary. He or she responds badly to authoritarian approaches of more control-oriented people, such as teachers, leading often to defiance, and even confrontation. Usually they are fearless. They respond very positively to challenges ("Can you really pull this off?").

DIGGING AWAY AT THE ASSUMPTIONS UNDERLYING THE TESTING RITUAL

Testing guru James Popham (2001) states an underlying rationale of testing: "Because the amount of knowledge and skills that teachers teach is typically too great to test everything, tests sample those bodies of knowledge or skills." Obviously. And, there's the rub.

The teacher wants to teach a pool of knowledge he or she *perceives* as essential or major. So far, so good. Then the teacher selects key items from that pool that he or she *perceives* as key elements to understanding the area under study. Thus, the instructor *assumes* that the student realizes that these very items are the essential elements that comprise the focus of the work. Or, at least teacher *hopes* that the student *should* realize this.

Popham provides a couple of illustrations. "For example, on the basis of a student's ability to write one or two persuasive essays on a given topic, *we can infer* the student's general ability to write a persuasive essay. *If* our interpretation of the student's skill in writing an essay *is accurate*, we have arrived at a valid performance-based inference about the student's mastery of the skill represented by the test." His next illustration continues "when a student scores well on a 10-item test consisting of multiplication problems with pairs of triple digit numerals, we *infer* that the student can satisfactorily do other problems of that ilk; hence, he or she *appears* to have mastered multiplying pairs of triple-digit numbers. *If* a test-based inference *is valid* and the teacher gets an accurate fix on students' current knowledge or skills" [italics added].

Critique Based on Constructivism

This set of assumptions ("*If* a test-based inference *is valid. . . . If* our interpretation of the student's skill in writing essays *is valid . . .*") is key. They are *assumptions*.

They often fly in the face of what we know about how all people construct knowledge. People simply perceive different facts, data, details, ideas, and concepts differently, and, often, many will not even see or perceive what others do. They will apply different perceptions, different ideas, and different interpretations, to the same experiences—

and will emerge with different conclusions than the teacher assumes and perceives as legitimate outcomes (often assuming that hers are the *only* legitimate outcomes).

Brooks and Brooks (1999, November) note, "Learners construct their learning. This simple truth lies at the heart of the constructivist approach to education." In their book, *The Case for Constructivist Classrooms* (1993, p.4), they state, "Each of us makes sense of our world by synthesizing new experiences into what we have previously come to understand."

So, how can we be sure what each learner learns from the same lesson, or even hears the same things? As a matter of fact we *know* that learners will emerge from the same shower of experiences with often vastly different perceptions, hear different things, emerge with different understandings. So, why not ask people what they have learned?

SPRINGING THE EVALUATION RITUAL'S TRAP: WHAT ABOUT CREATIVE AUTHENTIC EVALUATION ALTERNATIVES, SUCH AS, ASKING PEOPLE WHAT THEY HAVE LEARNED?

But, First: Portfolios

Portfolios are a recent example of the search for "authentic" assessment approaches and models. In actuality, many teachers over the years have employed it under other names, and have asked students to keep quality examples of their work, often for display, or for evaluative purposes. Portfolios are a useful alternative approach to evaluation, richly deserving the category of *"authentic assessment,"* in that a portfolio represents the work of the student over a period of time.

Two Additional Models of Insightful Quotes from the Mouths of Learners

The First Model: Asking at the End of Each Class: "Today, I Learned . . ."

Actually, asking learners what they have learned from a set of experiences is a somewhat different approach to finding out what people have learned—since it comes from their own mouths, so to speak. And it, too, is an "authentic assessment" tool.

How to pull this off?

Toward the end of a class, about the last three minutes or so, the instructor can ask the sentence stem, "Today, I learned . . ."

A sentence stem offers an invitation to finish it, so it presents an excellent opening to one and all to pitch in. By not making eye contact with anyone, no one is threatened by not responding, and by looking around casually, no one will feel a need to respond. Eventually, someone might jump in with what he or she has learned. Another important principle in working with this approach is to accept every contribution positively and absolutely to avoid evaluating any response negatively, since that will shut down virtually everyone. So, this usually invites an open-ended response, which can be an idea, a generalization, an emotional reaction, humor—in short, virtually anything.

Some examples:

I've learned to question what I do.—Enrique A. Boza
You learn how to trust your own judgment.—Chris Novak
This lets you go . . . break down old beliefs . . . be free.—Lori Thompson

One memorable response to "Today, I learned . . ." was a maverick, marginalized high school male senior, who, after we had studied gender roles in suburbia, said, "When I die, I want to come back as a suburban housewife." To the class's astonished questioning, he asserted, "Boy, do they have the life! Coffee klatches, husband bashing, what a way to live!" So, we were able to dig into over-generalizing, stereotyping. It provided a wonderful opportunity for everyone—and, provided him with a lot of recognition. My own estimation was that he kept the maverick role, but moved out of his marginalized status. People respected him for his intriguing insight.

A five-year-old: "I just figured out that a quarter (a twenty-five cent piece) is a quarter of a dollar."

The Second Model: "My Most Significant Learnings in This Class . . ."

This approach can be used about halfway through the semester or quarter and at the end of the semester. Any format can be utilized: an individual or group production; a skit or a play; a (traditional) paper; a poem; a video; a poster; a musical piece, such as a composed song; a piece of symbolic art work; and we've had poems accompanied with live or recorded music.

My wife asked me what were some of the best responses to that question I had ever heard.

One was: "In this class I learned to trust myself."

Two graduate students (Alex Dworzanski and Tim Hodak) came up with this creative response:

"Ten Commandments for a Constructivist Classroom"

    I. Satisfy Basic Needs: Comfort, Food
   II. Everyone Is Equal: Respect
  III. Value Differences
  IV. Discussion=Insight
   V. Why Create Pressure? We're All Professionals. Think, Speak, and Interact Freely
  VI. Everyone Is Involved
 VII. Useful, Recent Articles/Information
VIII. Have An Underlying Plan for Quality Performance and It Will Happen
  IX. Hot Topics That Cause Self-Analysis
   X. Today/Tonight I Learned . . .

Lets me question the way I think. It opens up a world of possibilities.—Kathryn Bylak Brady

This allowed me to see what changes I can make in my personality.—Denise Santiago

I have increased self-awareness and better understanding of people.—Mary A. Williams

I never understood why I did the wacky things I do until I got into this class. I never understood anything about personality styles until I took this class. I never understood why my husband and I clashed and why he became so angry at times. You helped me make my marriage more effective. We now understand each other. You made me believe in myself.—Elementary school vice-principal

We cite more intriguing responses in chapter 11 "From the Mouths of Students—Interactions with Constructivism."

SUMMARY

Briefly, we killed the ritual of testing. And, we suggested a couple of alternative models that work to stimulate higher-level thinking, motivate everyone, and are a lot of fun.

QUESTIONS

1. It's pretty clear that most educators think that we've gotten out of hand with this craze about testing. Why haven't the politicians and many of the public listened to us?
   A. What about testing gives it the "Motherhood and Apple Pie" aura?
2. What strategies can we develop to deal effectively with this movement?
3. What is it about rituals that we latch onto?
   A. Do you see testing as a ritual?
4. What do you think about the way we've analyzed how structured, sequential learners and the unstructured, more random learners react to tests?
   A. Which of these two kinds of learners are you? How do you react to testing?
5. What do you think of using an authentic assessment approach?
6. The alternative approaches, such as asking people what they've learned, is a lot more creative—and, a lot more insightful and fun—as can be seen in chapter 11 "From the Mouths of Students—Interactions with Constructivism."
   A. What is your thinking about trying that approach to see how it works? (Remember, don't look at the people in the class, and, if they're slow about responding, that's normal. Just be patient.)
7. Why has assessment become testing?
8. You might want to look at chapter 17 "Looking Up the Wrong End of the Horse: Our Testing Mania" for some further discussion of the testing movement.
9. What thoughts do you have about this phenomenon (of testing, that is)?

SOURCES

Brooks, M. G. & Brooks, J. Q. (1993). *The case for constructivist classrooms.* Alexandria, VA: Association for Supervision and Curriculum Development.

Brooks, M. G. & Brooks, J. Q. (1999, November). The courage to be constructivist. *Educational Leadership 57*(3), 18–24.

Dworzanski, A. & Hodak, T. (2000). In response to their "Most Significant Learnings," in Organizational Theories and Processes, Leadership Development Department, University of South Florida.

Kroeber, A. & Kluckholm, C. (1952). *Culture: A critical review of concepts and definitions.* Cambridge, MA: Harvard University Press.

Linton, R. (1955). *The tree of culture.* New York: Vintage.

Mathews. J. (2001, Jan. 9). Education's different drummer. *Washington Post.*

Popham, W. J. (2001, March). Teaching to the test? *Educational Leadership 58*(6), 16–21.

Popham, W. J. (2001). *The truth about testing: An educator's call to action.* Alexandria, VA: Association for Supervision and Curriculum Development.

Wasserman, S. (2001, September) Quantum theory, the uncertainty principle, and the alchemy of standardized testing. *Phi Delta Kappan 83*(1), 28–40.

CHAPTER 23

The Rigid New Principal and the Constructivist Teacher: Studies in Tension

All battles are won before they are fought.

—Sun Tzu

A SUDDEN EMERGENCY

When Alana Michelle, in shock, hung up her cell phone, confronted by the sudden and aching news that her longtime and favorite principal, Max Badour, had died suddenly the night before, she felt a terrible tear in her heart. She immediately called Mr. Badour's wife, only to get a busy signal. Four tries later she managed to get Mrs. Badour, who was even more in shock.

She then called several of her closest friends on the faculty who urged her to be the spokesperson for them and to contact the assistant principal, Marie Cross, to set up an assembly for the entire school sometime in the morning. Alana finally reached Mrs. Cross, who agreed to the idea.

Alana, however, came away from her conversation with a sense of unease, feeling that Mrs. Cross did not seem too devastated. Alana knew that Mrs. Cross was eager to head her own elementary school, not being comfortable with middle school kids and the widely acclaimed constructivist, decentralized, and team-taught model that the teachers and Mr. Badour had designed over several semesters.

As a matter of fact, the superintendent and Board of Education were extremely supportive of the school and its program, especially when the community came aboard after considerable involvement, and also became supportive. This had been reflected in the local newspapers, which had featured a number of articles about the school, "pointing with pride," as Alana, the team and other team leaders, such as Lynne Manners and Sue Sharp, had been pleased to note.

Alana tried to dismiss her feeling that the assistant principal was looking at the situation much differently than did she and the faculty.

MARIE CROSS—THE INTERIM PRINCIPAL, AND HER AGENDA

Within the next few days, the superintendent, with the consent of the Board of Education, appointed Mrs. Cross as interim principal. As the dust began to settle, Alana and her key social system became uneasier. They knew that Marie was more of a nuts-and-bolts person, more a manager than a leader or administrator, more of a person who thought in black-and-white contrasts than in the greys and nuances that were necessary to support and operate a constructivist school based on teams of teachers who were fairly autonomous, and who operated largely with consensus.

A Sense of Unease

A couple of weeks later in the teachers' lounge, Marie Cross commented that William Raspberry, the columnist, wrote that direct teaching got immediate results, and that he said that research showed that it was a superior approach. A couple of new teachers didn't say anything, but Alana pointed out that the teams had pondered long and deeply over their philosophy and approach and had decided by consensus that they would work to become constructivist. Direct teaching was the antithesis of constructivist learning, she noted, since the former aimed at the lowest level of cognitive thinking: recall. Alana further pointed out that a recent edition of *Kappan* (April 2001) in the Washington Commentary section noted that "teachers' instructional behaviors have more to do with student achievement than any other factor." And that means that the higher cognitive levels must be the focus. Mrs. Cross left quickly after a secretary called her to the office, but Alana and two of her team in the lounge, Janet Richards and Madeline Linkin, said that they felt very uneasy.

The Unease Spreads, Becomes Shared

At a team meeting they called the next day, Alana asked people how things were going, how they were working with Butch, a student whom everyone called "His Majesty's Loyal Opposition." They joked about Butch, and even though this was only a middle school, Janet remarked that Herbert Thelen, a group dynamics expert, had written that this role was highly respected in adolescent social systems (read, cliques), and that even if Butch abandoned that role or moved away, another kid would move in to adopt that respected role.

After a moment, as each was finishing her Danish, Alana asked how Marie Cross was doing filling in for Max Badour. An uncomfortable silence filled the room, until Janet asked how everyone would feel if Marie were appointed permanent principal. Alana had had some doubts about Marie, particularly whether or not she could trust the newly appointed interim principal. So, taking a deep breath, she asked whether Marie would support the constructivist direction that the middle school faculty had agreed upon two years earlier, just before Marie came into the school. People generally felt that this either was unclear, or that Marie was somewhat too rigid to be supportive.

One of the team, the outgoing Madeline, asked whether anyone had an idea about Marie's educational philosophy, since she concentrated so heavily on the managerial role she had been assigned to play. Feeling that they were dancing a bit around this issue, Alana questioned whether they could trust Marie to be supportive. Again, the consensus was that they were doubtful. Noting that the norm of everything said within the team was to be held in confidence (and that this always was carried out by the team), they left to begin their classes.

Social Unrest Begins to Be Felt

Alana and the team left feeling fairly uneasy. Alana, who had read in the field of elementary collective behavior in her sociology major, realized that they had begun to feel a sense of social unrest, that the individual feelings of unease were being shared by her teammates (Blumer 1951, rev.). She knew that as soon as individual unrest becomes shared, it becomes social unrest.

And it was becoming shared, although she was not sure how widespread it had become. She felt it was important to find out, but it had to be done quietly and subtly.

Two days later Janet approached Alana in their team planning space and asked her if she had read the Monday morning bulletin. Janet then noted that the bulletin had a very interesting item—and pointed to it. A member of the last team to approach moving into the constructivist model, which actually was to start in the coming year, was going to a conference on direct instruction.

Alana suddenly experienced a sinking feeling. She knew that that team was not supportive of direct instruction, but the team was composed of more-cautious, less-secure younger teachers who had not boldly moved into constructivism as strongly as her team had. By this action, Marie was clearly indicating that not only did she not support the direction of the faculty and school, but also that she was working to sabotage this hard-won effort. The social unrest was spreading.

More people were becoming more concerned, as they recognized the intent of that action and Marie's disregard of their previous decisions about the organization of the school and its approach to instruction.

Well, noted the two women, they had a problem. And they knew that it would get worse. It appeared that Marie had a tin ear when it came to listening to faculty. But, what to do about it?

It clearly meant that if the superintendent appointed Marie as permanent principal, their program, which they valued highly, was in jeopardy. The two women realized that they had better confront this in their meeting later in the morning.

Strategies

At the team planning session, Janet and Madeline pointed to the Monday morning bulletin and raised the issue. The pregnant silence was then broken by Janet. Should they get their ducks lined up and then question Marie? Should they contact people they trusted in the other teams before talking with Marie? Who were the linchpins in the other teams? Whom could they count on? Should they talk to the superintendent before turning to the considerable support they had generated in their parent group over the past two years?

The team realized that they were heading into a crisis and decided to think about it before rushing into any premature line of action. Maybe they should contact other teams and social systems.

More Social Unrest, and a Precipitating Event—
Problem or Opportunity?

The next morning, Lynne Manners, another highly respected veteran team leader who had been a unanimous choice for Teacher of the Year for the school, and had been nominated for Teacher of the Year for the district, quietly came over to Alana and asked her if she had a few minutes. When the two sat down off to one side of the team meeting area, Lynne told Alana that she was seriously considering leaving the school and would apply to another middle school, which had a team leader position that had just become open.

Incredulously, Alana asked what was the reason for this serious action. Lynne's response was that she and Marie and their team had crossed swords a couple of times, that she felt Marie was vindictive and would work to squelch the faculty site-based decision making they were working so hard to implement and maintain, and would try to take control of the school. Lynne felt that there would be an increasing and huge conflict as Marie pressed on with her agenda, and she, Lynne, didn't like or feel comfortable with this level of stress. Alana knew that Lynne, although well-organized, really operated a great deal on feelings, and valued harmony above all, hated conflict, and avoided it as much as possible.

Alana also knew that Lynne and her husband, Vince, had been instrumental in bringing a highly sophisticated, state-of-the-art program in technology into the school, a program that was beyond anything the entire region had developed. They had also conducted in-service programs to bring the faculty up to speed, and Lynne had written and been awarded a number of key grants to pull this off. Alana knew that this effort would collapse if Lynne left.

Alana realized that the faculty now faced another major issue, the potential loss of one of the primary figures in a key social system in the school, who was instrumental in the founding not only the school and its constructivist philosophy, but also its technological program. And, they would be losing an excellent teacher and person, a true indigenous leader. She knew that this impending event would shake the faculty up considerably. You do not lose such a key person blithely.

She felt that the morale of the faculty, which had been very high because of their success with their program and with the community, and which had been badly shaken with the death of the principal, might be dealt a major blow by Lynne leaving. No one had ever left the school voluntarily, especially such a key person as Lynne. She knew that another neighboring school had experienced a similar event, and the faculty had never recovered fully from the loss. Their morale and esprit de corps had been dealt a severe blow, which was felt for several years. People had felt abandoned, had really mourned the loss of such a key person who filled so many roles.

So, she said to Lynne that that action would play right into Marie Cross's hands, that if such a major and highly respected figure in the school would leave, Marie would readily conclude that she could bully the rest into whatever courses of action she would decide upon unilaterally. And it would be unilateral!

Lynne, looking upset, agreed not to act precipitously and to meet after school, off campus, to develop some alternative lines of action with other key people in other social systems and teams. She agreed with Alana that they were facing a crisis.

CONTEMPLATING ACTION

Planning

Alana, Janet, Madeline, Lynne, and Sue Sharp, another highly respected team leader, met at their favorite pizza parlor not far from school to talk over the situation and options. Sue thanked the others for inviting her, and recalled that Alana and Janet had been her team before she became a team leader in the school. They all congratulated her on her husband Asher's appointment earlier in the year as assistant superintendent of schools for instruction and administration, and joked about her newly acquired power and influence. Sue indicated that he, along with everyone else, was pretty jammed in their understaffed central office.

After ordering, they began talking about their situation, noting that everything said was to be held in total confidence. All three team leaders, as well as the teachers, shared their concern about Marie's ignoring the widely supported constructivist model of instruction, and her sending a member of another team to the in-service on direct instruction.

Lynne asked why they thought she was doing this. One response was that she definitely had a strong need to be in control; another was that she really didn't understand constructivism. Still another, as Alana noted, that she really did not feel comfortable with middle school kids and with the middle school in general, so, feeling insecure and perceiving that the constructivist model was essentially out of her control, she wanted to eliminate it.

Janet felt that she would bully people if they didn't stand up to her, a remark that the rest thought was insightful and from a person who was a people person with considerable intuition. All jumped on this insight, exclaiming that that was exactly what each had concluded in their own thinking about the problems they faced.

Alana was asked what her brother, Marc Douglas, as a middle school principal, thought about the situation. Alana's response was that he thought that Marie really had no heart for the middle school, saw herself as an elementary person, but that since becoming a principal was a longtime goal for her, she would take the job if she could get it. Alana, looking a bit uncomfortable, also added that he thought that Marie would work to change their middle school model to her own ideas of how the school should be organized, despite its strong support by the faculty and community.

Several chimed in to ask Sue what her husband's perceptions were, since they knew that as the assistant superintendent, this would be something he would be integrally involved in. They indicated that this was a sensitive subject, and that Sue did not have to respond if she felt uncomfortable. Sue indicated that was already becoming a difficult situation for her and for Asher, since the two were close partners, and did not want to be unprofessional in their conduct. Still, she noted that they shared virtually everything, and that Asher knew exactly what she thought and felt about the developing situation.

The question, they noted, was how to make sure that Marie was not chosen as permanent principal. Alana, intuitively noting that no search had been scheduled to this point, and that none seemed to be intended in the immediate future, thought that this was unusual.

Sue said nothing to this insight.

Potential Lines of Action

After a moment, a number of suggestions were made. Could they go to the central office, after ensuring that the great majority of the staff supported not choosing Marie? If so, what social systems should go? Should all the faculty go who were on continuing contract? Would they all go? Were they concerned or upset enough to go? If Lynne indicated that she was dissatisfied enough to leave, what would that do to faculty resolve and potential action?

Lynne mentioned that in a neighboring school district, an entire elementary faculty who had been saddled with a principal who was out-of-control and had done some outrageous things, had gone to the superintendent's office during the lunch period, had asked to see him, and had told him that he had to change the principal. And they had incidents to prove the oppression and poor treatment. Obviously, they were quite upset. The superintendent indicated that he had been aware of some aspects of the situation, and asked for information about the principal's actions. Although he tried to mollify them for a couple of minutes, he had recognized that they were so upset that some were in tears.

He replaced the principal immediately. This action had become well known in their district by both faculties and the administrators. So, there was precedent that had been set.

What about the PTO? The bulletin had been seen by the PTO president, who became quite upset after reading it—and said so. She even indicated that she had called a meeting of the executive committee of the PTO to discuss this portentous situation. But, Marie had not done too many outrageous things, yet. Should they wait for more incidents? Should they, as a group, ask for an informal meeting with the assistant superintendent, to get his take on the situation? Should they approach Board of Education members informally?

WHAT LINES OF ACTION WOULD YOU, THE READER, DEVELOP—AND USE?

What would you do?

- Wait? Let the social unrest build?
- Organize the teams and teachers?
- Informally contact the assistant superintendent?
- Make sure the PTO knew about the faculty's feelings about what was going on?
- Enlist their support?
- Go down in force to the central office, as in the neighboring district?
- Approach the Board and inform them of the problem?

RESOLUTION

An insecure person such as Marie would continue on her course of action, which she did. The team leaders called an informal meeting of all team leaders to make sure that everyone was on board. Interestingly, they were. All were extremely concerned that their model was being subverted actively by the interim principal.

Leaving Sue out of this line of action, they met informally with Asher, the assistant superintendent, to inform him of the by-now rapidly escalating situation, with people feeling increasingly outraged at the sabotage of their program and their feelings being ignored. Asher indicated that he, the superintendent, and the Board were aware of some of their concerns and issues, and at some of the incidents that were happening in the school.

After being asked if he, the superintendent, and Board intended to support the program in the school, he indicated that they absolutely would. He also asked those present to suggest a slate of members to serve on a search committee, particularly indicating that he would support their choices if they chose people who strongly championed the constructivist program, the decentralized team teaching model, and the middle school concept.

Those present suggested Lynne, Alana, Madeline, and Sue as key members. Asher noted that they needed a principal to serve, at which all present suggested Marc Douglas as the kind of principal who should serve. The PTO president and vice-president were also suggested.

Asher agreed to recommend these people to the superintendent and asked for their recommendations for another teacher or two from other teams to serve. They looked at each other and Lynne suggested Amy and Michelle, who were strong constructivists and taught in two different teams.

A LAST OPPORTUNITY FOR YOU, THE READER, FOR YOUR INPUT

1. What else would you, the reader, suggest? Did they miss any bases?
2. Would you have gone to Asher? Are you surprised that the whole faculty stood for their values, despite knowing that Marie was vindictive?
3. Have you ever seen a situation where the administrator pursues his or her own agenda without regard for the values and feelings of the faculty?
   A. What is it about Marie that she has such a tin ear? That she is going to have her own way with something as important as the model the school has chosen?
4. Whom would you have recommended for the search committee?
5. Would you want to serve on such a committee?
   A. What would be important to find out before making any decisions?
6. Can you think of any other ways of dealing with Marie?
7. What else would you want to add to this list of questions?

SOURCES

Blumer, H. (1951, rev.). Collective behavior. In A. M. Lee (Ed.) *Principles of sociology*. New York: Barnes & Noble.

Lewis, A. C. (2001, April).Washington Commentary. *Kappan 82(3)*, 567–68.

Thelen, H. A. (1960). *Education and the human quest*. New York: Harper & Row.

CHAPTER 24

Where Are the Students on Your School Board? A Case Study of an Alternative School's Student Board of Education

When all college athletic games were canceled the weekend after the World Trade Centers were destroyed, were the athletes consulted?

—Anon

THE SETTING

So, you have a few kids, often marginal, some very bright, who simply can't stand even the loose structure of a fairly relaxed high school. And, they're gumming up the works by their indifference to the way the place ought to operate.

What do you do?

OPTIONS

A. Ratchet up the pressure.
   Result: We create, from mostly marginal students, really alienated, angry adolescents.
   Analysis: Not so smart. Doesn't work, either.
B. Ignore things. Don't do anything.
   Result: They'll gum up the works even more.
   Analysis: Another bad idea. Also, doesn't work.
C. Redesign the structure and develop a zingier program, so that all students will benefit.

Result: This will work.

Analysis: Good idea.

But, it is a longer-range solution, requiring lots of skills, patience, involvement of and building allies in the faculty, administration, and student body, and thorough knowledge of change strategies. It also involves risk-taking.

Do it.

We did.

See the next chapter, "Designing Our Structures to Do Our Heavy Work: What a Curriculum Structure Can Do to Make Our Professional Lives *a Lot* Easier," for an innovative mechanism for doing this.

D. Create an alternative school to meet their needs.

Result: This will work (if you know what you're doing—and, involve the right teachers and kids).

Analysis: You can create a school-within-a-school, separated physically as much as possible from the main school. Or, if you're really lucky, you can find a small space outside the main building for these kids.

Good idea. We did this.

IMPLEMENTING IDEAS AND PROCEDURES

First Steps: Involvement and Developing the Concepts

- First, we talked the idea over with the principal and vice-principal of the school (if you're in the central office. If you are the principal, you're in pretty good shape). In our case, they got excited.
- Next, we talked it over with the key student leaders of the disaffected group. They got excited.
- Next, we were lucky in locating such a building. We had an old, abandoned Nike base on the edge of the school property that the school board had been deeded a number of years ago. It was in ruins—perfect!

  Principle: Don't get greedy—go small. We did.

  Principle: Get a teacher or a couple of down-to-earth, accepting teachers who relate to and like these kids, and who do not have any academic pretensions. We found such a marvel (actually, several).

Principle: We talked to a small, representative steering group of the kids we were interested in reaching about setting up a small school focused on meeting their interests and needs. What did they think about such an idea? They got excited.

Actually, they jumped at the idea. And, they suggested the teacher we had been thinking about, and another on a part-time basis, whom we also had thought about. The suggested teacher, Ellie, was a no-nonsense, down-to-earth person, who was comfortable with the kids in virtually any situation.

She jumped at the idea, and, so did John, a former combat Marine, who everyone thought would be excellent for their part-time needs. First, because John really identified with kids like these. (These faculty, themselves, were mavericks, often living on the edge, just like the kids.) And, second, because he had such a wide base of knowledge.

We (Ellie, John, the principal and vice-principal, the first smaller group of kids, and I) then met with a slightly larger group of the kids who we thought might like the idea. We asked the kids for their suggestions regarding who might be interested and who might benefit from the smaller, more informal structure and setting. They suggested some kids—and a good number of ideas.

Lots of ideas emerged:

- They wanted the two teachers.
- They thought the idea of keeping it small to make it work made a lot of sense.
- They were excited about the idea of having and then developing their own turf.
- Heavy discussion emerged regarding how to run the operation.
- Finally, we agreed to have a Board of Education consisting of the students (perhaps, after a while it could be representatives, but they liked the idea of total involvement), Ellie, John, and I as superintendent. Everyone thought that this was pretty unusual, but, then, the entire operation was hardly traditional.

Board Functioning

The Board's function, it was agreed, was to make and establish policy. An early area for focus consisted of admissions to the school. What were key criteria? Some students wanted a ban on anyone using drugs, actually, no druggies wanted. Fast and furious discussion ended based on the belief that we wanted to work with people, not eliminate them. Therefore, the policy was set that drugs were not to be used on campus.

The next major issue was the kids did not want any drunks to be admitted. Similar discussion led to the agreeing on the norm that no one was to arrive drunk, nor was any drinking to be permitted on campus.

The Visit, the Opportunity—and the Results

The group agreed to visit the Nike building to see what needed to be done. We all saw opportunity in the fairly ruined building: Plumbing had to be repaired; sinks, toilets had to be replaced; wiring had to be replaced, as did light fixtures; windows needed to be replaced; walls and ceilings needed a good deal of repair and painting; grounds needed to be worked on, grassed, planted; walks needed work; furniture needed to be acquired; and heating and cooling needed repairing.

This provided us with a golden opportunity to implement the model curriculum and structure that we thought ideal for this situation. Therefore, the instructional model developed with input by all participants was one that consisted of individuals or small groups of students establishing a contract with Ellie, John, or another faculty member, if needed. Students were expected with help from others or from the faculty to work on their contracts and to complete them.

The myriad opportunities opened up by the needs of putting the building into shape provided us with a huge range of projects for students and faculty to develop. The Nike School Board agreed that the overall school district Board of Education should not be approached for funds if at all possible. First of all, the district's budget had been set months earlier. Second, it seemed advisable to get our ducks in order before asking for any financial support. Another decision was that we should pull this off as a community. They wanted to reconstruct the building, with appropriate help from the vocational staff, who saw opportunity to expand their program in the operation, and to help kids who were becoming focused and interested in doing well in the setting.

An industrial arts teacher with construction skills and licensing proved an invaluable resource. He helped the kids pull off the reconstruction: They put in the windows; they repaired the roof; they rewired the electrical systems, but he made the final connections; they installed some of the phone lines, although the telephone people reconnected them; the walls, inside and out, were repaired and painted; plumbing was repaired with sinks and toilets scrounged from a variety of sources; the kids worked on the grounds and plantings; heating and cooling needed repair; and the students scrounged all sorts of furniture giving the place a homey, uncoordinated, sort of Salvation Army appearance.

The kids enjoyed the construction process a great deal, and were able to get school credits for their work, much to everyone's satisfaction. They also had their own place, their turf.

A friend of mine, a renowned architect, heard about our project and came by early in the process. He urged us to photograph the before and after, documentation that came in handy in due time.

FURTHER BOARD FUNCTIONING

The student Board of Education met regularly, as the regular Boards do. One major function consisted of admitting new students. The Board tended to be quite hard-nosed, not wanting to admit anyone who might compromise the program and its integrity. My role was to urge the Board to give students a chance, an obvious reason for the existence of the Nike School. The Board agreed to give students a chance, but to enforce the principles and norms collectively agreed upon (several noted earlier). Some required courses were provided by the regular high school, while others were handled by the Nike School.

Ellie and the students developed a variety of interesting projects. One money-raising effort was that the students planted, raised, and sold organic plants, including herbs, to the community. I bought some of the herbs. Many faculty members supported this effort, as did the community. The students felt extremely proud of the project and its outcomes.

Another student designed and built a trimaran as his project, much to everyone's astonishment.

ENDINGS

The district school Board became anxious to visit the school in the spring, and did so. They were quite impressed with the quality of the program (especially because we had the kids come before them at a Board meeting, explain their purpose and program and demonstrate some of the projects they had developed and were working on). When the Board saw the facility, they wanted to provide halfway decent furniture to replace what they considered a lot of really marginal, beat-up chairs, tables, and the like. We managed to indicate that that might change the ambience and the kids' perceptions of ownership. The Board saw that the students were quite proud of their work and operation, so our wisdom prevailed, and the Board members suppressed their good-hearted offer. One intriguing result was that the School Board included funding for the Nike School in the next year's operating budget, much to everyone's appreciation. This symbolized that a somewhat maverick operation was accepted by the mainstream.

Eight years later, Ellie was ready to retire. The Nike Board several years earlier had considered the possibility of replacing Ellie, and agreed on her replacement, a marine biology teacher with the same philosophy and ability to work with nontraditional, deviant kids. She agreed, and the school moved on smoothly.

The editor of *Nation's Schools*, a national journal focusing on K–12 education, reported on this unusual governance model, resulting, to our considerable surprise, in a number of requests for information and visits.

SOME PERPLEXING QUESTIONS

1. When I served on the building committee of my present university (we were involved in developing educational specifications to build a new facility), I suggested that we ought to get students on the committee. The woman operating as the link between the

architects and us said she'd do it, but it took three more meetings to get students onto the committee. And this was after an expensive study by Arthur Anderson concluding that we ought to be more student friendly. And, guess who came up with the most insightful ideas?

   A. So, why are we so reluctant to involve students in governance and other crucial endeavors?

   B. Is it lack of trust?

   C. Is it bias?

2. You will note in chapter 25 that we had students on our curriculum committees. This was considered a first. And, you will also find out that the students, once they trusted us and the system to have integrity, came through like gangbusters, offering numerous courses to be developed. And they were.

   A. Again, why this lack of confidence in our youth?

3. When I've been involved in recruiting teachers and administrators, particularly as a superintendent, again we involved students. We went so far as to send them to the candidates' home districts. Guess what? You could count on students to see through phonies all the time—and to get accurate information that determined whom we recruited.

   A. I know of few districts that do this. Does yours? Why? More importantly, why not?

4. How did students play out their role on the Board of Education of the Nike School?

   A. Were they as responsible as the adult Board? (Many felt that they were the adults.)

   B. When the students realized that they needed an infusion of some cash, what did they do?

   C. Similarly, in furnishing the buildings, again, what did they do?

5. We can ask more questions. Which do you want to kick in?

6. Is this an idea whose time may be coming?

CHAPTER 25

Designing Our Structures to Do Our Heavy Work: What a Curriculum Structure Can Do to Make Our Professional Lives a Lot Easier

If you fail to plan, you plan to fail.

—Anon

FIRST STEPS—ESTABLISHING THE DISTRICT'S (OR THE SCHOOL'S) GOALS

A couple of weeks after I became superintendent, I called a meeting of key people who were around to diagnose the school district's needs. (I knew that it would be crucial to develop a set of goals that would drive the system in some common major directions, instead of meandering in all directions—and going nowhere as a consequence.) We were able to get key teachers, administrators, community people including aides, and students from both the middle and high schools.

But First—A Very Angry and Disgruntled Teacher—with a Message

A tall, gravelly voiced teacher came up to me and angrily told me that he had tried to get an experimental course (determining the effect of chemical substances on white mice) into the summer school program for three years. He stated that he had killed himself in the process, and came up empty. His proposal had been blocked (he surmised by the department chairman, and possibly the principal).

His anger boiled out in the telling, and he ended up stating bluntly that he was giving up, that he was getting an outside job after school, where he could be more effective and would not have to face the intense frustration he felt at being ignored and treated like dirt. He started to leave with the rancid comment, "In this system it's who you know, not what you know that gets results."

(Incidentally, he was right on target, since I discovered early on that the system often made decisions for political reasons, not what was good for kids, or for teachers, or for the community. I was not used to this kind of foolishness, since in the Midwest, where I did most of my school work, decisions in the best interests of the kids came first.)

He started to listen when I told him that that's what I had figured out in my brief time with the district, and that I had an approach to get at the problem. He asked how, and my response was that it would take several months, probably four, to establish our district's goals in order to develop common purposes. Without common purposes, I said, people go off in every direction and you have exactly what was going on presently in the district's schools.

Once that was done, we would set up a districtwide curriculum structure to generate curriculum through the system as a *routine*, as we had done in my previous position.

I mentioned that if we treated developing curriculum as an *organized system*, it would be much easier to get a course developed and implemented, since changing a course or courses would become a *routine* aspect of the district's operation, instead of taking Herculean efforts to add or to change one course or part of it, as he had tried.

I added that changes would have to be professionally appropriate and meet required criteria (purpose, clear objectives, materials, timetable, budget, required in-service, etc.). He listened impatiently (probably not to offend this, in his eyes, optimistic and naive superintendent), growled, "Yeah, sure," and stalked off, not looking back. "O.K.," I thought. "As soon as we get the curriculum structure up and going, I'm going to approach him to work up his course and submit it to the committee."

This strong cynicism ran much more deeply than I had thought, leading me to think that my four-month guesstimate of the time needed to establish district goals might be much too long. People expected failure, and would simply give up if a major enterprise took too long. So, I cut the process.

ESTABLISHING THE STRUCTURE AND PROCESS TO DEVELOP THE DISTRICT'S GOALS

So, we focused on designing a structure and process to involve as much of the community, students, teachers, staff, and administrators as possible. Ultimately, we involved about twenty-one hundred people of the forty-one thousand in the community and schools, including all the kids in the junior and senior high schools who wanted to become involved, and all the faculties, aides, and staff. My role was to work with a steering committee to facilitate developing the structure and process for this, which was achieved in slightly more than two months.

ESTABLISHING THE CURRICULUM STRUCTURE AND PROCESS

Once that was accomplished, the first priority was to establish a curriculum structure whose mission it was to generate change through the system *as a routine*. The underlying rationale for this was illustrated by the enormous effort extending over three years by the enraged science teacher to get a pilot course approved for summer school. People become alienated as they labor to work through a resistant system whose culture unconsciously resists change—at which it is very effective. So, they eventually give up—and the people whose motivation usually is to work for the kids' interests become turned off—and lost.

And the district's curriculum badly needed to be updated, a belief shared by one and all, both inside and outside the district. The document produced in the effort to develop clear, believable, and achievable goals for the district called for designing and developing a curriculum structure. Fortunately, I had had a considerable amount of experience in designing and running such a structure, since, as an assistant superintendent in DeKalb, Illinois, that was a prime responsibility—to generate change in the system (Shapiro, Benjamin & Hunt 1995, pp.

233–39). And by some odd coincidence, a couple of the top teachers involved in designing curriculum in our previous district came to this district to work in the high school.

A small committee was then formed to work out a structure and process. The structure developed consisted of a Curriculum Steering Committee with four subcommittees in the humanities (social sciences, language arts, the fine arts), science-mathematics, special areas, and the practical arts. (See appendix 25A.)

In my former district we started with a subcommittee in each of the seven major areas (social sciences, language arts, science, mathematics, fine arts, practical arts, special areas), but none of us, including me, could keep up with the array of meetings that began to develop. So, we compressed the seven into four areas. The Curriculum Steering Committee was designed to have a majority of teachers on it and to be chaired by a teacher elected by each subcommittee. With the cynicism, hostility, and rampant distrust throughout the district and area, we thought it would be suicide to design a structure and process that would be taken over by administrators.

HOW THE PROCESS WORKS

The process was established so that anyone was able to suggest an idea, with the assistant superintendent being responsible to form a small committee to assist the person, team, learning community, or any group (teachers, administrators, aides, students, community members—anyone) to formulate the proposal in an appropriate format, including aims, goals, objectives, potential activities, budget, timetable, in-service provisions, and so forth.

The proposal was then taken to the relevant area committee, where it was analyzed and recommended for the Curriculum Steering Committee's consideration. Like the area committees, this body met once a month to review and to vote on proposals. In the spring, the Curriculum Steering Committee would prioritize all proposals with a 1, 2, or 3, the former being the highest priority for implementation.

For a district with a history of political favoritism, this process was carefully watched by one and all, including the Board of Education. Oh, yes, one more norm (read, rule) was established. No one, but no one, from Board of Education president to the department chairperson, could block any proposal from being considered by any area committee or the Curriculum Steering Committee itself. (See appendix 25A for all the rules.)

At first, presentations to the Curriculum Steering Committee tended to be somewhat haphazard and informal. After a short while, some of the presentations became very polished and complete by the more astute area committees. We knew from the grapevine that they were rehearsing (one of my two importees started this process)—and soon everyone took considerable care in developing and designing their proposals.

NEXT, THE ALIENATED SCIENCE TEACHER

One of my earliest forays, early in January, after the process and structure for designing and implementing curriculum was established and in place, was to visit the gravelly voiced science teacher to let him know that the curriculum development process was in place, and that he could submit his proposal to the Science/Mathematics Area Committee.

I also handed him the criteria the Curriculum Steering Committee had established. His cynicism and distrust was apparent in his curt "Yeah, sure." I asked him for a copy of his proposal and said I'd submit it if he still was distrustful and didn't want to, but that he had the right of first refusal to teach the course this coming summer, since it was his idea in the first place.

A Success

Well, we submitted it to the Natural Science Area Committee and to the Curriculum Steering Committee, it passed handily, of course, and he taught his mini-course successfully in the summer. Since we changed the structure of the high school curriculum into providing mini-courses (nine-week courses), as well as semester and yearlong courses, his pilot course was readily adapted into the regular curriculum the following year (we also submitted it through the structure), and he taught it during the year.

The science department now had at least one believer.

CREATIVITY EXPLODES

Since creative people lurk in the corners, woodwork, and back courts of virtually all organizations, they hungrily watch new leadership to evaluate whether it is safe or worthwhile to expose themselves with their ideas, often long-suppressed in heavily red-taped bureaucratically driven organizations. Obviously, we were able to convince some of these folks, since we began to get an avalanche of proposals from some of the area committees for consideration.

Social Studies and Language Arts—The Humanities

As with DeKalb, the social sciences and language arts took a strong lead. Courses in cultural anthropology and archaeology were suggested, including the Occult in Different Cultures, Stones and Bones (with a simulated and a real archaeological dig), and literally, a score of history courses, such as the Old West, The Civil War, The Atomic Age, The Roaring Twenties.

All of the history courses were designed to be interdisciplinary with the language arts by offering the literature of each course during the same session. For example, the Civil War and its literature were offered the same quarter (*Red Badge of Courage, Gone with the Wind*). The Roaring Twenties offered such literature as *The Great Gatsby*. All in all, eighty-five different courses were taught in each of these two areas.

Such courses as Criminology, the History of Political Thought and Dissent, Liberty in the American Culture were created and often tied in with another department, for example, language arts. Further, the creative members of the language arts faculty came up with Adolescent Love (featuring *Hamlet*), which in turn was tied into a social studies course titled Introduction to Adolescent Psychology, which was a big—no, a huge—attraction.

Science

The science department jumped into the model by offering a number of quarter courses, including the one on the impact of drugs on white mice, offered by the formerly angry science teacher. The Fetal Pig seemed to be as popular with both students and teachers, as was Lab Techniques.

MORE RESULTS—THE LAW OF UNINTENDED CONSEQUENCES (LUC) OPERATES—IN STRANGE WAYS

Students Participate

One such proposal came from a couple of students (remember, students, parents, teachers, administrators, aides served on all the committees), who proposed a mini-course in American humor, which they called, Dark Humor. Their planning astutely called for supervision by a teacher (so it could be taken for credit); the proposal was accepted, it was scheduled, and it was taught—and with considerable success.

More Interdisciplinary Programs

Numbers of other mini-courses began to surface, so that single courses were offered, as were numbers of other interdisciplinary proposals. The Good Earth was offered jointly by the language arts and home economics departments. A creative art teacher developed six mini-courses in ceramics, so we had to buy more wheels to throw clay pots.

Scheduling Options—for Student Decision Making

The school opened up opportunities for kids to take advantage of more creative and flexible scheduling by converting some classes (art, computers, vocational courses, etc.) into labs into which students could schedule themselves, work on their individual or group projects, and get credit by punching in their time cards to accumulate the required number of hours for Carnegie unit credits in that area.

Results of Standing Pat

But, one or two departments decided to stand pat, huffily deriding a "fun and games" mentality, which they claimed was overtaking some departments. I asked the foreign language department what would happen if their enrollment would plummet if some of the courses drew their clientele (suggesting that Criminology was a natural draw, as were Psychology and, equally, Adolescent Psychology), to which their reply was that their enrollment was stable and they would not suffer with competition. After the enrollment process was over in the spring, which was accompanied by a great deal of excitement by students and faculty, we had the foreign language department trying sadly and vainly to make the case that fifty or sixty students a day was a full load for a faculty member.

MORE LAW OF UNINTENDED CONSEQUENCES EXAMPLES

The Newspapers—and Adult Education

As a matter of fact, the major Long Island newspaper featured an article on the emerging programs offered by the high school, "Zingy Program Offered at Long Beach High School." As soon as this occurred, the community people in the adult education program began to ask, "Why can't we get a chance to take such terrific courses?" To this we said that we'd offer whatever courses they wanted. (Of course, they wanted courses from the high school curriculum.)

So, we began offering them the same courses, but in the evening. Interestingly, some of us began taking the courses, and my wife and I took one of the ceramics courses.

LESSONS LEARNED FOR CONSTRUCTIVISM— AND SUCCESSES

How Was This Constructivist?

A *system* (Deming 1982) was designed and implemented with maximum involvement of all social systems to *generate curriculum change* as a *routine* part of everyday functioning in the district. We made it an expectation of everyday operations that curriculum change would occur *routinely* in the schools of the district on a routine basis.

Consequently, a huge program was generated and offered for individual choice—for both students—and teachers. Note that this applied to teachers as well. (They were provided the *structure and the process* to design courses they *wanted to teach*, some of which were hobbies or longtime interests.) And did they jump in! So did students.

I overheard one student comment to another, "This is the first time I could ever take a course about me." He was talking about Adolescent Psychology. (And we tied it in with *Hamlet* in the language arts program, which, increasingly began to look like a collegiate humanities division in that teachers began to work across departmental lines and to communicate with each other, giving up "territorial ownership.") Students, faculty, community, aides—everyone who was interested was involved.

The basic structure of the school changed to accommodate this model, so that the high school became *nongraded*. That is, our thinking was that it did not matter if a student was a sophomore or junior or senior—or, even a freshman—if he or she wanted to take a course, although there were some prerequisites (overall American history before any of the specialty courses could be taken, etc.).

Developing a system so that kids could take a lab when they had time became important in student choice. One could work at an interest in free time, not be relegated to a study hall, thus, expanding individual autonomy.

Certainly, Maslow's third (Social Needs) and fourth (Esteem Needs) levels were met. Social Needs were met by the entire structure and process of curriculum development, which was essentially a social enterprise. Esteem Needs? Newspaper publicity, student reactions, the adult program changing radically to duplicate the high school program—these were clear signals that the high school was held in increasingly high esteem. The buy-in of the Teachers' Association was another signal.

In designing both the district goal development process and structure and the curriculum development process and structure, people took different roles within their groups. Oddly, the Goal Development Committee started with twenty-four people (eight students, eight community, and eight faculty and aides)—who watched to see if we really were serious. By the end of the process, twenty-nine people were attending regularly. Interest increased, rather than diminished, an unusual occurrence, especially for this district, which regarded their institutions with hostility and distrust.

More Constructivist Elements (Some of Which Are Unobtrusive)

We paid close attention to Barnard's (1938) three indispensable elements of any organization in our planning:

1. *Establish a clear mission and purpose.* The Goals Committee and process, involving over twenty-one hundred people, ensured this outcome, as did the heavy publicity of this process.
2. *Establish a system of communication to communicate the purpose.* A system of communication about curriculum development was established to communicate to everyone, in that minutes of all meetings of area committees and the Curriculum Steering Committee were sent to all schools in quantity. (See appendix 25A.) In addition, representatives of the Goals Committee met with all faculty, students, and community members in small groups to ensure input and communication. We also met with minority communities in their respective turfs. And, the materials were not only translated into Spanish for that ethnic group, but meetings were held with our Spanish teachers to interpret meaning, intention, and process. Needless to say, this community became supportive.
3. *Establish a system of cooperation to achieve the mission and purpose.* Pretty obviously, a system of cooperation was pulled off that worked. We made sure that the key social systems developed ownership through the system of participation that was established. Note in the appendix the crucial role of the teachers and the Teachers' Association. Thus, this group strongly supported the structure and the process.

A supportive culture was created and was itself supported by being written into the contract with the Teachers' Association, so that incoming administrators could not play mischief with the process and structure.

QUESTIONS—AND THE BIG PICTURE

1. Note that this was a *comprehensive* plan, first establishing goals for the district, then reviewing the structure of the school and curriculum, next establishing a structure to generate curriculum as a routine, and focusing on the content of the curriculum. How could this process be improved?
2. Have you been involved with any comprehensive curriculum development projects? If so, what processes were established to organize effort? How did it work?
   A. What rewards were built in so that all major social systems (teachers, administrators, supervisors, students, aides, community members) would want to participate over the long haul?
   B. Which Maslowian Hierarchy of Needs levels were involved?
   C. What other motivational needs were being met? Professional autonomy? Achievement? What others?
3. How do you react to the idea that we can design and establish organizational structures, such as the Curriculum Steering Committee structure, that can be used to support constructive change in our schools?
   A. What other structures could help us achieve our goals?
4. What do you think of the format, the membership, other factors in reviewing appendix 25A?
   A. Does it surprise you to see such careful attendance to involving the teachers' union? The administrators' union? The community? The students?
   B. Would you change the four subcommittees? If so, to what structure? Why?
   C. Would you change the composition of the overall Steering Committee and the working subcommittees? Again, if so, to what? Why?
   D. Would you change the operations and functions of the Steering Committee? If so, how?
5. In a larger district, how would you handle the issue of size? Would you develop curriculum committee structures and processes using feeder schools to decentralize the process to make it more workable?

6. How would you involve the major universities? The State Department? Minority communities?
7. How would you handle the anxiety? Would you have anxiety? If so, why?
8. What obvious areas and questions have I missed?

SOURCES

Barnard, C. I. (1938). *The functions of the executive*. Cambridge, MA: Harvard University Press.

Deming, W. E. (1982). *Quality, productivity, and competitive position*. Cambridge: Massachusetts Institute of Technology, Center for Advanced Engineering Study.

Maslow, A. H. (1954). *Motivation and personality*. (2nd ed.). New York: Harper & Row.

Shapiro, A. S., Benjamin, W. F., & Hunt, J. J. (1995, 233–39). *Curriculum and schooling: A practitioner's guide*. Palm Springs, CA: ETC.

APPENDIX 25A: TWO CURRICULUM COMMITTEE STRUCTURE MODELS AND SUGGESTED RULES FOR OPERATION

CURRICULUM COMMITTEE STRUCTURE AND RULES

I. PURPOSE
   A. The purpose of the *area committee* is to review and recommend to the Steering Committee all changes in curriculum related to their area. The stimulus for change comes from work groups. The area committee will concern itself with content and behavioral concepts.
   B. The purpose of the *Steering Committee* is similar to that of the area committee but on a much broader basis. The Steering Committee will review and recommend to the upper administration and Board of Education all changes in curriculum. The members of the committee cannot be expert in all curricular areas; however, some group must be responsible for the ever-changing curricular process. The main judgment will be in terms of a priority, which is best for the total school district.

II. STRUCTURE
  A. A committee to be established for each of the major curriculum areas, these to be known as area committees: [See attached diagram]
    1. Humanities, including social studies, English-language arts, fine arts (music, art, drama)
    2. Mathematics—Science
    3. Applied Arts, including business, home-economics, industrial arts, vocational courses, physical education, health and safety
    4. Special Areas, including outdoor education, slow learner and special education, accelerated learner, evaluation, preschool education, educational media, extra-curricular performance activities (athletics, drama, speech, etc.)

  Each area committee may select work groups for carrying out specific tasks—responsible to the parent committee. The entire staff will be considered a committee of the whole to be drawn upon as needed by the individual area committees and subcommittees.

  B. Each area committee to be composed of three (3) teachers each from elementary, middle, and high schools plus one (1) principal and the assistant superintendent for instruction. (The Applied Arts Committee shall be composed of four (4) teachers plus one (1) principal and the assistant superintendent for instruction.)

  This structure may be altered only in rare instances to conform to what is needed at a particular time.

  C. Membership on each area committee to be by preference; final selection to be made by the assistant superintendent, chairman of each respective committee (plus one member selected by both) with the advice of the principals and the approval of the superintendent. Membership of the Curricular Steering Committee to be composed of:
    1. Two (2) representatives appointed by DCTA president, and 3 teachers to be selected at large (1 elementary, 1 middle, 1 high school) by the assistant superintendent for instruction, one principal, and DCTA president.

(4) Chairmen, one from each area committee

(3) Principals

(1) Director of research

(1) Assistant superintendent of instruction

(1) Assistant superintendent for pupil personnel

(1) Superintendent (Ex-Officio)

D. Principals to choose the committee they will work on according to interest and/or competency. They are not eligible to serve as chairmen or may not be elected recorder but are requested to serve on work committees.

E. Chairman from previous school year to act as chairman pro tempore until new permanent chairman for the year has been elected. If no chairman, present principal to serve as chairman pro tempore until permanent chairman is elected.

F. Chairman to work with the principals on the respective committees and communicate with the total committee through the principals, who will work directly with the assistant superintendent and through the assistant superintendent's office. Minutes will be typed by building secretaries.

G. The agenda, minutes, and proposals for each area committee are to be approved by the chairman and sent in final form to the assistant superintendent for curriculum and instruction's office where they will be duplicated and distributed to all principals and committee members, DCTA building representatives, representatives of the special services council, the assistant superintendent, superintendent, and Board of Education.

H. Meetings to be held once a month from 3:45 to 5:00 P.M. on a regular school day with overall Steering Committee meetings once a month on the first Tuesday, at 3:45 P.M. The agenda and minutes of the Steering Committee and all proposals to be considered by them shall be sent to all committee chairman and principals, DCTA building representatives, representative of the special services council, the assistant superintendent, superintendent, and Board of Education.

I. Prior to the establishment of work groups the prospective proposal must be submitted to the area committee and the assistant superintendent for instruction.

III. RULES

A. The only matters to be considered by the Steering Committees are those that are associated with curriculum, as defined by IIA.

B. All members of the Steering Committee are voting members.

C. Two-thirds of the members of the Steering Committee shall constitute a quorum.

D. Recommendation shall be approved by the Steering Committee when they receive a positive vote by two-thirds of the membership of the committee. The record of the vote on a particular recommendation shall not be recorded when it is approved and sent to the administration and Board of Education.

E. When a recommendation fails, it is returned to the recommending committee for reconsideration with any explanation necessary. It may be resubmitted.

F. Recommendations that are approved by the Steering Committee are submitted to the administration and Board of Education for action.

G. Recommendations received during the school year will be tentatively approved or rejected and returned to the recommending committees. Those that are tentatively approved will be collected through the year when they will be given priority ratings by members of the Steering Committee.

H. Any recommendations for changing curriculum offerings must be submitted through the area committee to the Steering Committee *prior to the Steering Committee's first meeting in April.* All proposals shall have a first reading at a Steering Committee meeting and then may be approved at the next meeting.

I. Priority ratings of tentatively approved proposals will be made on the basis of a 1 (top rating); 2 (second priority); or 3 (low priority). Recommendations reported out of the Steering Committee will be placed in one of the three categories for action by the administration and Board of Education.

J. A final report shall be filed by each area committee incorporating all subcommittee and area committee work for the next year. This final report shall include:

(a) A summary of the year's work in all areas;

(b) Findings from the study and recommendations for improvement;

(c) Direction studies should take for the ensuing year.

The total report, which will include the rating of recommendations, will be made available to every school and area chairman. A short-form report summarizing actions on recommendations and final reports will be made available to every staff member in the school district and the Board of Education.

K. Recommendations not implemented shall be returned to the recommending committee for reconsideration and resubmission.

L. The following format shall be the standard for all recommendations submitted to the area and Steering Committees.

Format to Be Used for Preparing and Submitting Recommendations for Curriculum Improvement

1. Introduction—Rationale stating purpose, goals, and objective—stated behaviorally, if possible

2. Required materials, staff, other
   (a) Immediate
   (b) Long range

3. Justification for recommendations

4. Cost implied by recommendations

5. Method of evaluation

6. Mode of dissemination

7. Other

   All statements to be dated. Fifteen copies of every recommendation shall be provided when the proposal is submitted.

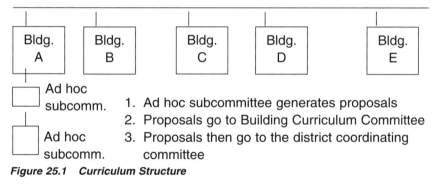

Curriculum Coordinating Committee

1. Two representatives from each Building Curriculum Committee
2. Administrations
3. CTA representatives

| Bldg. A | Bldg. B | Bldg. C | Bldg. D | Bldg. E |

Ad hoc subcomm.

Ad hoc subcomm.

1. Ad hoc subcommittee generates proposals
2. Proposals go to Building Curriculum Committee
3. Proposals then go to the district coordinating committee

Figure 25.1   Curriculum Structure

Curriculum Steering Committee

(5) 2 representatives appointed by CTA President and 3 teachers to be selected at large (1 elementary, 1 middle school, 1 high school) by Ass't Supt. for Instruction, one Principal & CTA President
(4) Chairmen of Area Committees
(3) Principals
(1) Director of Research
(1) Assistant Superintendent for Instruction
(1) Assistant Superintendent for Pupil Personnel
(1) Superintendent (Ex-Officio)

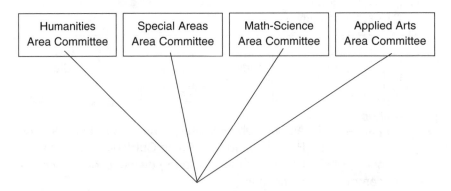

Humanities Area Committee	Special Areas Area Committee	Math-Science Area Committee	Applied Arts Area Committee

(9) teachers—(3 from each of) - - - - - - elementary, middle, and high school-(1) Principal and Assistant Supt. for Instruction.

Work Groups → ◄—Assistant Superintendent—► ◄—Work Groups

Figure 25.2   Curriculum Structure

Developing and Running a Pupil Personnel Services Council: Making Our Structures Work for Us

When I became the assistant superintendent of the DeKalb Unified School District #28 in DeKalb, Illinois, the new superintendent of schools, Dr. Ronald Simcox, who had been the assistant superintendent, stated that one of his highest priorities was to continue the Pupil Personnel Services Council and its structure and process.

For one, I had never heard of such a structure and process. So, of course, Ron explained its purpose and how it worked—I became a believer instantly.

HOW IT WORKED

Every other Tuesday morning, the assistant superintendent would chair what we called a "staffing" of students about whom someone was concerned. Issues could range from kids perceived as having speech problems or psychological concerns to kids who might need special education intervention to those who might have severe reading difficulties, behavior problems, and learning disabilities.

However, a range of other concerns or problems anyone in the schools or a parent perceived as issues could be the starting point of a recommendation for Pupil Personnel Services Council consideration. Obviously, we had a number of professionals inside and outside the district who could be involved to help with the diagnosis and remediation.

These included: two pediatricians who attended every meeting; the recommending person; the student's teacher and team leader; usually the involved psychologist; usually the involved social worker (who largely worked with families, and often with faculty); the co-op teacher (if a high school kid was in this program); the special ed teacher; the speech pathologist; the nurse; the administrator, if necessary; the parent; the counselor; and often, the student, if appropriate.

Roles

The counselor was responsible to pull the paperwork together and to send out an agenda. These were to be sent to all involved people the Thursday prior to the Tuesday meeting to make sure everyone was on the same page. The counselor also took minutes, which were to be distributed by the Friday following the meeting. We rarely had any corrections to these documents. And, of course, they were confidential.

Procedures/Rules

Each case was given full attention, and was finished to everyone's satisfaction. We did not finish until all participants were satisfied. The DeKalb model was to evaluate each student carefully and (generally) to the satisfaction of all participants. Obviously, a psychological workup was often the basis for discussion. At times, a social work analysis and report were essential. The student's counselor was always involved. (DeKalb had the first counselor in the state of Illinois, early in the last century.)

OUTCOMES

Then, a series of potential programs were evaluated for their appropriateness for the students. In short, an Rx, or a prescribed program, was developed for that student.

These might include:

- Work with a speech therapist
- Treatment for a medical condition
- Referral to a psychiatrist
- Referral to a psychologist

- Placement in a gifted or other special education program
- Placement in a co-op work program
- Placement in a variety of academic, business, or vocational programs
- A workshop for psychologists, social workers, or other personnel with a psychiatrist or other specialists according to the needs of one or more cases, and the education of personnel.

The Structure of the Schools Facilitated This

Since the high school was based on a modified Trump (1959) model (large-group lectures, small-group seminars, independent and small-group work in an immense instructional resource center) it provided an enormous variety of potential independent study programs and courses, many of which could be constructed to appeal to an individual student who might have a special interest. For example, someone who might become stimulated by studying a different culture could find a faculty member who would work with him or her (not by accident, we had several faculty with anthropological and sociological backgrounds). Those who could be stimulated by work in the arts could find willing support, if not within the faculty, within the local rather large and major university and/or the community. And we developed middle schools with extensive intramural programs in the two former junior high schools.

In my succeeding position in another district as superintendent of schools, when I introduced a Pupil Personnel Services Council with a similar structure and process, we found that the psychologists in the district often were prescribing programs that did not exist in the school, and so had become somewhat fatalistic, even noting in their prescription that the district did not offer the recommended program for the student. One could detect a sense of anger and futility in such behavior.

The development of the Pupil Personnel Services Council structure gave them a voice and a vehicle to deal with their frustration and emotional reaction. This enabled them (and others) to generate a variety of programs through the Pupil Personnel Services Council and the Curriculum Steering Committee.

The DeKalb model involved a process by which professionals could recommend programs as a prescription for whatever the outcome of the diagnosis, and then, if the academic program did not exist, to bring them to the Curriculum Steering Committee for their consideration. If it was a program in the Student Personnel area, then the possibility of developing such a program was considered, and if approved, was developed.

Usually, by the middle of April, all the referrals in the district were finished. We then worked with other districts in the immediate area to provide them with diagnoses for their students, plus recommendations for dealing with the special needs of their students. They even publicized this cooperative venture.

CONSTRUCTIVIST ELEMENTS

- A *system* (Deming 1982) was established to pull off a vital function.
- A *structure and process* were introduced to *generate change as a routine* in the district's systems.
- Barnard's (1938) three indispensable elements for any organization were carefully attended to.
  - Establish a clear mission and purpose. The purpose was clear.
  - Establish a system of communication to communicate the purpose.
  - A system of communication was instituted that involved everyone.
- The parties were informed of the agenda prior the meeting, and minutes distributed the same week as the meeting.
- A system of cooperation must be established to achieve the mission and purpose.
- A system of cooperation was established, in which relevant people functioned.

Successes

- The structure and process were clear.
- It worked. The newspapers even reported on it, so that the neighboring districts wanted us to utilize our structure and process with their kids needing services. This we did.

- Everyone was involved who needed to be involved.
- A small group composed the basic continuing core, consisting of the assistant superintendent, the two local physicians, the directors of social work, psychology, and guidance.
- Everyone was informed; no one was left out.
- Meetings were confidential, so safety was assured, one of Maslow's Hierarchy of Needs (1954).
- Meetings were regular as clockwork every other Tuesday morning, so a routine was established.
- Programs could be generated to meet individual and group needs, both in the Pupil Personnel Services and academic areas.
- A supportive culture was created among the personnel involved, and certainly within the district and the surrounding county.
- Social needs were met, as were esteem needs (shades of Maslow). People in the system and in the community were proud of the functions of this group.

We even publicized some of its functioning and action in the local paper, and received complimentary letters to the editor. The Teachers' Association strongly supported this process, knowing full well that it helped teachers and kids considerably. As a matter of fact, the Teachers' Association was often our strongest ally.

THE WRAPAROUND MOVEMENT

Recently, a movement has surfaced in social work called "Wraparound" (Malysiak 1997; Malysiak-Bertram et al. 2000) models, which are essentially collaborative, strengths-based and family-centered in nature in which all the specialties and agencies involved in working with a family combine to provide a unified approach. The method relies on the strengths of the family and individuals, rather than on perceiving individuals and families as lacking in strengths and resources to deal with their problems and issues.

The latter is a deficit-based model (look at these people with all these problems) versus a strengths-based model (this family has some abilities and talents that we can use as starting points in developing programs with them to resolve their concerns, problems, and issues).

The DeKalb model was a precursor of this movement, as Dr. Malysiak-Bertram has observed. (R. Malysiak-Bertram, personal communication, March 15, 1997.)

QUESTIONS FOR THOUGHT

1. What do you think of the idea that we can support change initiatives through developing supportive structures such as the ones in this chapter and in chapter 25?
   A. Have you seen any in your professional experience? If so, how have they worked? Could you design and/or use it?
2. To whom would you make such a structure, as the one in this chapter, responsible?
   A. Should it be at the very top of the organization, as in DeKalb?
   B. If it isn't, how would you assure solid support from the very top of the organization? (Or, have I answered the question?)
3. Who should be the responsible administrator?
   A. Should it be the appropriate assistant superintendent, thereby assuring support at the very top of the organization?
4. How would you build a pupil personnel services structure?
   A. What would be your starting steps?
   B. Whom would you approach first?
   C. Whom would you include?
   D. What rules of operation would you develop? Whom would you involve in this enterprise? Why?
5. Does the size of the district make a difference?
   A. If so, would you use a decentralized model? For example, have a Pupil Personnel Services Council for each cluster of feeder schools?
6. How would you inform the district and the community about its operation in order to build support and cooperation?
7. What other questions would you ask?

SOURCES

Barnard, C. I. (1938). *The functions of the executive*. Cambridge, MA: Harvard University Press.

Deming, W. E. (1982). *Quality, productivity, and competitive position.* Cambridge: Massachusetts Institute of Technology, Center for Advanced Engineering Study.

Malysiak, R. (1997). Exploring the theory and paradigm base for wraparound. *Journal of Family and Child Studies 6*, 399–408.

Malysiak-Bertram, R., Bertram-Malysiak, B., Rudo, Z., & Duchnowski, A. (2000). What maintains fidelity in the wraparound approach? How can it be measured? In C. Liberton, C. Newman, K. Kutash & R. Friedman (Eds.). *The 12th annual conference proceedings, a system of care for children's mental health: Expanding the research base* (February 21 to February 24, 1999), pp. 197–202. Tampa: University of South Florida, The Louis de la Parte Florida Mental Health Institute, Research and Training Center for Children's Mental Health.

Maslow, A. H. (1954). *Motivation and personality.* (2nd ed.). New York: Harper & Row.

Trump, L. (1959). *Images of the future: A new approach to the secondary school.* Urbana, IL: Commission on the Experimental Study of the Utilization of the Staff in the Secondary School, National Association of Secondary School Principals.

CHAPTER 27

National Standards—The Good, the Bad, the Ugly

Bracey's Paradox: Test scores mean something only when you don't pay any attention to them.

—Gerald W. Bracey, *Phi Delta Kappan*, October 2001

The standards movement: If it moves, test it.

—Selma Wasserman, *Phi Delta Kappan*, September 2001

The states are becoming more unlike one another. . . . Therefore, to have a single national standard, measured by a single national test, with a single national cutting score—which is very unlikely to happen, I believe—would not be a good thing for America. . . . The richness of American education is its diversity, and I cannot imagine how we could fail to acknowledge that diversity.

—Harold Hodgkinson, Demographer, ASCD's *Education Update*, January 2002

THE VALUE OF A BROAD BASE OF EXPERIENCE

I've taught as a substitute all over the northern two-thirds of the Chicago Public Schools—from slums to suburbs, including vocational-technical high schools for boys. I've taught and principaled in suburbs so ritzy no faculty could afford to live there. I've taught in a rural community's university lab school, and later became assistant superintendent there, but in the school district's schools. I've been an administrative intern in Chicago's inner city, worked in an inner-city school that

Tad Lincoln had attended (a long while before, to be sure), where the median I.Q. was 83. I've been a principal in a school where the median I.Q. was 118, and taught in John Dewey's old laboratory school at the University of Chicago, where the median I.Q. was 135.

I've been a director of secondary education in both a rural and an urban district. And I've been a superintendent of schools where one group of upper-middle-class students got into some of the best colleges in the land—while others had trouble getting one square meal a day and staying in school—and where people still lived on dirt floors. And, I've worked in major universities teaching undergrads, as well as master's and doctoral students

THE POINT? (REGARDING NATIONAL STANDARDS)

We Have Immense Differences

The schools, the kids, the faculties, the cultures—all were phenomenally different. They had different needs, different interests, different cultures, lived in different worlds. How, then, can we set up national standards for *all* kids? Or even state standards for all the kids in one state? But national standards for *all* kids? (This reminds me of my conversation with the director of testing for Iran's educational system, when she pointed out that at that time [10:20 A.M.], all the sixth graders were on a certain page in mathematics. I asked, "Even the very low academic kids?") And my experience doesn't include Native Americans with their needs, kids in Aleut villages in Alaska, kids in border towns in the Southwest, Hawaiian kids with diverse cultural, racial, and ethnic backgrounds, immigrants from all over the world.

That's the first point. Schools in the United States are replete with differences and divergent purposes. Do national standards make sense? How will all these kids handle tests cooked up by people who know nothing about them (Ohanian 2001). Demographer Harold Hodgkinson is quoted as observing, "All of the demographics suggest that we need to give states more leeway in how they accomplish their (educational) objectives. Different states will need to use different strategies, and they won't get the same results" (2002, January).

HOW ABOUT STATE STANDARDS?

The Thomas Fordham Foundation's study (1998 [Finn et al.]) in which each state's standards were graded using a 4.0 grading scale, showed most states falling far, far short of implementing meaningful standards. As a matter of fact, the overall cumulative Grade Point Average (GPA) for the states' standards was D+. In addition, the study pointed to the nebulous and vague nature of the standards, which lack clarity and precision due to several reasons. One is that it is difficult to achieve consensus on standards since multiple constituencies are chosen for inclusion in the committees to achieve the task. Certainly, another is that the committees really do not know what the various districts and schools teach, and attempts to develop precision tend to break down.

HOW ABOUT A SAMPLE OF A FEW TESTS? (YOU'LL LOVE THIS)

Arizona

Arizona's Standard 1 (Ohanian 2001) states that students analyze the human experience through time, recognize the relationships of events and people, and interpret significant patterns, themes, ideas, beliefs, and turning points in Arizona, American, and world history. For students in *grades six through eight* [italics added] this includes:

- Assessing the credibility of primary and secondary sources and drawing sound conclusions from them.
- Examining different points of view on the same historical events and determining the context in which the statements were made, including the questions asked, the sources used, and the author's perspectives (p. 189).

Like California's, Arizona's Standardistos insist that seventh graders will:

- Describe the geographic, political, economic, and social characteristics of the ancient civilizations of Egypt, Mesopotamia, and China and contributions to later civilizations.

- Describe the political and economic events and social and geographic characteristics of Medieval European life and their enduring impacts on later civilizations (pp. 189–190).

Pretty stiff? Unrealistic? Wait until you read some test items in the
famous Massachusetts Comprehensive Assessment System (MCAS).

Massachusetts

Susan Ohanian reports on that state's testing mania: Massachusetts
has released the questions on the Massachusetts Comprehensive Assessment System (MCAS), which were inflicted on students in grades
four, eight, and ten. The questions in history and social science for
grade eight cover prehistory to 1000 B.C., classical civilizations from
1000 B.C. to A.D. 500, the growth of agricultural and commercial civilizations from A.D. 500 to 1500, the United States from its Colonial
beginnings to 1650; its settlements, colonies, and emerging identity
from 1600 to 1763; the American Revolution; the expansion, reform,
and economic growth of the nation from 1800 to 1861; the Civil
War and Reconstruction up to 1877.

Here is a typical question: Many modern historians cite all the following as reasons for the decline of the Roman Empire in the West except:

A. political crises
B. decline in population
C. barbarian invasions
D. the abolition of slavery (2000, January, p. 346).

The absurdity of this for most kids, if not all, is all too self-evident.

Chicago's Turn

Next, Gerald Bracey, a former director of testing for the Virginia Department of Education, and now in his eleventh annual publication of
"The Condition of Public Education" for *Phi Delta Kappan*, comments
on the Chicago Academic Standards Examinations (CASE):

These tests were more than just a set of "trivial pursuit" items, although most of the items were that, too. The test contained items that had no right answer, items that had multiple right answers, and items to which the official right answer was wrong. It also contained items for which an earlier item cued the answer for a later one. In short, these tests were garbage. (p. 157)

Bracey goes on to state that when he was director of testing for the Virginia Department of Education, if he had produced tests as defective as these, "The department would have summarily sacked me and deservedly so" (p. 157). Bracey then graciously points out what standardized tests do not measure: "creativity, critical thinking, resilience, motivation, persistence, humor, reliability, enthusiasm, civic-mindedness, self-awareness, self-discipline, empathy, leadership, and compassion" (p. 138).

I can think of adding analytic ability. What else can *you* add?

Student Reactions to This Stress

Selma Wasserman (2001, September) reports on some of the reactions of her working-class suburban New York *first-grade* class to standardized tests. When I first read her article, I had to check back to confirm that she was talking about standardized, regimented tests in the *first grade*.

Then I read on. She pointed out that the class was heterogeneous, and that about three-quarters had finished pre-primers and primers and were considered to be reading at the "first-grade level." She notes:

The test began with a list of vocabulary words that the children were to define by blacking-in the space for the correct choice from among four options. Jimmy Tully, one of the better readers in the class, took his time, carefully decoding the words in the first column of the test booklet. I could see him struggle with the unknown words, bravely sounding them out and finding the appropriate match. By the time he had gotten to the seventh word on the list, his anxiety level had peaked and he had turned a deep rose. I touched his shoulder to comfort him, and, in response, he laid his pencil down, lowered his head, and wept.

Torn between my human feelings and the detailed prohibitions about
test-taking, I felt like a killer teacher. (p. 30)

ASSUMPTIONS OF THE "WE NEED STANDARDS MOVEMENT"

First, let's take a look at the assumptions used in arguing for national
(or even state) standards. The first, according to Cuban (1997, April 13)
is that if we increase schools' productivity, the larger economy will improve. The second is that so-called poor U.S. performance on international tests is caused by having no national standards.

Cuban notes, "Both assumptions are false."

The first assumption started being bruited about when we were in re-
cession in 1990. However, history is clear: our productivity increased
considerably in the 1990s. But, I haven't noticed the media crowing
over the wonderful work the schools have done to increase our productivity. Actually, we still find the critics blaming the schools for poor
performance. Linking test scores and productivity is still a sham, as
Cuban writes. Actually, a great deal of the success in economic productivity results from university research, which leads to new products
and inventions, all contributing to greater productivity.

The second assumption, that lack of national standards is causing
poor scores, is equally demolished by the evidence. Cuban notes that
some countries with national standards score above us and some score
below us. And some countries without national standards (like the
United States) score above us and some score below. And, some countries with decentralized curricula also score above nations that have set
national standards. It seems that standardized tests are not the panacea.
Another one-cause cure-all bites the dust. But, our policymakers still
haven't figured this out.

THE TEST-DRIVEN CURRICULUM

Before we turn to the impact of the standards movement on constructivist education, let's first take a look at what William Benjamin of the
University of South Florida, in a remarkably prophetic article written
in 1989, predicted what he labeled, "The Test-Driven Curriculum."

The test-driven curriculum appears to be in control. The very practice of testing students' achievement and then making immediate adjustments in curriculum and instruction gives a powerful message to the public. It says that the schools are in control of the situation and that educators know how to make kids smarter. (p. 3)

It's pretty obvious that we are in the midst of the curriculum being test-driven. Bracey (2001, October) concurs with this. "If 2000 was the year that testing went crazy, 2001 was the year it went stark, raving mad" (p. 158).

IMPACT OF THE STANDARDS MOVEMENT ON CONSTRUCTIVIST EDUCATION

The Association for Supervision and Curriculum Development's monthly newsletter, *Education Update*, dealt with this issue in a May 2001 article titled *Trying Too Hard? How Accountability and Testing Are Affecting Constructivist Teaching.*

The increasing accountability that has accompanied the reliance on high stakes testing—test results are used for everything from determining student placement to teacher and administrator pay raises and school funding—has profoundly affected the content of classroom teaching, according to many education experts. Teachers and administrators have reported sweeping changes in several states, including the cancellation of entire subject areas—not just arts and music but also traditional "hard areas" like math and science—so teachers can devote more time to preparing students for state tests. (p. 1)

"When I taught third grade a couple of years ago, we took practice tests called 'testlets' every day," says Karen Lounsbury, a prekindergarten teacher in Lincoln County, NC. "Instead of teaching reading and writing skills, I found I was teaching the testlets themselves. The children could not apply anything they had learned because all they wanted to know was, 'Will this be on the test?' It created a climate where the test was all that mattered." (p. 4)

In talking with teachers in Florida, they angrily reported that because the Florida Comprehensive Assessment Test (FCAT) was also used to give each school a grade, and because it only dealt with arithmetic, reading, and writing, many schools and districts abandoned teaching science and social studies. They were extremely concerned that their kids were scientifically illiterate—and knew nothing about the social science subjects. But, they assured us, there was hope. The state was going to add science to the testing pudding in a couple of years.

Alfie Kohn's book, *Punished by Rewards* (1993), states that intrinsic motivation gets replaced by extrinsic motivation when rewards (M&Ms, pizza parties, and the like for good grades) begin to become widely used to motivate kids. We begin to work for the reward and, after a while, find it harder to work when no reward exists. Kohn indicates that this is an effective strategy to reduce intrinsic motivation, as Karen Lounsbury points out on the previous page.

THE "STANDARDISTOS"

If you love sarcasm, you'll love Susan Ohanian's article, "Goals 2000: What's in a Name?" (2000, January). Ohanian terms those who support standards "Standardistos," generally businessmen, such as Louis Gerstner, CEO of IBM, and others, who love—no—who worship, the bottom line mentality brought into the schools by such illustrious educators as Ross Perot. She notes that this mentality insists on measuring school productivity with "unequivocal yardsticks" (p. 69). "They speak of the need for national tests and absolute standards, insisting that schools must compare themselves to each other the way 'Xerox, for example, compares itself to L.L. Bean for quality control'" (p. 70).

Snorts Ohanian, "Now, that's a fine notion: teaching as quality control" (p. 346).

What we have is the business mentality looking at the human enterprise of schooling, and trying to reduce it into business terms. For example, she points out that

> Gerstner and his cronies got to name the problem as well as define the solutions: claiming the need for choice, competition, and technology in the schools; defining students as human capital and the teaching/learning compact as a "protected monopoly" offering "goods and services"; describing the relationship between teachers and the communities they serve as that of "buyers and sellers." (p. 345)

Any human enterprise is a highly complex enterprise, which is considerably more difficult to measure than mere profit and loss.

GOALS 2000

Ohanian scathingly criticizes the eight goals of Goals 2000 by pointing out both left-wing and right-wing concerns. Don't forget that these were supposed to be accomplished by the year 2000.

My own take is to view them simply as mythology. For example:

Goal 1: All children are going to start school ready to learn.

Really? With one of the largest poverty levels in any industrialized nation?

Goal 2: The high school graduation rate will increase to at least 90 percent.

Not if we kick up standards. And because we did, it's actually dropping.

Goal 5: United States students will be first in the world in mathematics and science achievement.

Not even worth commenting on, with our poverty levels.

Goal 7: Every adult American will be literate . . .

The absurdity of such propaganda becomes clear with time.

In her next two books dealing with nonstandardized (read, socially, intellectually, or emotionally challenged) kids, Ohanian asks what seems a simple question: What happens when nonstandardized kids collide head-on with a standardized curriculum? Both her *One Size Fits Few* (1999) and *Caught in the Middle: Nonstandardized Kids and a Killing Curriculum* (2001) deal with this. But, the kids she teaches, low socioeconomic and minority, are not really able to succeed in a world that defines success as passing the standardized tests. As with Wasserman's accounts, many of the students do not fare too well in this hypercharged testing environment.

An example will do. In Ohanian's seventh- and eighth-grade class, a boy named Arnold spends a month studying George Washington. When it comes time to make his oral report, Arnold has a dickens of a time trying to start. After considerable cajoling from the other seven students, he starts talking. "When George was born," he begins, "his father looked at the dollar bill and said, 'I think I'll call him George Washington,' and that's how the baby got his name."

"I [Ohanian] must have looked startled because Arnold addresses his next remarks to me, 'You have seen his picture right there on the dollar bill, haven't you?' He reaches into his pocket, pulls out a dollar, and holds it up. 'That's how he got his name. Right off the money.' Now, this is after a month of work."

A FINAL COMMENT

If standards and goals are to work, they must have two characteristics: They have to be *believable—and achievable*. These are not.

QUESTIONS FOR REFLECTION

1. Arguments for state and national standards are based on one-size-fits-all assumptions.
    A. Do you believe that we should develop national standards?
    B. How about in your state, should we develop state standards?
    C. Will they work?
    D. What are positive and negative results of such actions?
2. How can state and national standards (which by nature imply uniformity), be supported in the face of so much diversity among students and teachers?
3. What factors lead such a majority of educators to question national and state standards so vehemently?
4. And on the other side of the coin, what makes the idea of national or state standards so attractive to the public and politicians?
5. Cuban points out that two assumptions underlie the national standards movement. The first is that increasing schools' productivity will increase economic growth and power.
    A. Do you believe this to be valid? To what evidence does Cuban point?
6. The second is that so-called poor performance on international tests is due to lack of national standards.

   A. What evidence does Cuban's article use to destroy that argument?
7. William Benjamin writes prophetically that we are generating a test-driven curriculum. Do you concur? What is your own experience in this area?
8. Alfie Kohn's *Punished by Rewards* states that intrinsic motivation gets replaced by extrinsic motivation when too much focus is placed on the latter, so that people start to work for the reward. Does this apply to the standards movement? If so, how?
9. What's your take on this movement? Is it part of the bottom-line mentality that business leaders use in their economic mind-set?
   A. Does it fit into educational thinking?
   B. What does it do to the educational process?

SOURCES

Benjamin, W. F. (1989, Spring). From the curriculum editor. *Florida ASCD Journal 5*, 3–5.

Bracey, G. W. (2001, October). The eleventh Bracey report on the condition of public education. *Phi Delta Kappan 83*(2), 157–69.

Cuban, L. (1997, April 13). Debunking national academic standards. *Saint Petersburg Times*.

Finn, C. E., Jr., Petrilli, M. J., & Vanourik, G. (1998, July). *The state of state standards*. Washington, DC: The Fordham Report, Thomas B. Fordham Foundation.

Gerstner, L., Jr., Semerad, R., Doyle, D., & Johnson, W. (1994). *Reinventing education: Entrepreneurship in America's public schools*. New York: Dutton.

Hodgkinson, H. (2002, January). Standards and the students of the future. Alexandria, VA: *Education Update 44*(1), 7.

Kohn, Alfie (1993). *Punished by rewards: The trouble with gold stars, incentive plans, A's, praise, and other bribes*. Boston: Houghton Mifflin.

Ohanian, S. (1999). *One size fits few*. Portsmouth, NH: Heinemann.

Ohanian, S. (2000, January). Goals 2000: What's in a name? *Phi Delta Kappan 81*(5), 345–55.

Ohanian, S. (2001). *Caught in the middle: Nonstandard kids and a killing curriculum*. Portsmouth, NH: Heinemann.

Wasserman, S. (2001, September). Quantum theory, the uncertainty principle, and the alchemy of standardized testing. *Phi Delta Kappan 83*(1), 28–40.

Part III

RESEARCH

Science is the attempt to make the chaotic diversity of our sense-experience correspond to a logically uniform system of thought.

—Albert Einstein
Out of My Later Years

Without question, there are widespread indicators that constructivist views of learning have captured the current zeitgeist in today's educational arena.

—Applegate, Huber & Moallem
The High School Journal

The Latest Research (about Constructivism) Part I: Different Approaches to Constructivism—What It's All About

The overwhelming consensus as the twentieth century closed has been that knowledge is constructed.

—D. C. Phillips, *Constructivism in Education*

Constructivism has suddenly exploded onto our present educational and academic stage with a potency that hardly could be imagined, let alone predicted, in 1990 (although in science and mathematics the "science wars" about constructivism started somewhat earlier). We'll get to this shortly.

ORGANIZATION OF THIS CHAPTER

This chapter starts with a (mercifully) *very* brief overview of the origins of constructivist thinking among philosophers. We will then look at perceptions of the major kinds or forms of constructivism, based on the assumption that it's probably useful to know what we are talking about.

By this time, some of us may be anxious in our quest to find out what constructivism actually is. So we'll try to rope it in (but not tie it down) with several definitions, or approaches. We'll even describe models of what constructivist classrooms or teams might look like by suggesting essential elements. We then move on and compare and contrast constructivist education with several of the more passive and popular forms of classroom instruction. This will help us to dig into current research on constructivism. It's useful to have everyone on the same page, that is, that we are talking about the same thing to avoid adding further confusion to our complex and interesting world. Hopefully, it will shed some insight into the impact of constructivist approaches on student, teacher, and administrator growth and learning!

And we continue in the following chapter ("Part II") with a quick overview of major and key research on constructivist teaching and leadership.

A QUICK PEEK AT THE CONSTRUCTIVIST LANDSCAPE— THE PHILOSOPHERS

Somewhat of a consensus has developed that constructivist thinking started with the eighteenth-century German philosopher, Immanuel Kant. Kant, as D. C. Phillips (2000, p. 8) noted, "argued that certain aspects of our knowledge of the physical universe (time and space, for example) were the products of our own cognitive apparatus—we 'construct' the universe to have certain properties, or, rather, our faculty of understanding imposes those temporal and spatial properties on our experience."

Rene Descartes, a French philosopher and mathematician of the seventeenth century, is famous for his claim that he had examined all of his beliefs, and started with the very basic "I think, therefore, I am." In this process he claims that he dumped all of his beliefs that did not meet his "light of reason" test. This test focused on starting knowledge from propositions of indubitable certitude.

Jean-Jacques Rousseau and Johann Pestalozzi contributed to the development of constructivist thought. Rousseau believed that students learn through their senses, their experience, and their activity. "Pestalozzi . . . believed that the student's mind receives impressions through observation and experience and that these impressions produce ideas and an organized mental structure that the student uses to compare, examine, separate, sort, and conclude" (Marlowe & Page 1998, p. 17).

We now jump to the twentieth century for the next major thinker, the founder of empirical developmental psychology, Jean Piaget. He worked with children to determine how they formed basic concepts, research which is described in *The Construction of Reality in the Child*

(1954). Since he asserts that the child constructs his own reality, Piaget can be considered constructivist in his thinking. So is Bruner (1961), for whom discovery is at the core of thinking, as Marlowe and Page (1998) assert. "Whatever a person discovers himself is what he truly knows. From discovery . . . comes increased intellectual ability, including the ability to solve problems."

Several other major contributors to constructivism will be discussed as we move along, including John Dewey, George Herbert Mead (the founder of contemporary social psychology and a friend, colleague, and contributor to Dewey's thinking), Lev Vygotsky, Howard Gardner, and other key thinkers.

MAJOR FORMS OF CONSTRUCTIVISM

The major constructivist approaches have *fundamental* implications and applications for education.

Psychological Constructivism

Phillips (2000) points to two different constructivist approaches: psychological and social constructivism. The former

> refers to a set of views about how individuals learn (and about how those who help them to learn ought to teach). Roughly, this . . . type of constructivist view is that learners actively construct their own ("internal," as some would say) sets of meanings or understandings; knowledge is *not* [my italics] a mere *copy* of the external world, nor is knowledge acquired by passive absorption or by simple transference from one person (a teacher) to another (a learner or knower). In sum, knowledge is *made*, not *acquired*. (p. 7)

Phillips then indicates why he considers this approach, psychological constructivism:

> Some constructivists of this broad type go on to stress that we cannot be certain any two individuals will construct the same understandings; even if they use the same linguistic formulations to express what they have learned, their deep understandings might be quite different. . . . In previ-

ous papers I have used the expression *psychological constructivism,* because the center of interest is the *psychological understandings of individual learners.* (p. 7)

Translated into common, everyday words, this implies that each of us sees the world around us differently by reason of our different upbringings, experiences, and personalities. We have different successes and traumas, and we react differently to the same conditions. We perceive the world differently, often quite divergently, from others.

One may argue that this hardly applies to twins. But, doesn't it? My wife, who is a twin, can recognize nine out of ten times who is the older in another pair of twins. She looks for more assertive behavior, more dominant behavior on the part of one twin—more get-up-and-go—and she hits it almost all the time. But, she is attuned to it—I am not. Nor is her younger twin sister. So, not only do my wife and I perceive the world of twins quite differently, the twins see the world differently. As a matter of fact, my wife will pick up on twins way ahead of me, because they are a significant object for her.

As for families within families, the first child enters a world of two parents. The second child does not enter the same two-world-set-of-parents. He or she enters a family of three, with different dynamics than a two-adult world develops. Note these examples point out how each of us constructs his or her own world differently.

In the book *Radical Constructivism: A Way of Knowing and Learning,* Ernst von Glasersfeld states:

> Radical constructivism . . . starts from the assumption that knowledge, no matter how it is defined, is in the heads of persons, and that the thinking subject has no alternative but to construct what he or she knows on the basis of his or her own experience. What we can make of experience constitutes the only world we consciously live in. . . . All kinds of experience are essentially subjective, and though I may find reasons to believe that my experience may not be unlike yours, I have no way of knowing that it is the same. . . . Taken seriously, this is a profoundly shocking view. (1995, p. 1)

Von Glasersfeld *is* right since he is asserting that since you and I never fully share the same experiences, we never see the same things similarly. And his view is quite radical, but he misses the key processes that make us human, that make us social animals. What he misses is the enormity, the power of culture and its underpinning vehicle, language, in impacting each of us who lives in the same culture. For example, we speak the same language—no accident. We have many of the same customs (we drive on the right side of the road). In addition, von Glasersfeld avoids confronting the fact that the mind, the self, and society are socially formed, as George Herbert Mead (1934) recognized.

Social Constructivism

Now, in tackling his *second* kind of constructivism, social constructivism, Phillips states:

> "Constructivism" embodies a thesis about the disciplines or bodies of knowledge that have been built up during the course of human history. I have described this thesis as, roughly, that these disciplines (or public bodies of knowledge) are human constructs, and that the form that knowledge has taken in these fields has been determined by such things as politics, ideologies, values, the exertion of power and the preservation of status, religious beliefs, and economic self-interest. This thesis denies that the disciplines are objective reflections of an "external world." (p. 6)

So, understanding even our most sacrosanct fields of knowledge, such as the sciences, has to turn to the question of how we construct knowledge. We'd better take a hard look at this—a very hard look. What does this mean? As with psychological constructivism, a considerable range of thought is covered by the term, *social constructivism*. And this is the exact ground over which the "science wars" erupted.

Moderate Social Constructivism—Very Briefly

A more moderate form of social constructivism holds that, without question, the *social world* is socially constructed. The social construction of the social world is fairly self-evident. When I first saw the title of Berger and Luckmann's (1966) book, *The Social Construction of Reality*, it stopped me cold. It was a huge revelation to me! The title says it all, that we construct our social worlds, that they are not ready-made to be put on like a suit of clothes or a pair of jeans.

For example, we talked about rituals in life and in school in chapter 22 on testing, "Our Evaluation Ritual Trap: And How to Spring It." Our customs, our rituals, our norms, usually come into existence without our becoming aware of them. Why do we drive on the right-hand side of the road? By the time the colonists arrived in North America, knighthood not only wasn't flowering, it had withered. So, there was no reason to sidle off to the left when we would meet another person on the road in case he wanted to show the world what a macho lad he was. So, we drive on the right side of the road. The Brits still drive on the left, a holdover from half a dozen centuries ago.

How did homecoming rituals enter the high schools (and later the junior highs)? They were borrowed from the universities. But high school homecoming and football games take place on Friday night, while the college model takes occurs on Saturdays. (And the pros play football on Sunday—and since the last three decades, one game is played Monday evening.) Since the first public high schools were formed a little over 150 years ago, a lot of customs and rituals have developed within them.

So, the social world *is* socially constructed.

Another example? How about how family customs start? For over a decade my wife and I sojourned down to a resort island for Thanksgiving. But, this year we decided to abandon the custom since a close friend we made left the area for a better life. Goodbye, this custom. But, where to go for Thanksgiving? Behold! The start of a new family custom.

The Radical Social Constructivists—A Major Threat to the Assumed Objectivity of Science and Mathematics?

At the other extreme, the more radical social constructivists push the envelope a lot further—and here is where the so-called "hard sciences" feel gored. These sociologists, labeled "the Strong Program in the sociology of knowledge," hold

> that the form that knowledge takes in a discipline can be *fully explained*, or *entirely accounted for*, in sociological terms. That is, . . . what is taken to be knowledge in any field has been determined by sociological forces

including the influence of ideologies, religion, human interests, group dynamics, and so forth . . . this group of thinkers wishes to deny that so-called knowledge is in any sense a reflection or copy of that "external reality" that the community in question is investigating. (Phillips, pp. 8–9)

What these radical social constructivists are stating is that even the hard sciences are socially constructed and cannot claim objectivity. In other words, the structure and knowledge of the sciences and mathematics are determined by social forces, and therefore the vaunted objectivity our culture ascribes to science and mathematics is a delusion. The implications of this radical approach are absolutely fundamental, for if you take this viewpoint, how can you tell science from nonsense? If science has no validity or objectivity, where are we?

As you can imagine, natural scientists and mathematicians have gone ballistic over this contention. That's why these are called "the science wars." Yet, if we give it a moment of thought, it is obvious that the major concepts of the sciences did not appear like manna from heaven. *They were—and are—developed*, as Phillips notes:

The concepts we use in everyday life or in the scholarly disciplines, did not descend—fully formed—out of the blue. There was a time when the concepts of "energy" or "mass" or "molecule" or "psychosis" or "working class" did not exist; and the halting and interactive process can be traced whereby these concepts and the very things or categories themselves were developed." (p. 88)

Some Common Sense Examples to This

Certain ideas are so commonplace, so embedded in our culture and our thinking, that we think they were here for all time. But have they been around that long?

I remember visiting Paul Revere's house in Boston and being amazed that he could raise twelve kids in such a tiny house. Apparently, the colonials didn't have much of a sense of privacy. We do now. "Privacy" has become a constitutional right. When and how did it develop?

We could spend a little more space on the development of major ideas we take absolutely for granted, as if they have existed for all time. But, of course, they haven't. They are recent discoveries, although we accept them as if they have been here forever. For example, in education, Piaget's (1954) work on discovery learning has had a great impact on the practice of education. He popularized this very practical idea. Next, Vygotsky (1978) noted that "we construct intelligence, meaning, and thought in interaction with others and that this construction is also historically cumulative and socio-cultural, thereby shaping our relationships over time" (Lambert 1995, p. 192).

In actuality, George Herbert Mead (1934), who founded contemporary social psychology, was by far the more profound thinker for he worked on the interrelationships of the processes forming the human mind, the self, and society. Mead dissected the processes that lead to objects becoming significant or social through *interaction.* For example, a piece of paper, if we crumple it up, can become a "ball" if it is treated as a ball. In other words, the symbol of paper has changed to the symbol of "ball." Mead is the father of Symbolic Interaction, a major field of contemporary social psychology. Mead's work led to the understanding that a person's "self" is formed through social interaction, the self being that part of us which permits us to interact with ourself, such as treating ourself as an object. For example, we talk to ourselves—few other animals do that. (Maybe some gorillas do.)

Later, in discussing an early book on constructivist leadership by Lambert et al. (*The Constructivist Leader*, 1995), we will see that she perceives that the "most important factor in schools is *relationships*" [my emphasis] (p. 35), thus, espousing Symbolic Interaction as a keystone of her theory of constructivist leadership. Gardner (1983) furthered our thinking about intelligence by pointing to seven different forms of intelligence in humans. Lately, he seems to think an eighth may exist. These are all ideas that were recently formulated. This leads to the fundamental question being addressed here: Are all ideas socially constructed?

The more moderate social constructivists do not espouse the more extreme viewpoints of the radical constructivists, but they do "think that the public bodies of knowledge, or the disciplines, are *public* and hence are socially constructed" (Phillips 2000, p. 89).

More Thinking: Enter Thomas Kuhn and His "The Big Picture" Approach—Paradigms!

Lest we think that social constructivism was hatched in the ivory towers of a few discontented academics, let's review Kuhn's (1970) contributions to our thinking about science. Before Kuhn, generally, scientists considered science as objective, certain, and immune from personal, cultural, or scientific bias. Scientists thought that if they used the same methods, the results of their research would be objective, and, therefore, the same.

Kuhn, however, asserted that scientists tended to march along the same conceptual railroad track, merely filling in spaces, dotting their i's and crossing their t's. They tended to stay inside their conceptual parameters (their boxes). His perceptions were that scientists, like all of us, tended generally to follow widely accepted processes, concepts, beliefs of accepted thinking, often rejecting radically new theories, ideas, and those mavericks in their fields who stray from the mainstream. He noted great changes in thinking, paradigm shifts, in scientific thinking, such as Darwin's theory of evolution, Freud's theory of the unconscious, the atom being divisible (my older cousin was taught that the atom was indivisible—and then came the atom bomb), and the discovery of the gene as examples. What can *you* think of as great shifts in paradigms?

I never heard anything about quarks in my high school physics classes. DNA was not dreamt of in my biology classes, nor were tectonic plates mentioned in geology classes. These, and many more, theories represent quantum leap (a recent word in physics) paradigm shifts.

John Casti (1989) affirms that "what is taken to be true at any moment is more a matter of social convention in the scientific community than it is a product of logical methods and procedures." In its history, science changes radically over the long haul. Thus, all science is colored by the perspectives, assumptions, values, culture, and paradigms of the present. Science often resists radical, new ideas.

Can a Theory Map "Reality"?

The above discussion should make us a bit queasy about holding too strongly the idea that science actually "maps" reality. So, let's take a

brief shot at this. We can go back to James Conant (1952), a highly respected scientist, for some interesting views about this:

> Scientific theory should not be regarded as an objective map that de-
> scribes and explains reality, but rather, as "a policy—an economical and
> fruitful guide to action by scientific investigators."

Percy Bridgman, a respected physicist, drives a dagger into the heart
of the notion that science transcends human factors in stating:

> Scientific, empirical-rational methods had shown that scientific theory
> was not, as had been thought, a value-free, objective description of real-
> ity, but a construct invented to advance human endeavors.
>
> Theory regarded as a map, as mentioned earlier, purports to tell us
> what the world is really like. It implies *discovered* knowledge, which lit-
> erally represents an uncovering of the nature of reality. By contrast, mod-
> ern scientific theory—that is, theory regarded as a policy for action—
> claims only to tell us what are the best *representations* of the work in
> terms of present experience. Knowledge from this point of view is re-
> garded as *constructed*, that is, fabricated on the basis of human experi-
> ence for particular ends-in-view . . . theory may vary accordingly as pur-
> poses for which it is constructed may vary.
>
> As we noted in a previous paragraph, all of the evidence available
> seems to indicate that the revolution in modern physics has rendered the
> "map" concept of scientific theory both an illusion and a presumption.
> Scientific theory not only *does not* describe the nature of reality, but it
> *cannot*. The reason, some physicists contend, is that theory is a product
> of human thought processes, and modern physics suggests that human
> thought processes may not correspond sufficiently to the structure of na-
> ture to permit us to think about it at all. (1952, pp. 86–87)

Put another way, the nature of reality and the concept of existence
are meaningless, not because of the nature of the world, but because of
the construction of the human organism. It is simply impossible for
man to transcend the human reference point. "We cannot even express
this in the way we would like . . . . It is literally true that the only way
of reacting to this is to shut up" (Bridgman 1952).

As Margaret Bogan notes, "All science is colored by the perspectives
(and assumptions, values, and culture) and understandings of the re-

searchers. . . . No human enterprise is an objective experience, and science is a human enterprise" (Shapiro et al. 1995, p. 34).

Another Formulation of Constructivist Thinking

Michael Matthews (2000) suggests three different major constructivist traditions: educational, philosophical, and sociological constructivism. Interestingly, he places both psychological and social constructivism under the educational label.

Matthews then gives constructivism a huge scope in human knowledge, citing:

- Theory of cognition
- Theory of learning
- Theory of teaching
- Theory of education
- Theory of personal knowledge
- Theory of scientific knowledge
- Theory of educational ethics and politics
- Worldview (p. 163).

To this, one might add the possibility that constructivism provides a:

- Theory of instruction
- Theory of administration and supervision.

THE CONSTRUCTIVIST LANDSCAPE: GETTING A HANDLE ON ITS NATURE—FINALLY

Martin Brooks and Jacqueline Brooks (1999, November, p. 18) define constructivism as "a theory of learning that describes the central role that learners' ever-transforming mental schemes play in their cognitive growth." Further on they note, "Learners control their learning. This simple truth lies at the heart of the constructivist approach to education" (p. 19).

They then point to five central tenets, or instructional practices, that are basic to constructivist teaching and learning. First, constructivist teachers seek and value students' points of view. Knowing what students think about concepts helps teachers formulate classroom lessons and differentiate instruction on the basis of students' needs and interests. Second, constructivist teachers structure lessons to challenge students' suppositions. Third, constructivist teachers recognize that students must attach relevance to the curriculum. As students see relevance in their daily activities, their interest in learning grows. Fourth, constructivist teachers structure lessons around big ideas, not small bits of information. Finally, constructivist teachers assess student learning in the context of daily classroom investigations, not as separate events.

Lambert and Walker (1995, p. 1) assert that "constructivism is a theory of learning, and it is also a theory of knowing." They quote Catherine Fosnot as pointing "out that constructivism is at once a theory of 'knowing' and a theory of 'coming to know'" (p. 167).

Brooks and Brooks (1999, November, p. 23) further explain: "State and local curriculums address *what* students learn. Constructivism, as an approach to education, addresses *how* students learn. The constructivist teacher, in mediating students' learning, blends the *what* with the *how*."

So, How Do We Tell a Constructivist Classroom or Team from a Traditional One?

Just as we might diagnose a quality restaurant by its elegant and quiet atmosphere, white tablecloths, reservations necessary for admission, well-dressed servers, quality service, table-side flaming of certain desserts, and the like, so we might scan the classroom or team to determine whether it has constructivist elements.

For example: Are the students engaged in active learning? Are they active or passive? Do they sit and listen, for the most part? (Dewey would love it if they were very active.) What is the organizing vehicle of the class? Are groups the basis? (In other words, do students interact openly with each other, with the teacher?) Or, do they sit in rows? Is the approach experiential? How about the use of inquiry as a major vehicle? Do the students have a voice in what and how they study? Do they have the opportunity to make choices? Are different learning styles and approaches used? Are students' views and thinking respected? Do the students develop projects? Do the students feel safe in the class or in the team? Do the teachers? If the students are mostly sitting listening passively, it isn't constructivist. These are some key elements of constructivist education.

How do they match with Dewey? [Note that the title of this chapter is "The Latest Research (about Constructivism)" and here we're talking about Dewey, who wrote early in the last century.] Here's what Phillips (2000) has to say about Dewey's thinking:

> Dewey was a constructivist of sorts. He stressed that learners must be active. He advocated the use of projects and inquiry methods, he attacked the acquisition by students of "cold storage knowledge" (knowledge that was acquired passively or by rote and students did not know how to use). He regarded learning as best proceeding in social contexts, and he wanted the classroom to be seen as an interactive community. He also was aware of the issue outlined above, namely that students have to learn the bodies of knowledge that are represented in the curriculum. He would not regard a student as being scientifically educated if he or she did not know the "funded wisdom" that is represented in the discipline publicly recognized as science. (p. 14)

COMPARING CONSTRUCTIVIST AND TRADITIONAL APPROACHES

Passive and Active Theories of Learning

Eric Bredo (in Phillips 2000, p. 132) points to constructivism as having two implications for education. First, "a concern for students' having an active role in learning, and second, "their being allowed to redefine or discover new meanings for the objects with which they interact."

Traditional direct instruction, which qualifies for being classified as a passive approach, is contradicted by these two criteria. Indeed, therein lies its emptiness. Traditionally, direct instruction is used in education for disadvantaged kids, usually minorities, on the grounds that they: need more discipline; need more structure; need more basics; are slower developmentally—and any other excuse we can dredge up.

The reality is that kids who are described in this way are being stereotyped. It is they who need much greater doses of active, experiential learning—which direct instruction will not provide. In direct instruction, there is little role for student activity. Not only that, but it does not permit students to redefine or build new meanings for the objects with which they come into contact. So, the upshot of this approach is that the kids will be further disadvantaged. Some gift!

Lecture

We studied how long high school kids could handle a lecture. The answer—at the outside—is 27 minutes. A psychiatrist asked to evaluate the program at a major college of medicine once analyzed lecturing as dictating a book to very poor stenographers.

Very limited. Forget it.

Object Lessons

Ditto.

Skinnerian Conditioning

This, indeed, is an active approach. But, it is hardly constructivist, since instruction is directed by a master designer totally outside of the students' control. The only student decision making is whether or not to participate, and to decide on how fast or slow to go. Not much activity is assumed—and little freedom is given to explore finding new meanings, except over a highly constricted turf decided upon by the master designer. In this model the learner has little freedom to construct his or her own meanings.

Problem-Solving Approaches

Closer, but still missing the core of the apple.

Bredo notes that problem-solving approaches "tend to presuppose a fixed problem definition at base that is not up for reorganization. . . . Since these procedures and related 'objects' may not be reconstructed, such approaches are not fully constructivist, at least according to this definition" (in Phillips, p. 132).

Cooperative Learning Approaches

Cooperative learning approaches are not necessarily constructivist. Some cooperative learning methods involve a teacher-dominated method and are concerned with the learning of basic skills involving right and wrong answers. Sharan's Group Investigation method, however, focuses on higher level learning. (Marlowe & Page 1998, p. 22)

Active Learning Approaches

On the mark! People working on projects that relate to goals they participated in developing would be one model. Obviously, others can be developed, such as: *students* developing a skit or a play; *students* writing a poem or a short story; *students* designing and producing a poster; *students* planning and carrying out an activity related to the goals; *students* developing a report; and *students* designing and building any model, such as a medieval village. "The more actively students are involved in the learning process and take personal responsibility for their learning outcomes, the greater are the learning results" (Davis & Murrell 1993).

SUMMARY

We have now discovered that constructivism takes a number of forms, about which scientists often disagree. Thus, the field is complex. But, constructivism in whatever form makes a good deal of sense—certainly the more moderate positions would appeal to the majority of us. We also described some key elements found in a constructivist class and team, and we compared constructivist and traditional teaching models.

The next chapter deals with research findings, first, on instruction and then on leadership. A huge literature is building on constructivism and teaching and instruction. However, if you expect a similarly large literature on constructivism and leadership, you will be disappointed.

QUESTIONS FOR THE CURIOUS

1. Does this satisfy your interest in the nature of constructivism? Its philosophical roots? Its historical beginnings so recent? Its foundations in theory and its introduction to major theorists? Or, would you have preferred more?
2. Does moderate psychological constructivism sound valid to you? Ernst von Glasersfeld's radical psychological constructivism (in the earlier section of this chapter)?
3. What is your reaction to moderate social constructivism, which speaks to the issue of the social construction of reality? Does it appear valid?
   A. How about radical social constructivism, which states that all knowledge is socially constructed?
4. Which of the components of constructivist practice (active learning approaches, experiential learning, groups as the normal organizing vehicle, use of inquiry, student choice and decision making, dealing with different learning styles, safety in your classroom or team or school) are you using?
5. How close are you to becoming a constructivist teacher or administrator/supervisor?
6. Is this something you want professionally and personally? If so, why? If not, why?
7. Does changing mean that one has to stretch? Is this important for our personal and professional growth?
8. What questions would you ask that have not been put down on paper?
9. Would some of these questions offend people in education whom you know?
   A. Why?

SOURCES

Berger, P. L. & Luckmann, T. (1966). *The social construction of reality*. Garden City, NY: Doubleday.

Bloor, D. (1976). *Knowledge and social imagery*. London: Routledge & Kegan Paul.

Bogan, M. (1992). Personal Communication.

Bridgman, P. W. (1952, February). Philosophical implications of physics. *American Academy of Arts and Sciences Bulletin*, 86–87.

Brooks, M. G. & Brooks, J. G. (1999, November). The courage to be constructivist. *Educational Leadership 57*(3), 18–24.

Bruner, J. S. (1961). The act of discovery. *Harvard Educational Review 31*(1), 232.

Casti, J. L. (1989). *Paradigms lost: Images of man in the mirror of science.* New York: Morrow.

Conant, J. B. (1952). *Modern science and modern man, 97.* New York: Columbia University Press.

Davis, T. M. & Murrell, P. H. (1993). Turning teaching into learning: The role of student responsibility in the collegiate experience. [Abstract]. In *Active learning, critical thinking, learning styles, and cooperative learning.* Washington, DC: George Washington University, 1993 ASHE-ERIC Higher Education Reports; Report 8.

Dewey, J. (1938). *Experience and education.* New York: Macmillan.

Fosnot, C. (1992). Constructing constructivism. In T. M. Duffy & D. H. Jonassen (Eds.). *Constructivism and the technology of instruction: A conversation* (pp. 167–76). Hillsdale, NJ: Lawrence Erlbaum.

Gardner, H. (1983). *Frames of the mind: The theory of multiple intelligences.* New York: Basic Books.

Gergen, K. (1994). *Realities and relations: Soundings in social construction.* Cambridge, MA: Harvard University Press.

Kuhn, T. (1970). *The structure of scientific revolution.* Chicago: University of Chicago Press.

Lambert, L. (1995). Toward a theory of constructivist leadership. In L. Lambert, D. Walker, D. P. Zimmerman, J. E. Cooper, M. D. Lambert, M. E. Gardner, & P. J. Ford Slack (Eds.). *The constructivist leader.* New York: Teachers College Press.

Marlowe, B. A. & Page, M. L. (1998).*Creating and sustaining the constructivist classroom.* Thousand Oaks, CA: Corwin.

Matthews, M. R. (2000). Appraising constructivism in science and mathematics education. In D. C. Phillips (Ed.). *Constructivism in education: Opinions and second opinions on controversial issues.* Ninety-ninth Yearbook of the National Society for the Study of Education, Part I. Chicago: University of Chicago Press.

Mead, G. H. (1934). *Mind, self, and society.* Chicago: University of Chicago Press.

Pestalozzi, J. H. (1898). *How Gertrude teaches her children.* (L. E. Holland &

F. C. Turner, Trans.). New York: C. E. Bardeen. (Original work published 1801).

Phillips, D. C. (Ed.). (2000). *Constructivism in education: Opinions and second opinions on controversial issues.* Ninety-ninth Yearbook of the National Society for the Study of Education, Part I. Chicago: University of Chicago Press.

Piaget, J. (1954). *The construction of reality in the child.* New York: Basic Books.

Rousseau, J. J. (1957). *Emile.* (B. Foxley, Trans.). New York: E. P. Dutton. (Original work published 1762).

Shapiro, A., Benjamin, W. F., & Hunt, J. J. (1995). *Curriculum and schooling: A practitioner's guide.* Palm Springs, CA: ETC.

von Glasersfeld, E. (1995). *Radical constructivism: A way of knowing and learning.* London: Falmer Press.

von Glasersfeld, E. (1998). Why constructivism must be radical. In Larochelle, M., Bednarz, N. & Garrison, J. (Eds.). *Constructivism and education.* Cambridge, UK: Cambridge University Press.

Vygotsky, L. S. (1978). *Mind in society: The development of higher psychological processes.* Cambridge, MA: Harvard University Press.

Walker, D. (1995). The preparation of constructivist leaders. In L. Lambert, D. Walker, D. P. Zimmerman, J. E. Cooper, M. D. Lambert, M. E. Gardner, & P. J. Ford Slack (Eds.). *The constructivist leader.* New York: Teachers College Press.

CHAPTER 29

The Latest Research (about Constructivism) Part II: On Instruction and Leadership

A new scientific truth does not triumph by convincing its opponents and making them see the light, but rather because its opponents gradually die, and a new generation grows up that is familiar with it.

—Max Plank, *Scientific Autobiography and Other Papers*

MORE RESEARCH FINDINGS—ON INSTRUCTION

A Web search for the key words "constructivism and teaching" produced 1,397 hits (in comparison with 77 on "constructivism, education, and leadership"). We will select those in both areas most germane to the purposes of this book.

A Pioneer: A Singular Focus on the *Individual Classroom*

One of the earliest, most fundamental, and most influential books on constructivism in the classroom was Brooks and Brooks, *In Search of Understanding: The Case for Constructivist Classrooms* (1993). A basic premise of the book is "that in order for learning to take place in schools, teachers must become constructivist . . . they must provide a learning environment where students search for meaning, appreciate uncertainty, and inquire responsibly" (p. v). Successive chapters titled, "Seeking and Valuing Students' Points of View" and "Adapting the Curriculum to Address Students' Suppositions" inform us of the authors' viewpoint. They also perceive the fundamental unit of reform

345

and movement toward constructivism to be the *individual classroom* unit, noting:

> While the philosophies and mission statements of many schools purport to want students to be thinking, exploring individuals who generate hypotheses and test them out, the organization and management structures of most schools militate against these goals. So, if autonomy, initiative, and leadership are to be nurtured, it must be done in individual classrooms. (p. 103)

Fascinatingly, the authors perceive the organizational structures of the schools as so constrictive and limiting that they abandon even considering working with the school as an entity and prefer to work with teachers, who can control what they can do in their classes. We'll deal with this more directly in the section titled "More Research Findings—On Leadership."

Designing the Constructivist Classroom

In a paper titled "Creating the Culture of Constructivist Classrooms in Public and Private Schools" (1996) and later published as "Creating Culture for a Constructivist Classroom and Team" (2000, May), I laid out a constructivist approach to designing and implementing a highly effective constructivist classroom and team that was based thoroughly on theory. A major focus of the piece comprises procedures to *create the culture of the class deliberately*, rather than letting the culture of the organization develop by accident, by hit or by miss. The article provides clear directions for creating the culture one desires, instead of being a helpless (and, often a hapless) bystander unaware of the slowly unfolding, possibly resistant culture surrounding us. A classroom (indeed, any organization) inevitably creates a subculture as it develops.

The question for us becomes, why not shape the culture? And, what I'm saying here is that organizations such as classrooms and schools develop a culture, about which we normally are serenely unaware.

I rested my classroom design in part on implementing Maslow's (1954) Hierarchy of Needs, which consists of basic human needs. People learn much better if they feel safe. If the teacher can provide a setting in which social needs are met, more needs are satisfied. Hence, the key vehicle of the class or team is the small group. As Walker and Lambert (1995) note, "Learning is a social activity that is enhanced by shared inquiry" (p. 18). So, we work in small groups. Esteem needs are met by acceptance of all thoughts and ideas as valuable contributions to the processes of inquiry being carried on.

Lewin's (1952) findings comparing the group's impact versus individual attempts to change behavior over time are crucial in the model I designed. Lewin's experiments concluded that decisions to change attitudes and behavior are considerably more effective when participants make them publicly in a small group than in either a lecture or a one-on-one format. People who commit publicly will tend to do what they say they will do. Thus, it becomes obvious that the small group becomes the vehicle for constructing the constructivist educational process. Other theoretical sources included Mead (1934), cited earlier as a fundamental source for understanding the construction of the self, and for pointing out the crucial nature of social interaction in that process.

I use Bloom's (1956) Taxonomy to move to the higher cognitive levels. For example, at the end of every session, the group is asked to respond to the sentence stem, "Today, I learned . . ."

People come up with the most interesting statements. In the middle of each semester, and at the end, students analyze "My most significant learnings in this class . . ." with any format they may wish, from producing their own response to developing group responses. Results can range from creating a paper to a skit, a videotape, a poster, a poem, a model, and so forth.

Other people, such as Goffman (1967) for his work on *The Presentation of the Self in Everyday Life*, Johnson and Johnson (1984) for their work on cooperative groups, Linton (1955) and others for their work on the nature of culture, Thelen (1949) for his work on the effective size of working groups, and others, have been useful in developing this design.

Gagnon and Collay (2001) tease out six essential elements they believe make constructivist classrooms work. These are: developing situations, organizing groupings, building bridges, asking questions, arranging exhibits, and inviting reflections. The focus, appropriately, is on organizing for student learning, rather than on teacher telling, presenting constructivist perspectives on structuring the classroom to facilitate student learning.

An Expanded Focus: From the Classroom, Team, Learning Community—to the Total School

Seeing opportunity to expand the constructivist idea and process to an entire organization, such as a school, or a school district, I suggested strategies to constructivize the total school, as well as the classroom, team, or learning community. As a consequence, I spent a good deal of time in the book, *Leadership for Constructivist Schools* (2000), first exploring constructivist teaching, and comparing and contrasting it in actual case studies with more traditional models. Most chapters then deal with teachers *and* leaders as they deal with the elements and dynamics of both classroom *and* organizational constructivism.

The book first gets at the guts, the key elements and dynamics of both constructivist teaching and leadership, such as using the group as the fundamental vehicle for teaching. It provides readers with the underlying dynamics of classrooms, teams, learning communities, and schools, and then presents models and approaches for readers to design and develop effective change strategies to implement constructivism in classrooms, learning communities, and whole schools, on the assumption that people at those levels have a more intimate and better knowledge of the needs and interests of those they serve. I strongly endorse decentralizing approaches, which constructivist approaches themselves entail, as one basis for educational reform. The section on leadership digs into this.

Further Studies on Instruction/Teaching

We'll sum up a major conclusion about research on constructivist teaching: "The research as a whole shows active learning methods to be superior to teacher-dominated approaches in measures of academic, affective, and skill learning" (Marlowe & Page 1998, p. 19).

Marlowe and Page point to two major studies in the pre-1950 era, the Winnetka Schools Project approach and the Progressive Education Association's Eight-Year Study (which was actually longer than that). The Winnetka Schools Project compared kids in their schools who worked on projects for the first half of the day with kids from three comparable towns who had a traditional education and who went to the same regional high school.

Guess what? The students who worked on the projects scored above the others in all major subject areas.

The Famous Eight-Year Study (That Actually Was Longer)

The Eight-Year Study found similar results comparing thirty high schools using progressive program ideas with those from traditional high schools. In the study, "the authors concluded that graduates of the progressive schools were 'on the whole' (Aiken 1942, p. 149) more successful than others in their cohort and that students whose high school programs were most different from traditional programs were much superior to their traditional school counterparts (Aiken 1942; Darling-Hammond 1993; Greene 1942; Walten & Travers 1963)" (Marlowe & Page 1998, p. 20).

Active Learning

Two other large qualitative studies support active learning processes, according to Marlowe and Page (1998). They point to Page's (1992) study "of the National History Day Program, a grade 5–12 program grounded in active learning . . . [which] showed that the participating students developed their own conclusions and their own knowledge" (p. 23).

Gonzales (1995) applied social construction theory in her study regarding how multicultural education is implemented in the classroom. Social constructivist theory holds that individuals' perceptions of the world of reality in which they are immersed shapes their ideas and their practices. Gonzales's findings were that teachers shifted their educational approaches as various factors impinged upon them.

Condon and others (1993) studied the development of an alternative teacher education program, which resulted in the students concluding that *learning to teach is a process of constructing meaning*. Additionally, they also realized that children learn through constructing ideas about themselves and the world. In an early article on constructivism, Brooks (1986–1987, December-January), asserts that utilizing a constructivist approach in designing curriculum enables students of all ages to learn more effectively.

In "The Many Faces of Constructivism," Perkins (1999, November) points to the notions that "different kinds of knowledge invite different constructivist responses" (p. 6). Perkins cites the philosopher D. C. Phillips (2000) as identifying three distinct roles in constructivism: the active learner, the social learner, and the creative learner. In the first, "The active learner: Knowledge and understanding are actively acquired . . . The social learner: Knowledge and understanding as socially constructed. . . . The creative learner: Knowledge and understanding as created or recreated." This presents the teacher and administrator a wide range of options to choose from in their armamentaria of strategies, processes, and models to utilize in educational and change processes.

Constructivism Offers More Options for Teacher and Student Choice

By this time, we should have generalized the idea that constructivist approaches offer great ranges of options to teachers and leaders to construct and design in their professional practice, much as the invention of the "man in motion" revolutionized opportunities for coaches and quarterbacks to develop greatly enlarged options when the "T" formation was developed by Clark Shaughnessy and used by the Chicago Bears football team in the early 1940s.

The "T" formation revolutionized football. Constructivism is revolutionizing education.

In an interesting article, "The Courage to Be Constructivist," Brooks and Brooks (1999, November) discuss the negative impact of high-stakes testing on constructivist classroom practices (cited in the chapter on testing titled, "Looking Up the Wrong End of the Horse: Our Testing Mania"). A simple sentence strikes a chord when they state, "Learners control their learning. This simple truth lies at the heart of the constructivist approach to education" (p. 21).

More Heresy—and Insights

Regarding Students

Grace (1999, November) titles her article "When Students Create Curriculum." While this may astound some of us, in actuality a goodly number of people have secretly—and not so secretly—been doing exactly that for a number of years. The funny thing is, although I've been allowing students to create curriculum for years, in every class people generally want to learn the same subject matter I perceive as fundamental in the context of the course. And, often, their interests exceed my thinking in interesting and creative ways. Oddly, it always occurs, although the more rigid (read, structured) people in the class seem dumbfounded by the process—and suspicious that I'm kidding them when I say that their interests should also form the basis for the curriculum.

Grace does acknowledge that providing opportunities for students to generate their own curriculum requires risk and courage. But, the risk is worth it as this process also generates a good deal of motivation. Grace concludes:

> Constructing curriculum with students is a lively process that can lead to high levels of independent learning and great leaps of individual knowledge. Giving students the freedom to explore their world confidently and routinely is one of the most important learning experiences that schools provide. (p. 52)

To that, I can add, if the teacher uses the group as the organizing vehicle for the class, it may lead to powerful learning and to "great leaps" of creating knowledge jointly, as students learn from each other and from other groups.

This insight composes the guts of social constructivism.

"Underlying the constructivist theory and its goals is a recognition of the value of the student as a thinker." This quote of Richetti and Sheerin (1999, November, p. 59) explains the title of their article, "Helping Students Ask the Right Questions." They cite Cecil:

> Students attain significantly higher levels of thinking when they are encouraged to develop skill in generating critical and creative questions and when they are provided opportunities for dialogue with classmates about the questions posed and conclusions derived from information they encounter. (1995, p. 36)

The Swedish Model (Read, Approach)

A recent doctoral study of education (Nordgren 2001) in Sweden points up the strongly constructivist nature of the model of schooling developed in the three schools he studied. Consisting of case studies of an elementary, a middle, and a secondary school (in which attendance is voluntary) in a small city of fifty thousand in Sweden, the researcher found that the model structured schooling so that every student was responsible for planning his own learning. The vehicle was a "planning-book" that every child had on his or her desk or table starting in the first grade of school. On every Monday morning, each child would write in the book what he or she expected to learn during that week. The function of the faculty was to facilitate accomplishing that plan for learning.

Thus, the *child was responsible* for his or her own learning. According to Nordgren, faculty trust the child to be responsible and to learn, students trust each other, the administration trusts faculty, and the community trusts the schools. The child can work alone if he or she wants to do so, or can work with others. A great deal of flexibility has developed since 1994 when the entire centralized educational program was reformed and decentralized to reflect this focus.

Oddly for Americans, the Swedish curriculum is increasingly decentralized, while ours is racing headlong into state and national conformity. The Swedes are focused first on developing values they hold dear, then academics—and, yet their results on international tests are first-rate. Thus, the Swedish educational system is focused on instilling democratic values such as shared power, trust, and building responsibility in students first, over academics. The results exemplify their success. They also are very pragmatic, with sixteen different programs available for student choice in secondary schools, fourteen of the sixteen being vocational.

When the researcher, R. D. Nordgren, asked the secondary students (who were there voluntarily) why they wanted to go to school, they responded, "It's my responsibility to learn," and went on with their self-chosen studies.

The Swedes seem to have pulled off developing constructivist schools, which, they told Nordgren, was difficult.

What did the Swedes find when they visited American schools? *Control.* The teachers controlled the kids. The principals controlled the teachers, the system controlled the principals, and the state controlled the districts and systems.

Constructivism and Brain Research

Abbott and Ryan (1999, November) state:

Four of the greatest predictors of eventual success at the university level are achieved before a child even enters school: namely, the quantity and quality of discussion in the child's home, the clarity of value systems, the level of peer group support, and the amount of independent reading. (Abbott & Ryan, 1999)

They note that:

We now can see why learning is much more than just the flip side of good teaching and schooling. Instead of thinking of the brain as a computer, researchers now see it as a far more flexible, self-adjusting entity—a living, unique, ever-changing organism that grows and reshapes itself in response to challenge, with elements that wither if not used. (pp. 66–67)

Wilson and Daviss also deal with the mainspring of constructivism, noting that:

In constructivist learning, each individual structures his or her own knowledge of the world into a unique pattern, connecting each new fact, experience, or understanding in a subject in ways that bind the individual into rational and meaningful relationships to the wider world. (1994, p. 176)

Fosnot (1996) provides an interesting insight into developments in the major subject matter associations. "Most recent reforms advocated by national professional groups are based on constructivism. For example, the National Council for Teachers of Mathematics published a series of position papers in the 1980s describing mathematics instruction as engaging learners in: (1) meaningful problem solving; (2) arguing and proving their own solutions; and (3) constructing their own algorithms and formulae" (pp. ix and x). She also cites the National Science Teacher's Association as "arguing for an inquiry science approach" (p. x). The implications of these insights are more appropriate for the later section "More Research Findings—On Leadership."

SUMMARY OF MORE RESEARCH FINDINGS—ON CONSTRUCTIVIST INSTRUCTION

The elements of constructivist instruction/teaching were discussed above. Active learning and heavy student involvement in their own learning, indeed, in designing their own learning, are major keys.

Constructivism is seen as ultimate decentralization, with student and teacher able to make decisions regarding what and how they learn. Thus, constructivist education generates responsibility, trust, and, hopefully, democratic values. Grace's article points up the value of students designing their own curriculum. This is why I've included a brief discussion of a recent study of schooling in Sweden in this section.

The Swedish educational system was cited as a system developing a constructivist model of education, with students learning to take responsibility for their own learning and being trusted to do so. Democratic values of shared power, trust, and responsibility are strongly held and implemented.

My visit to a Swedish elementary school substantiated Nordgren's findings. Students took responsibility for their own learning. The faculty were relaxed and trusted the kids, who essentially designed their own curriculum and learning.

I've visited several thousand schools in my educational career. This was patently one of the very best. Indeed, I told the reporters who interviewed us after the visit that I would gladly send my own kids there if I lived in the area. This comment was quoted in the headlines in the papers.

MORE RESEARCH FINDINGS—ON LEADERSHIP

A Surprisingly Limited Menu of Offerings

Oddly, this section on research on leadership will prove to be relatively short. Not much research can be cited on constructivism and leadership, because little research has occurred. This latter area comprises a vast, fertile field for further investigation.

In 1995, Lambert, Walker, Zimmerman, Cooper, Lambert, Gardner, and Slack published a pioneer book on constructivist leadership, titled *The Constructivist Leader*. In it, Walker notes:

Constructivist learning has received a good deal of attention recently, if book titles and journal articles are an indication of interest. The impact of constructivist approaches can be seen most clearly in K–12 education, professional literature, state curriculum frameworks, and school reform provisions. At the university level, interest in constructivist learning and leading appears to be in the infancy stage; that is, professors of educational leadership are aware of the theory, may see its promise, but have yet to introduce constructivist approaches in any systematic way across university programs. (p. 179)

This view of administrative preparation lagging behind teacher training programs is supported by Danzig (1996). This analyst notes the growing gap between the knowledge and skills that most teachers must learn in their preparation programs, and the knowledge and behavioral categories that school administrators employ to evaluate teacher performance and to understand the criteria by which teachers assess their students.

Three University Leadership Preparation Programs Cited as Constructivist

Walker (1995), in *The Constructivist Leader*, cites three university leadership preparation programs that have moved toward constructivism: California State University at Hayward (CSUH), the University of Hawaii, and the Department of Educational Administration at Wichita State University in Kansas. Some common elements to all three programs include "use of cohorts to integrate the curriculum and to build among students a sense of collegiality and collaboration" (p. 185). In other words, creating a learning community, and, thus changing the cultural norms and roles of participants, involving students in developing the curriculum and program, changing the professor's role to move toward being a facilitator, attempts to apply theoretical learnings to actual school situations, and a more active role for students, among others.

Walker notes that "content is imbedded in the processes that exemplify constructivist learning and leading" (p. 176), for the CSUH program, but it is clear that different constructivist elements are being implemented in all three programs.

Leithwood (1996) studied eleven university-sponsored leadership preparation programs. Interestingly, constructivist teaching strategies had a significant impact on changing the practice of leadership in the schools, as perceived by both graduates and teacher colleagues.

In the same book cited above (1995), Lambert contributed a chapter titled, "Toward a Theory of Constructivist Leadership," noting that "it was discovered that the most important factor in schools is *relationships*" (p. 35). She notes, *"Reciprocal relationships* [my emphasis], the meanings of which must be discussed and commonly construed in schools, are the basis through which we make sense of our world, continually define ourselves, and 'coevolve,' or grow together" (p. 36). This is the core of George Herbert Mead's Symbolic Interaction discussed in a previous chapter. Another chapter in that book views the constructivist leader as being a leader of conversations, the thesis focusing on "the vital role of language in the construction of meaning and knowledge" (p. xiv).

A Focus on the Dynamics of Systems and the Decentralizing Power of Constructivism

My book, titled *Leadership for Constructivist Schools* (2000), explores the dynamics and processes involved in creating constructivist classes, teams, learning communities, and schools. I am concerned that people interested in constructivism grasp the key dynamics, the essential elements of schools and change strategies, since I view both teachers and leaders as potential and actual change agents. These underlying dynamics (how organizations really work [such as the operative social systems, norms, roles, culture, and structure that develop], the nature and impact of power and symbolism, the teacher and leader shifting their roles to become change agents and facilitators, evaluation models using feedback loops) are essential to constructing effective change strategies to move learning communities and entire schools toward a constructivist philosophy and practices.

I view and have utilized constructivist approaches on a "big picture" scale as an effective tool to deal with the ever-increasing impersonality and size of both institutions and society. We can utilize constructivism to return decision making to the local level by decentralizing schools and even to the individual teacher, team, or learning community, making such decision making more sensitive to student, teacher, and community needs and interests.

Actually, constructivism also provides a great deal of thrust to decentralizing down to the individual student level, since decision making by students is considerably respected—and enhanced. Creating a supportive subculture in the organization is a major vehicle to accomplish constructivist processes and goals.

Brooks and Brooks (1993) in their early pioneer work focus on constructivism in the classroom, an appropriate target for an early work in a field, since any work must have limitations.

Their conclusions as quoted in the previous section in constructivist instruction are so startling that they deserve special note. They write:

> The organizational and management structures of most schools militate against these goals (of becoming thinking, exploring individuals who generate hypotheses and test them out). So, if autonomy, initiative, and leadership are to be nurtured, it must be done in individual classrooms. (p. 103)

This constitutes a serious indictment of the rigid structures of the schools, and can be considered relatively astounding. As a consequence of this insight, they abandon any efforts at schoolwide reform with this position, and state that educational reform lies with individual efforts of classroom teachers *in their classrooms*, a position counter to most reform literature and strategies.

It is worthwhile to compare and contrast this viewpoint with that of my approach, in *Leadership for Constructivist Schools* (2000). Note the above analysis of this work as focusing on moving toward constructivism not only in the classroom, but also in teams, learning communities, and, indeed, in the whole school, and even in the district. Thus, I present the vision and hope and provide the insights into organizational dynamics, as well as the appropriate tools to redesign not only classes, but also total organizations. These tools include a highly individual change strategy that first diagnoses, then analyzes, issues and concerns people develop in their organization, and digs away at underlying themes. Further, the strategy, which is presented in chapter 20 "Moving Orange Blossom Trail Elementary School toward Constructivism," is designed to stimulate developing potential lines of action and their underlying rationale, and then to evaluate consequences of the actions taken. Hopefully, this can help those interested in changing their organizations into taking the risks necessary to venture forth and achieve some measure of success.

The approach runs counter to the present race to reform education from the top down, often through state-mandated initiatives, utilizing a one-size-fits-all approach. The dynamics of schools and school districts are too complex to yield to such centralized initiatives, a view that experience and literature abundantly support.

Further Thinking of Teachers as Leaders

Lambert (1997) explores the role of teachers as leaders in her thinking about the future of schooling. She views constructivist leadership as one of four themes of teaching (the others being human learning and development, learning communities, and systemic change), and utilizes a chapter in this document to deal with constructivist leadership and constructivist leading.

Levin (1999) asserts that supporting constructivist teaching constitutes a challenge to educational administrators. It certainly does, since results and processes are unpredictable. Structured administrators (as many administrators tend to be) often find constructivist teaching "messy," making them uncomfortable. See R. D. Nordgren's chapter 6, "My Development as a Constructivist Teacher," pointing to the all-too-common experience of an administrator not recognizing constructivist approaches, and saying that she'd return when Nordgren was teaching.

Abbott and Ryan (1999, November), in their article "Constructing Knowledge, Reconstructing Schooling," deal with brain research and its implications for social constructivist education. They begin by asking questions about our current national model (read, approach) to school reform.

> We must now ask deeper questions about the institutions of schooling than have so far been raised in the school reform movement, with its short-term panaceas of more accountability, site-based management, standardized tests, prescribed curriculums, and longer hours for teachers and students. We have to accept that we are dealing with a deep systemic crisis. Constructivism collides head on with so many of our institutional arrangements for learning. (p. 68)

They point to behaviorist models of learning that conflict with adolescents' desires to be independent, and pose one conclusion as "Constructivism is open-ended, as is the neural structure of the brain. Education that focuses on specific outcomes and national curriculum targets does not support genuinely creative or entrepreneurial learners" (p. 69).

The Law of Unintended Consequences (LUC) Once Again

Jones and Whitford (1997) report:

> [In Kentucky] there has been a rebound effect. Pressure generated by the state test for high-stakes accountability has led school-based educators to pressure the state to be more explicit about content that will be tested. This in turn constrains local school decision making about curriculum. This dialectical process works to increase the state control of local curriculum. (p. 278)

SUMMARY OF RESEARCH ON CONSTRUCTIVIST LEADERSHIP

Surprisingly, few studies and books can be found on leadership and constructivism. And equally few exist on leadership preparation programs. And those that exist are very recent. It seems that we in leadership are not only behind the curve, but haven't even seen the curve on the horizon. The few studies point up the considerable value of moving toward constructivism in leadership, for example, in noting the power of constructivist leadership in decentralizing schools, and even classes or teams—and producing effective results.

More generally, the constructivist perspective can be deployed to critique the shallow roots of the current wave of top-down educational reform.

THE FINAL SET OF QUESTIONS AND REFLECTIONS

On Instruction

1. What do you think of using Maslow's or another psychologist's or social psychologist's theories to deal with people's needs in the

classroom? Why don't these psychologists use one or more of these theories in their classroom teaching models?

2. Have you seen active learning used by teachers? What were the results? How much active learning do you use?

   A. Note in chapter 6, Dr. Nordgren refers to how long it took him to move into constructivist practices, and the social pressure to conform. Is there social pressure for us to conform to present practices? How does this affect you?

3. How do you react to the idea of students participating in developing curriculum? Have you seen it done?

4. How do we build responsibility without providing experiences for people to learn to take responsibility?

5. Did this chapter provide adequate research findings on constructivism focused on teaching and instruction? What further information do you need?

6. What further questions would you ask about constructivist instruction, since these questions are so limited?

On Leadership

7. The first book on constructivist leadership was published in 1995. Why are we able to find so few studies on constructivist leadership?

8. One researcher found only three educational administration or leadership preparation programs that had moved toward constructivist models. Why is this?

9. In this book, chapter 19 "A Day in the Life of a Constructivist Principal," deals with a move toward becoming a constructivist school, as does chapter 20. Are you familiar with any other school moving deliberately toward one of these models?

10. Why are Brooks and Brooks so pessimistic about an entire school moving toward constructivist practices? I was taken aback by their insistence that constructivism can only be nurtured in individual classrooms. Are you?

    A. Have we explored any organizational structures in this book to help with this process? Does developing a curriculum structure, as in chapter 25, constitute one such device that can help us in such a course of action?

11. How about developing a Pupil Personnel Services Council, as described in chapter 26?

12. What about the change strategies used in chapter 16 and chapter 20? Are they relevant, and can they help us?

A. How do you react to the notion that structures we can design can provide prodigious help in moving our organizations in constructive (and constructivist) directions?

13. What does constructivism have to say about our current efforts toward national reform?

SOURCES

Abbott, J. & Ryan, T. (1999, November). Constructing knowledge, reconstructing schooling. *Educational Leadership 57*(3), 66–69.

Aiken, W. M. (1942). *The story of the eight year study* (vol. 1). New York: Harper & Row.

Bloom, B. (Ed.). (1956). *Taxonomy of educational objectives, Handbook I: Cognitive domain.* New York: McKay.

Bredo, E. (2000). Reconsidering social constructivism: The relevance of George Herbert Mead's interactionism. In D. C. Phillips (Ed.). *Constructivism in education: Opinions and second opinions on controversial issues.* (pp. 127–57). Ninety-ninth Yearbook of the National Society for the Study of Education, Part I. Chicago: University of Chicago Press.

Brooks, M. (1986–1987, December-January). Curriculum development from a constructivist perspective. *Educational Leadership 44*(4), 63–67.

Brooks, M. G. & Brooks, J. G. (1993). *In search of understanding: The case for constructivist classrooms.* Alexandria, VA: Association for Supervision and Curriculum Development (ASCD).

Brooks, M. G. & Brooks, J. G. (1999, November). The courage to be constructivist. *Educational Leadership 57*(3), 18–24.

Cecil, N. (1995). *The art of inquiry: Questioning strategies for K–6 classrooms.* Winnipeg, Canada: Peguis.

Condon, M. W. F., Clyde, J. A., Kyle, D. W., & Hovda, R. A. (1993, September-October). A constructivist basis for teaching and teacher education: A framework for program development and research on graduates. *Journal of Teacher Education 44*(4), 273–78.

Danzig, A. (1996). Educational leadership: Stories of administrative practices with implications for a standards-based education system. (ERIC Document Reproduction Service No. ED401615).

Darling-Hammond, L. (1993). Reframing the school reform agenda: Developing capacity for school transformation. *Phi Delta Kappan 74*(10), 752–61.

Davis, T. M. & Murrell, P. H. (1993). Turning teaching into learning: The role of student responsibility in the collegiate experience. [Abstract]. In *Active learning, critical thinking, learning styles, and cooperative learning.* Washington, DC: George Washington University, 1993 ASHE-ERIC Higher Education Reports; Report 8.

Dewey, J. (1938). *Experience and education.* New York: Macmillan.

Fogarty, R. (1999, November). Architects of the intellect. *Educational Leadership 57*(3), 76–78.

Fosnot, C. T. (Ed.). (1996). *Constructivism: Theory, perspectives, and practice.* New York: Teachers College Press.

Gagnon, G. W., Jr. & Collay, M. (2001). *Constructivist classrooms.* Thousand Oaks, CA: Sage.

Goffman, E. (1967). *The presentation of self in everyday life.* Garden City, NY: Doubleday Anchor.

Gonzales, M. R. (1995). Multi-cultural education in practice: Teachers' social constructions and classroom enactments. (ERIC Document Reproduction Service No. ED 390851).

Grace, M. (1999, November). When students create curriculum. *Educational Leadership 57*(3), 49–52.

Greene, K. B. (1942). Activity education. *Review of Educational Research 12*(3), 280–88.

Johnson, D. W. & Johnson, R. T. (1984). *Circles of learning: Cooperation in the classroom.* Alexandria, VA: Association for Supervision and Curriculum Development (ASCD).

Jones, K. & Whitford, B. I. (1997, December). Kentucky's conflicting reform principles: High stakes accountability and student performance assessment. *Phi Delta Kappan 78*(4), 276–81.

Lambert, L. (1995). Toward a theory of constructivist leadership. In L. Lambert, et al. (Eds.). *The constructivist leader.* New York: Teachers College Press.

Lambert, L. (1997). *Who will save our schools? Teachers as constructivist leaders.* Thousand Oaks, CA: Corwin.

Lambert, L., et al. (1995). *The constructivist leader.* New York: Teachers College Press.

Larochelle, M., Bednarz, N., & Garrison, J. (Eds.). *Constructivism and education*. Cambridge, UK: Cambridge University Press.

Leithwood, K. (1996, May). Preparing school leaders: What works? *Journal of School Leadership 6*(3), 316–42.

Levin, B. (1999, October). What is educational administration, anyway? *Educational Administration Quarterly 35*(4), 546–61.

Lewin, K. (1952). Group decision and social change. In G. E. Swanson, T. M. Newcomb & E. L. Hartley (Eds.). *Readings in social psychology* (rev. ed.). New York: Holt.

Linton, R. (1955). *The tree of culture*. New York: Random House.

Marlowe, B. A. & Page, M. L. (1998). *Creating and sustaining the constructivist classroom*. Thousand Oaks, CA: Corwin.

Maslow, A. H. (1954). *Motivation and personality*. New York: Harper & Row.

Mead, G. H. (1934). *Mind, self, and society*. Chicago: University of Chicago Press.

Nordgren, R. D. (2001). *Shared power, trust, student responsibility, and global workforce competence*. Unpublished doctoral dissertation. University of South Florida.

Page, M. (1992). *National History Day: An ethnohistorical case study*. Unpublished doctoral dissertation, University of Massachusetts, Amherst.

Perkins, D. (1999, November). The many faces of constructivism. *Educational Leadership 57*(3), 6–11.

Phillips, D. C. (Ed.). (2000). *Constructivism in education: Opinions and second opinions on controversial issues*. Ninety-ninth Yearbook of the Society for the Study of Education, Part I. Chicago: University of Chicago Press.

Richetti, C. & Sheerin, J. (1999, November). Helping students ask the right questions. *Educational Leadership 57*(3), 58–62.

Shapiro, A. S. (1996). Creating the culture of constructivist classrooms in public and private schools. In *Global–Local Articulations*. The Society for Applied Anthropology (SfAA), 1996 Annual International Conference, Baltimore, MD.

Shapiro, A. S. (2000, May). Creating culture for a constructivist classroom and team. *Wingspan 13*(1), 5–7.

Shapiro, A. S. (2000). *Leadership for constructivist schools*. Lanham, MD: Scarecrow.

Sharan, S. (1985). Cooperative learning effects on ethnic relations and achievement in Israeli junior high school classrooms. In R. Slavin (Ed.). *Learning to cooperate, cooperating to learn* (pp. 313–44). New York: Plenum.

Slavin, R. E. (1989). Cooperative learning and student achievement. In R. Slavin (Ed.). *School and classroom organization* (pp. 129–58). Englewood Cliffs, NJ: Lawrence Erlbaum.

Thelen, H. A. (1949, March). Group dynamics in instruction: The principle of least group size. *School Review*, 139–48.

von Glasersfeld, E. (1998). Why constructivism must be radical. In Larochelle, M., Bednarz, N. & Garrison, J. (Eds.). *Constructivism and education*. Cambridge, UK: Cambridge University Press.

Walker, D. (1995). The preparation of constructivist leaders. In L. Lambert et al. (Eds.). *The constructivist leader*. New York: Teachers College Press.

Walker, D., Lambert, L., Zimmerman, D. P., Cooper, J. E., Lambert, M. D., Gardner, M. E., and Ford Slack, P. J. (Eds.). (1995). *The constructivist leader*. New York: Teachers College Press.

Walten, N. E. & Travers, R. M. (1963). Analysis and investigation of teaching methods. In N. E. Gage (Ed.). *Handbook of research on teaching* (pp. 448–505). Chicago: Rand McNally.

Wilson, K. G. & Daviss, B. (1994). *Redesigning education*. New York: Holt.

About the Author

Arthur Shapiro, with three degrees from the University of Chicago, is professor of educational leadership and policy studies at the University of South Florida in Tampa. He has worked as a teacher, principal, director of secondary education, assistant superintendent, and superintendent in inner-city, rural, and suburban settings, all in nationally visible districts. He directed an advanced doctoral center in Chattanooga, Tennessee, and chaired the College of Education of George Peabody College in Nashville, Tennessee, and two departments in Tampa.

He is coauthor of the first theory of supervision and coauthor of the first theory of curriculum and a theory of oganizational decision making. His latest book is *Leadership for Constructivist Schools* (Scarecrow Press, 2000). Shapiro is working with schools using a highly individualized diagnostic, analytic, and implementation change strategy called organizational mapping. He writes, consults, and speaks widely on numerous issues in education. He is also a fellow of the Society for Applied Anthropology.